MAPPING THE

MIND

Rita Carter is an author, journalist and lecturer who specializes in neuropsychology and neuropsychiatry. She contributes to a very wide range of newspapers and magazines in the UK and USA, and has twice been awarded the Medical Journalists' Association prize for outstanding contribution to medical journalism. *Mapping the Mind* was shortlisted for the Rhône-Poulenc Prize for science books.

Chris Frith is Emeritus Professor of Neuropsychology at the Wellcome Centre for Neuroimaging at University College London (UCL) and Niels Bohr Visiting Professor in the Interacting Minds project at the University of Aarhus in Denmark. Since completing his PhD in 1969 he has been funded by the Medical Research Council and the Wellcome Trust to study the relationship between the mind and the brain. He is a pioneer in application of brain imaging to the study of mental processes. He has contributed more than 300 papers to scientific journals and is known especially for his work on agency, social cognition, and understanding the minds of people with mental disorders such as schizophrenia. For this work he was elected a Fellow of the Royal Society in 2000.

Acknowledgements

My thanks to those explorers of the human mind who have been kind enough to enhance this book with their written contributions or by making time to talk to me about their work. Particular thanks to Chris Frith, whose unerring ability to spot a fragile speculation has (I hope) ensured that everything here is grounded in good science; to Malcolm Godwin, whose right-brain talents have made the book beautiful, and to my brilliant assistant Priya Rallon, for her conscientiousness, dedication and curiosity.

MAPPING THE
MIND

Revised and Updated Edition

RITA CARTER

Consultant: Professor Christopher Frith

UNIVERSITY OF CALIFORNIA PRESS
BERKELEY LOS ANGELES

University of California Press, one of the most distinguished university presses
in the United States, enriches lives around the world by advancing scholarship
in the humanities, social sciences, and natural sciences. Its activities are supported
by the UC Press Foundation and by philanthropic contributions from individuals
and institutions. For more information, visit www.ucpress.edu

University of California Press
Berkeley and Los Angeles, California

Published by arrangement with Weidenfeld & Nicolson

Library of Congress Control Number 2010922392

ISBN 978-0-520-26628-5

Designed and illustrated by MoonRunner Design Ltd

Printed and bound in China

18 17 16 15 14 13 12 11 10

9 8 7 6 5 4 3 2 1

Contents

Acknowledgements   2

Preface to the second edition   6

Introduction   7

Chapter One ~ THE EMERGING LANDSCAPE   10

Chapter Two ~ THE GREAT DIVIDE   34

Chapter Three ~ BENEATH THE SURFACE   54

Chapter Four ~ A CHANGEABLE CLIMATE   80

Chapter Five ~ A WORLD OF ONE'S OWN   106

Chapter Six ~ CROSSING THE CHASM   136

Chapter Seven ~ STATES OF MIND   158

Chapter Eight ~ HIGHER GROUND   180

References   208

Bibliography   216

Index   220

PREFACE TO THE SECOND EDITION

I WROTE THE FIRST edition of this book because at that time – the late 1990s – there was nothing like it and I thought there should be. The previous decade had seen the emergence of functional brain imaging, from fuzzy PET scans of monkey brains to pixel-precise fMRI studies of human cognition. For the first time we could see the mechanisms that generate our subjective worlds.

I thought then (and still do) that this inside view of a world which most would have assumed would always remain inscrutable, was the most exciting revelation in the history of science. At that time, though, the picture was maddeningly fragmentary. *Mapping the Mind* was an attempt to pull the pieces together and place them in a broad psychological and evolutionary framework.

I likened the result to an early map of the earth, complete with dragon-strewn *terra incognita*. Twelve years later the map is much more detailed, and in this edition I have filled in areas that were previously empty or sparse, sharpened up contours that have withstood further exploration and redrawn those where new work has shown early assumptions to be wrong. Some of the muddy images that came from early scanners have been replaced with sharper versions, including some of the brilliant diffusion tensor images that are clarifying neural tracts and connections. And I have added sections on major new areas of discovery such as mirror neurons and the brain's 'default' activity.

The first edition was written for people who, like me, are insatiably curious about how the human mind works and want a broad-brush but up-to-date account of the latest research for no reason other than that they find it the most fascinating topic on earth. It came to be used, however, by students in a wide variety of disciplines and this edition maintains, I hope, that balance between general and text book.

George Bush, in 1998, declared the years 1990–2000 to be the Decade of the Brain. The advances made in those years were certainly astonishing, but looking back it can be seen that modern neuroscience was only just getting under way. The notion of identifying the neural impulses that give rise to 'higher' faculties, such as altruism, empathy, or morality; of using brain scans to detect lying, or of feeding the electrical output from someone's head into a computer and then watching the visual content of that person's mind pop up on a screen seemed like science fiction. Today we can do all of this, and the practical and commercial applications of such work are starting to be felt. What we do with them remains to be seen. The Decade of the Brain may be over but the Decade of the Mind is about to begin.

INTRODUCTION

THE HUMAN BRAIN has been slow to give up its secrets. Until recently the machinations that give rise to our thoughts, memories, feelings and perceptions were impossible to examine directly – their nature could only be inferred by observing their effects. Now, however, new imaging techniques make the internal world of the mind visible, much as X-rays reveal our bones. In the twenty-first century functional brain scanning machines are opening up the territory of the mind just as the first ocean-going ships once opened up the globe.

The challenge of mapping this world – locating the precise brain activity that creates specific experiences and behavioural responses – is currently engaging some of the finest scientists in the world. This book brings news of their discoveries in a way that will make them comprehensible even to those with no knowledge of, or specific interest in, science.

Everyone should be enthralled by this venture because it is giving us greater understanding about one of the oldest and most fundamental of mysteries – the relationship between brain and mind. It is also providing fascinating insights into ourselves and shedding light on aberrant and bizarre behaviour. The biological basis of mental illness, for example, is now demonstrable: no one can reasonably watch the frenzied, localized activity in the brain of a person driven by some obsession, or see the dull glow of a depressed brain, and still doubt that these are physical conditions rather than some ineffable sickness of the soul. Similarly, it is now possible to locate and observe the mechanics of rage, violence and misperception, and even to detect the physical signs of complex qualities of mind like kindness, humour, heartlessness, gregariousness, altruism, mother-love and self-awareness.

The knowledge that brain mapping is delivering is not only enlightening, it is of immense practical and social importance because it paves the way for us to recreate ourselves mentally in a way that has previously been described only in science fiction. Rather as knowledge of the human genome will soon allow us to manipulate the fundamental physical processes that give rise to our bodies, so brain mapping is providing the navigational tool required to control brain activity in a precise and radical way.

Unlike genetic engineering, gaining this control does not depend on the development of tricky new technology – all it will take is a little refinement of existing methods and techniques like drugs, surgery, electrical and magnetic manipulation and psychological intervention. These are limited only in that, at present, they are (literally) hit-and-miss. When our brain maps are complete, however, it will be possible to target psychoactive treatments so finely that an individual's state of mind (and thus behaviour) will be almost entirely malleable. It may even be possible to alter individual perception to the extent that we could, if we chose, live in a state of virtual reality, almost entirely unaffected by the external environment.

This is an old ambition, of course, reflected in our perpetual attempts to alter our consciousness through drugs, sensation-seeking and self-entrancement. What is new is that brain mapping may soon make it possible without any of the usual drawbacks. The personal, social and political implications of this are awesome, and one of the most serious ethical questions we will face in the new century is deciding how this powerful new tool should be deployed.

Those who are actually engaged in brain mapping loathe this sort of talk. For people at the leading edge of scientific research, where findings are often hyped in the scramble for funding, they are oddly reticent about the potential uses of their work. One reason for this is that modern behavioural neuroscience is a new discipline and its practitioners have come into it from many different fields: physics, radiology, neurology, molecular biology, psychology and psychiatry – even mathematics and philosophy. They have yet to develop a group mentality or a commonly agreed purpose beyond their immediate task of charting brain function. Many neuroscientists are also terrified of what might happen if their work is ever subjected to the tabloid treatment that has been meted out to their opposite numbers in genetics. The Human Genome Project has led to endless apocalyptic headlines, and as a result the geneticists are now closely scrutinized and controlled. Brain researchers can do without that sort of attention. At a brain mapping conference in 1997 (at which I was the sole reporter) a *Time* magazine cover about neuropsychology was held up by a speaker as a warning of what could result from loose talk to outsiders. The story to which the cover related was not inaccurate or sensational – its fault seemed to be its very existence.

The result of this reticence is that while we all debate and fret about the ethical and practical implications of genetic engineering, brain mapping tends to be regarded as the geeks' corner of psychology – interesting, no doubt, for those who like that sort of thing, but of no practical importance. When news leaks out it tends to be in isolated blips: one tiny piece of brain tissue is found to be the source of fear; the connection between the two hemispheres appears to be denser in women than in men; damage is found in the frontal lobes of a disproportionate number of murderers on Death Row. Each of these stories generates a brief flurry of speculation, but their full significance is rarely elucidated.

One of the purposes of this book is to draw attention to the social implications of what at first sight may seem a purely technological advance. Another is to examine the extent to which behavioural neuroscience is contributing to the age-old brain/mind conundrum and the puzzle of consciousness. Brain mapping is, of course, only one part of the current task. Along with it goes exploration of the workings of individual brain cells, the ebb and flow of neurotransmitters and the phenomenally complex interactions of the brain's various parts – things that are merely touched upon here but are of no less importance.

The more optimistic of today's brain explorers believe that when, or if, all of this is brought together – when each minute brain component has been located, its function identified and its interactions with each other component made clear – the resulting description will contain all there is to know about human nature and experience. Others think this reductionist approach will never fully explain why we feel and behave as we do, let alone yield the secret of the brain's most extraordinary product – consciousness. By their lights, a map of the brain can tell us no more about the mind than a terrestrial globe speaks of Heaven and Hell.

The work described here does not settle the debate about the nature of existence, but it seems to me to provide tantalising clues about it. Please remember, though, that these are the early days of mind exploration and the vision of the brain we have now is probably no more complete or accurate than a sixteenth-century map of the world. Most of what you will read is actually more complicated than I might make it appear, and some of it will almost certainly turn out to be wrong. This is because many of the findings are too new to have been replicated. There are also huge areas where very little is known and – as is the nature of leading-edge science – everyone is essentially guessing. Some of the foremost scientists in this venture have been generous enough to offer their thoughts and theories for inclusion here, and the diversity of their opinions demonstrates how far we still are from consensus in this field.

The cartographers who produced those early world maps filled the gaps in their knowledge with the medieval equivalent of scientific bluster. 'Here,' wrote one map-maker confidently, 'be Dragons.' I have tried to keep the dragons out of this chart, but others are bound to spot them, along with misleading signs and dubious landmarks. Such things are, I suspect, unavoidable on virgin territory, so those who prefer to travel only on well-worn paths should wait for the tourist guides that will be along later. Those who want to explore, read on and I will show you some strange and wonderful things.

CHAPTER ONE

THE EMERGING LANDSCAPE

The human brain is made of many parts. Each has a specific function: to turn sounds into speech; to process colour; to register fear; to recognize a face or distinguish a fish from a fruit. But this is no static collection of components: each brain is unique, ever-changing and exquisitely sensitive to its environment. Its modules are interdependent and interactive and their functions are not rigidly fixed: sometimes one bit will take over the job of another, or fail, owing to some genetic or environmental hiccup, to work at all. Brain activity is controlled by currents and chemicals and mysterious oscillations; it may even be subject to quantum effects that distort time. The whole is bound together in a dynamic system of systems that does millions of different things in parallel. It is probably so complex that it will never succeed in comprehending itself. Yet it never ceases to try.

I F YOU PLACE A FINGER ON THE NAPE of your neck then edge it up and outwards, you will come across a bump formed by the base of your skull. Have a little feel. According to Franz Gall, the founder of phrenology, this particular protuberance marks the location of the Organ of Amativeness, 'the faculty that gives rise to the sexual feeling'. Now slide your finger an inch or so further up towards your crown. You are now passing over the Organ of Combativeness.

Those of a warm and peaceful disposition should, in theory, find the second area of their skull flatter than the first. But don't be too concerned if your bumps do not match your self-perceptions – Gall arrived at the Amativeness Organ by seeking out the area of greatest heat in the skulls of two recently widowed and 'emotional' young women, and he fixed the Organ of Combativeness by observing that area's smallness in 'most Hindoos and Ceylonese'.[1] It was dubious methodology even for the early nineteenth century.

Bump-reading was nonsense, anyway, because the soft tissue of an individual brain generally has no effect on the shape of the skull. Yet it wasn't all wrong. Feel your skull again, on top this time, just a little forward and to the left of the crown. This is where Gall placed his Organ of Mirthfulness. A few years ago surgeons at the University of California Medical School applied a tiny electric current near to this part of the left brain of a 16-year-old girl.

The patient had intractable epilepsy and the stimulus was part of an established procedure designed to locate the foci of her seizures prior to their removal. She was conscious, and as the stimulus passed through this particular part of her cortex she started to laugh.[2] It was no empty rictus but a genuine, humour-filled chortle, and when the surgeons asked her what was so amusing she had an answer: 'You guys are just so funny – standing around.' The doctors applied the current again and this time the girl suddenly saw something comic in a picture, which happened to be in the room, of a perfectly ordinary horse. A third time she was struck by something else. The surgeons seemed to have come across a part of the brain that creates amusement, however unpromising the circumstances. Gall's pinpointing of it nearly 200 years ago was no doubt accidental. Yet his basic idea – of a brain made of functionally discrete modules – was prescient.

Phrenology's downfall came, ironically, from the discovery of *real* brain modules. Towards the end of the nineteenth century a craze for biological psychiatry took root in European universities, and neurologists started to use localized electrical brain stimulation and animal lesion experiments to find out which bits of the brain did what. Others observed the association between certain behaviour and certain brain injuries. Many important landmarks were identified during this first era of brain mapping, including the language areas discovered by the neurologists Pierre Broca and Carl Wernicke. Embarrassingly for the phrenologists, these areas were found in the side of the brain, above and around the ear, while Gall's Organ of Language was firmly located near the eye.

The language areas identified by Broca and Wernicke still bear those names today. If early

Language area discovered by Broca

Language area discovered by Wernicke

Phrenologists' language area

twentieth-century scientists had continued the search for functional brain areas, today's charts might now be crowded with the names of other long-dead individuals instead of the dull labels – primary auditory cortex, SMA , V1 – now attached to each newly discovered region. Instead scientific brain mapping fell out of fashion along with phrenology, and the modular brain theory was largely abandoned by scientists in favour of the theory of 'mass action', which held that complex behaviour arose from the action of all the brain cells working together.

On the face of it, the mid-twentieth century should have been a bad time for anyone with ambitions to use physical methods to treat mental illness or alter behaviour. Yet psychosurgery flourished. In 1935 the Lisbon neurologist Egas Moniz heard about some experiments in which aggressive, anxious chimps had certain fibres in the front of their brains lesioned.[3] The operation – leucotomy – made them quiet and friendly. Moniz promptly tried it on similarly afflicted humans and found it worked. Frontal leucotomy (which later evolved into the more radical frontal lobotomy) rapidly became a standard treatment in mental hospitals, and during the 1940s at least 20,000 such operations were carried out in America alone.[4]

Looking back, the approach to brain surgery at that time seems shockingly cavalier. It was used for almost any mental disorder – depression, schizophrenia, mani – even though no one then had a clue what was causing the symptoms or why making cuts in the brain should relieve them. Travelling surgeons went from hospital to hospital with their implements in the back of their cars, knocking off a dozen or so operations in a morning. One surgeon described his technique like this:

'[There's] nothing to it. I take a sort of medical icepick… bop it through the bones just above the eyeball, push it up into the brain, swiggle it around, cut the brain fibers and that's it. The patient doesn't feel a thing.'[5]

Unfortunately, the lack of feeling extended, in some patients, to a long-term flattening of emotion and a curious insensitivity that left them seemingly only half-alive. It didn't always cure aggression either: Moniz's career was brought to an end when he was shot by one of his own lobotomized patients.

On balance, the mid-century craze for cutting up the brain probably relieved more suffering than it caused, but it created a deep sense of unease in the medical profession and a profound and still-lingering suspicion of psychosurgery among lay people. When effective psychotropic drugs came along in the 1960s, surgery for mental disorders was almost entirely abandoned.

Today the idea of altering behaviour and relieving mental anguish through direct brain manipulation is creeping back. This time, though, the tinkering is based on much greater understanding of how that organ works. Modern imaging techniques such as functional MRI allow researchers to explore the living, working brain.

Frontal leucotomy involved cutting through fibres which connect the unconscious brain, where emotions are generated, to the cortical area where they are consciously registered.

What they have learned from this has provided a wealth of insight into both mental illness and the nature of our everyday experiences.

Take, for example, pain. Common sense might predict a specialized pain centre in the brain, connecting, perhaps, with another bit that registers sensation in the affected part of the body. In fact, scans show that there is no such thing as a pain centre. Pain arises as much from the activation of brain areas associated with attention and emotion as from those directly concerned with sensation. Seeing what pain is, in terms of neurological activity, it becomes clear why we feel it so much more when we are emotionally stressed and why we often don't notice it – even when our bodies are quite badly injured – when more pressing things have captured our attention.

While apparently simple functions like pain are showing themselves to be more complex than might be expected, some seemingly imponderable qualities of the mind are looking to be surprisingly mechanistic. Morality, altruism, 'spiritual' and religious experiences, aesthetic appreciation – even love – have generally been thought of as being beyond scientific exploration. Yet all these seemingly impenetrable mysteries are now revealing their physiological roots, and in some cases they can be manipulated simply by the touch of a perfectly-placed electrode. Implanted brain 'pacemakers', for instance, can transform the meaningless darkness of depression, once assumed to be a sickness of the 'spirit'[6] and eradicate compulsive and obsessive thoughts where all conventional means of stopping them has failed.[7] Feelings of disembodiment, timelessness – even a sense of spiritual transcendence – can be produced on cue if the right bits of brain are tweaked in the right way. You can even buy a helmet which offers you a choice of 'intense spiritual experiences' by sending electronic waves through your skull to turn the grey matter beneath on and off. Dubious as the claims for it might at first seem, the helmet is based on legitimate scientific research. In a series of pioneering studies, started in the 1980s, the Canadian neuroscientist Michael Persinger discovered that disturbing electrical activity in the brain (especially around the temporal lobes) produces weird subjective states in a majority of people. They include out-of-body experiences and the feeling of being in the presence of an invisible but sentient being.[8] What all this demonstrates is that feelings such as amusement, awe, love, terror and spirituality can be experienced independently of the external circumstances with which they are generally associated. You don't need a love object to feel desire, you don't have to be under threat to feel fear, and you don't need a supernatural being to feel haunted. Given an appropriate prod, your brain can produce more or less any experience on its own.

So how does it do it? How does the conglomeration of neuronal clumps and cat's cradle wiring actually generate experience, as well as controlling the rest of the body? All experience arises from electrical discharges in the type of brain cells known as neurons. But the firing of a single neuron is not enough to create the twitch of an eyelid in sleep, let alone a conscious impression. It is when one neuron excites its neighbours, and they in turn fire up others, that patterns of activity arise that are complex and integrated enough to create thoughts, feelings and perceptions.

Millions of neurons must fire in unison to produce the most trifling thought. Even when a human brain is idling a scan of it shows a kaleidoscope of constantly changing activity – a default

A TOUR OF THE TERRITORY

The human brain is as big as a coconut, the shape of a walnut, the colour of uncooked liver and the consistency of chilled butter. It has two hemispheres, which are covered in a thin skin of deeply wrinkled grey tissue called the cerebral cortex. Each infold on this surface is known as a sulcus, and each bulge is known as a gyrus. The surface landscape of each individual's brain is slightly different, but the main wrinkles – like nose–mouth grooves and crow's feet on an age-ing face – are common to all and are used as landmarks. At the very back of the main mass of brain, tucked under its tail and partly fused to it, lies the cerebellum – the 'little brain'. Aeons ago, this was our mammalian ancestors' main brain but now it has been superseded by the larger area, the cerebrum.

Each half of the cerebrum is split into four lobes, their divisions marked by various folds. At the very back lies the occipital lobe; the lower side, around the ears, is the temporal lobe; the top section is the parietal lobe; in front of that is the frontal lobe. Each lobe processes its own clutch of things: the occipital lobe is made up almost entirely of visual processing areas; the parietal lobe deals mainly with functions connected with movement, ori-entation, calculation and certain types of rec-ognition; the temporal lobes deal with sound, speech comprehension (usually on the left only) and some aspects of memory; and the frontal lobes deal with the most integrated brain functions: thinking, conceptualizing and planning. They also play a major part in the conscious appreciation of emotion.

If you slice the brain in half down the centre line so that the two hemispheres fall apart, you see that beneath the cortex lies a complex con-glomeration of modules: lumps, tubes and chambers. Some of them can be likened in size and shape to nuts, grapes and insects, but many of them look like nothing you have ever seen. Each one of these modules has its own function or functions, and they are all interconnected by criss-crossing ropes of axons. Most modules are greyish – a colour lent by the densely packed neuron bodies. The bands that connect them, however, are lighter because they are covered in a sheath of white substance called

Dendrite

Cell body

Axon

Synapse

Axon

Vesicle

Mitochondrion

Membrane

Dendrite

myelin, which acts as insulation, allowing electricity to flow swiftly and directly along them. Apart from a single little bit – the pineal gland in the centre base of the brain – every brain module is duplicated in each hemisphere. Throughout this book each module is referred to in the singular but in fact there are always two. When it is necessary to distinguish between the two it is made clear which one is indicated.

Looking sideways on at the sliced brain, the most noticeable thing is a curved band of white tissue that forms a curvaceous division between the folded cortex and the mass of modules beneath. The corpus callosum itself joins the two hemispheres and acts as a bridge between them, constantly shunting information back and forth so that most of the time they are effectively one. The modules that nestle beneath the corpus callosum are generally known as the limbic system. This area is older than the cortex in evolutionary terms and is also known as the mammalian brain because it is thought to have first emerged in mammals. This part of the brain – and the even older areas below it – is unconscious, but it has a profound effect on our experience because it is densely connected to the conscious cortex above it and constantly feeds information upwards.

Emotions – our most basic cerebral reactions – are generated in the limbic system, along with most of the many appetites and urges that direct us to behave in a way that (usually) helps us to survive. But the limbic modules have many other functions besides: the thalamus is a sort of relay station, directing incoming information to the appropriate part of the brain for further processing. Beneath it the hypothalamus, together with the pituitary gland, constantly adjusts the body to keep it optimally

The Limbic System
The main modules

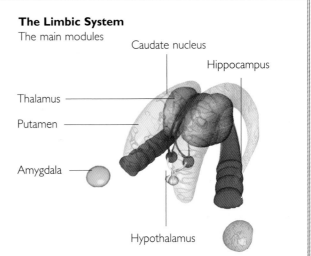

adapted to the environment. The hippocampus (named after a seahorse – a likeness that can only be discerned when the organ is seen in cross-section, using a lot of imagination) is essential for the laying down of long-term memory. The amygdala, in front of the hippo campus, is the place where fear is registered and generated.

Going down even further you get to the brainstem. This is the most ancient part of the brain – it evolved more than 500 million years ago and it is rather like the entire brain of present-day reptiles. For that reason it is often called the reptilian brain. The brainstem is formed from the nerves that run up from the body via the spinal column and it carries information from the body into the brain. Various clumps of cells in the brainstem determine the brain's general level of alertness and regulate the vegetative processes of the body, such as breathing, heartbeat and blood pressure.

Zoom in close enough on a section of brain and you will see a dense network of cells. Most of them are glial cells – relatively simple-looking structures whose main purpose is to glue the whole construction together and maintain its physical integrity.

Glial cells also play a role in amplifying or synchronizing electrical activity within the brain – they heighten nerve pain, such as sciatica, for example, by exciting the neurons that transmit pain signals.

RIGHT HEMISPHERE of the **Cerebral Cortex**

Gyrus

Corpus callosum

Medial view cut away to show the fan-shaped connective fibres of the cerebral cortex

Sulcus   'White matter'

Limbic System

Pineal gland

Amygdala

Thalamus

Hippocampus

Hypothalamus

Midbrain

Cerebellum

Pons

Medulla
Spinal cord

Spinal cord

LEFT HEMISPHERE of the **Cerebral Cortex**

The cells that actually create brain activity – about one in ten of the total – are neurons, cells which are adapted to carry an electrical signal from one to another. There are long thin ones that send single snaking tendrils to the far reaches of the body; star-shaped ones that reach out in all directions; and ones that bear a dense branching crown like absurdly overgrown antlers. Each neuron connects with up to 10,000 neighbours. The bits that join up are the branches, of which there are two kinds: axons, which conduct signals away from the cell nucleus, and dendrites, which receive incoming information.

If you zoom in even closer, you will see that there is a tiny gap where each axon meets a dendrite. This gap is called the synapse.

In order for the current to cross the synapse each axon secretes chemicals, called neurotransmitters, that are released into the space when the cell is suitably fired up. Some of these chemicals cause neighbouring cells to damp down their activity, but other make their neighbours fire, too, and the resultant chain effect produces simultaneous activity in millions of connected cells.

The things that happen down here among cells and molecules create the foundations of our mental lives and it is by manipulating them that most existing physical psychiatric therapies work. Antidepressants, for example, work on neurotransmitters – mainly enhancing the action of 'amines' such as serotonin, dopamine and noradrenalin. Research into microscopic brain processes is currently helping to develop drugs to relieve dementia, Parkinson's disease and stroke damage. Some scientists believe the secret of consciousness is to be found here or even at a more fundamental level – in the quantum processes thought to occur in the tiniest recesses of brain cells.

ONE BRAIN, ONE MIND, ONE LIFE

PAUL BROKS
Senior Clinical Lecturer,
University of Plymouth, UK

Though we may acknowledge, intellec-tually, that life finishes when we die, the notion that our mind can float free of our brains and survive our physical demise is peculiarly persistent. Neuropsychologist, writer, and play-wright Paul Broks examines the under-pinnings of that peculiar delusion.

We are incapable of imagining absolute noth-ingness. Our mental apparatus is tuned to states of being in the world. Non-being is simply beyond our ken. All of this is of no con-cern to those who believe in an afterlife. The conscious personality just floats on elsewhere. That most people hold to this bizarre belief is not simply due to religious indoctrination. The separateness of body and mind is a primordial intuition. It has sprung from our evolution as social beings and coalesced into the hardware of the central nervous system. Human beings are natural born soul makers, adept at extract-ing unobservable minds from the behaviour of observable bodies, including their own. Taking the next, false step, if mind and body are con-ceived as separate entities, it is easy to see the possibility of a mental life after physical death. This leads me to 'Broks's paradox': we are inclined to believe in mind-body dualism even though we understand it to be wrong. Neuroscientists are not exempt. Consider the following thought experiment, devised by the philosopher Derek Parfit. Some years hence you find yourself taking business trips to Mars. Teleportation is the usual mode of transport. It works like this. A scanner records the states of your body in atomic detail and digitally encodes the information for radio transmission. Your body is destroyed in the process but recon-structed on Mars using locally available materials as soon as the radio signals are decoded. The replication is perfect: identical body and brain, identical memory stores and patterns of mental activity. It is 'you'. You are in no doubt. Most neuroscientists say they would readily submit to this process. Why should they worry about destruction and reconstruction of the body? As good materialists, they know that 'the self' (secular cousin to the soul) is no more than a pattern of experiences and dispositions bundled together by the operations of the central nervous system. Now imagine this. There is a teleporter malfunction. You have been scanned and the information transmitted, but this time your body was not vaporised in the usual way. Your replica was automatically constructed and is going about its business. Worse still, the faulty scanner has left you with a fatal heart condition. You will be dead within days. Which would you rather be, the Martian replica or the moribund earth-bound version? It should make no difference to a true materialist. In scenario two, the vapori-sation process has been delayed, that is all. The personal trajectory of the individual arriving on Mars is the same for both scenarios. Psychological continuity has been maintained, as it is via the oblivion of sleep from one ordinary day to the next. But very few rest easy with scenario two. It shatters one's complacency about unprob-lematic teleportation (and therefore material-ism): 'If the replica's not me now...'

One might dismiss all this as 'angels on a pin-head' stuff. But it has great significance because belief in an afterlife divides the world. Rather than clinging to the notion that consciousness might survive death, we should treasure it all the more for its transience.

THE MIND MADE VISIBLE

SEMIR ZEKI
Professor of Neuroesthetics,
University College London

The recognition of beauty seems to be the most subjective, unquantifiable thing of all. Yet even this can be seen on a brain scan – and is no less marvellous for it.

Most people wonder at the fact that brain imaging techniques demonstrate with fair certainty that specific experiences – seeing red, say, or hearing a particular tone – correlate with activity in a specific area of the brain. But imaging techniques have gone way beyond that. Things that were thought to be outside the realm of objective observation are now the target of experimental studies which are proving hugely successful. Fear, expectation of reward, the experience of love and of beauty – all of them thought until recently to be unverifiable, or not easily verifiable, subjective experiences – have been shown to have neural correlates specific to them. To ascertain that someone is in love, for instance, I need only show them the picture of their [suspected] lover and note whether there is any activity in the brain areas that have been shown to correlate with feelings of love. In 2004, Hideaki Kawabata and I published a paper showing that the experience of beauty correlates with activity in the orbito-frontal cortex, a part of the brain that is linked to reward.

Hence the subjective experience could be localized and quantified. Ours is not the only study to show that the activity in specific parts of the brain is often quantifiably related to the declared subjective experience. At least two dozen other studies have shown the same result for different subjective experiences. This, it seems to me, is a major achievement of brain imaging studies. It brings subjective experiences firmly into the realm of measurable science.

The sensory impact of something in the outside world alters our subsequent perception of it, which in turn creates an altered impact, which further alters our perception …

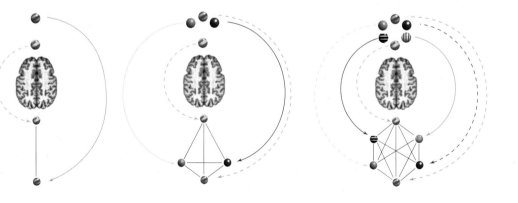

External stimulus

Internal links

mode which is associated with daydreaming, introspection and rumination. Sometimes, when a person undertakes a complex mental task or feels an intense emotion the entire cerebrum lights up.

Every incoming sensation stimulates a new pattern of neuronal activity, some of which create physical changes which allow them to be repeated in the form of memories. Most of these configurations, however, linger for just a fraction and then disappear, consigning to oblivion the experience they fleetingly incorporated.

Patterns that linger may in turn connect with, and spark off, activity in other groups, forming associations (learned knowledge) or combining to create new concepts. In theory, each time a particular interconnected group of neurons fires together it gives rise to the same fragment of thought, feeling or unconscious brain function; but in fact the brain is too fluid for an identical pattern of activity to be repeated – what actually happens is that similar but subtly mutated firing patterns occur. We never experience exactly the same thing twice.

Little explosions and waves of new activity, each with a characteristic pattern, are produced moment by moment as the brain reacts to outside stimuli. This activity in turn creates a constantly changing internal environment, which the brain then reacts to as well. This creates a feedback loop that ensures constant change.

Part of the brain's internal environment is a ceaseless pressure to seek out new stimuli and to gather information, especially about future events. As well as being useful as a guide for action, information-gathering is its own reward because it stirs a response in the neurons which create a feeling of pleasurable anticipation.[9] This greed for information is one of the fundamental properties of the brain and it is reflected in our most basic reactions. People can have the brain regions that support consciousness totally destroyed, yet their eyes will still scan the room and lock on to and track a moving object. The eye movements are triggered by the brainstem and are no more significant of consciousness than the turning of a flower to the sun. Yet even when you know this, it is deeply disturbing to have your movements followed by the eyes of a person you know is for all intents and purposes dead.

The loop-backs between brain and environment are a bootstrap operation *par excellence*. Computer simulations of neural networks show that the simplest network can develop phenomenal complexity in a short time if it is programmed to replicate patterns that are beneficial to its survival and junk those that aren't. Similarly, brain activity evolves in the individual.

This process – sometimes referred to as neural Darwinism – ensures that patterns that produce thoughts (and thus behaviour) that help the organism to thrive are laid down permanently while those that are useless fade. It is not a rigid system – the vast majority of brain patterns we produce are quite irrelevant to our survival – but overall this seems to be the way that the human brain has come to be furnished with its essential reactions.

Some of this furniture has been built in at genetic level. Certain patterns of brain activation – even quite complex ones like speech production – are so strongly inherited that only an extraordinarily abnormal environment can distort them. The pattern of brain activation during, say, a word retrieval task is usually similar enough among the dozen or so participants who typically take part in such studies for their scans to be overlaid and still show a clear pattern. This is how brain mappers can confidently talk of a chart of 'the' brain, rather than 'a' brain.

This is not to say that everyone thinks alike. Thanks to the infinitely complex interplay of nature and nurture no two brains are ever exactly the same. Even genetically identical twins – clones – have different brains by the time they are born because the tiny divergence in the foetal environment of each is enough to affect their development. The cortex of human twin babies is

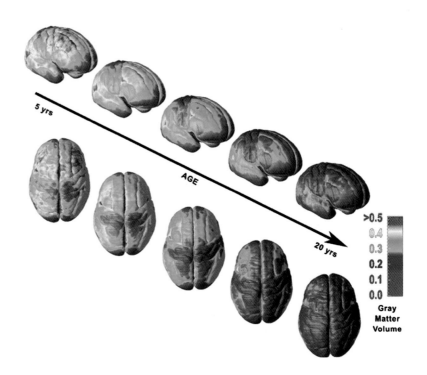

Right: *The brain develops from the back — areas mainly concerned with sensation and movement — through to the front, the areas concerned with decision-making, judgement and planning. Grey matter becomes thinner with maturation, as excess neurons are pruned away but the connections between the remainder become increasingly dense and efficient as they become sheathed by the fatty tissue known as myelin.*[10]

Below, right: *As the brain matures it becomes increasingly dense and develops a complex pattern of bulges (gyri) and valleys (sulci).*

visibly different at birth, and structural variations inevitably produce differences in the way brains function.[11] Indeed, the brain structure of so called identical twins is actually less similar at birth than later, suggesting that genes have a stronger effect in later life than at first. Hence twins may become more alike in their behaviour as they age, rather than less.[12, 13]

During foetal development the brain develops, bulb-like, at the upper end of the neural tube that forms the spine. The main sections of the brain, including the cerebral cortex, are visible within seven weeks of conception and by the time the child is born the brain contains roughly the same number of neurons – some 100 billion – as it will have as an adult.

These neurons are not mature, however. Many of their axons are as yet unsheathed by myelin – the insulation that allows signals to pass along them – and the connections between them are sparse. Hence large areas of the infant brain, and particularly in the cerebral cortex, are not functioning. Brain imaging studies of babies' brains show the most active areas are those associated with bodily regulation (the brainstem), sensation

25 week   30 week   33 week

TERM   ADULT

(thalamus) and movement (deep cerebellum).[14]

The uterine environment has a profound effect on the wiring of the infant brain. Babies born to drug addicts are frequently addicted at birth, and those born to mothers who eat curries or garlic while they are pregnant take to spicy food more readily than others,[15, 16] suggesting that their tastes are primed by exposure to the residue of such foods in their mothers' blood.

Life in the womb provides a good example of how genes and environment are inextricably combined. A male foetus, for example, has genes that provoke the mother's body to produce a cascade of hormones, including testosterone, at certain times in its development. This hormonal deluge physically alters the male foetus's brain, slowing the development of certain parts and speeding the development of others. The effect of this is to masculinize the foetal brain, priming it to produce male sexual behaviour. It also creates many of the typical differences seen between the sexes, like girls' superiority at speech and boys' at spatial tasks. If a male foetus does not get the appropriate pre-birth hormone treatment, his brain is likely to remain more typically female; if a female foetus gets exposed to a male-pattern hormonal sequence, she is likely to be more typically masculine.[17]

Inside the developing brain individual neurons race about looking for a linked team of other neurons to join as though in some frantic party game. Every cell has to find its place in the general scheme, and if it fails it dies in the ruthless pruning process known as apoptosis or programmed cell death. The purpose of apoptosis in the immature brain is to strengthen and rationalize the connections between those that are left, and to prevent the brain becoming literally overstuffed with its own cells. This 'sculpting' process, though essential, may also have a price. The connections that get killed off during it include some that may otherwise confer the sort of intuitive skills we label gifts. Eidetic (photograph) memory, for example, is quite common among young children but usually disappears during the years of cerebral pruning. Incomplete apoptosis may also account for synaesthesia, the 'cross-wiring' that bonds one sensory experience (feeling blue, say) to another (hearing a tone) so that when one is experienced , so is the other. Conversely, apoptosis that runs wild and strips out far too many connections is thought to be one of the causes of impaired intelligence in Down's syndrome[18] and autism.[19] It is also probably the reason why Down's people are more likely than others to develop Alzheimer's disease.

Newborn   6 months   2 years

The connections between neurons are sparse at birth (above, left)*, but new links are made at a terrific rate during infancy, reaching maximum density around the age of six. Thereafter they thin out again as unused connections die off, leaving only those which are useful.*

Adults can increase neural connections throughout their life by learning new things. But if the brain is not used the connections will become further depleted. New brain cells are made throughout life — a process called neurogenesis — and some new cells are incorporated into existing networks, especially those concerned with memory and learning.

Climbing to consciousness

A baby's brain contains some things that an adult's does not. There are, for example, connections between the auditory and visual cortices, and others between the retina and the part of the thalamus that takes in sound. These connections probably give the infant the experience of 'seeing' sounds and 'hearing' colours – a condition that occasionally continues into adulthood and is known as synaesthesia. Babies show emotion dramatically, but the areas of the brain that in adults are linked to the conscious experience of emotions are not active in a newborn baby. Such emotions may therefore be unconscious.

'Unconscious emotion' sounds like a contradiction in terms – what is emotion if not a conscious feeling? In fact, the conscious appreciation of emotion is looking more and more like one quite small, and sometimes inessential, element of a system of survival mechanisms that mainly operate – even in adults – at an unconscious level.[20]

This does not necessarily mean that early traumas do not matter. Unconscious emotion may not be, strictly speaking, experienced, but it may lodge in the brain just the same. We cannot remember things before the age of about three because until then the hippocampus – the brain nucleus that lays down conscious long-term memories – is not mature. Emotional memories, however, may be stored in the amygdala, a tiny nugget of deeply buried tissue that is probably functioning at birth.[21] The way a baby is treated during those first amnesiac years may even alter the way that their genes function. The genes of baby rats that are well-nurtured behave differently to those in identical twins who are neglected, and the difference causes changes in the brains of the nurtured animals which results in them showing less anxiety. A study of brain cells taken from adult suicide victims who had been abused in childhood suggests that a similar thing occurs in people.[22]

As the baby gets older myelinization creeps outward and brings increasing numbers of brain areas 'on-line'.[23] The parietal cortex starts to work fairly soon, making babies intuitively aware of the fundamental spatial qualities of the world. Peek-a-boo games are endlessly intriguing once this part of the brain is working because babies then know that faces cannot really disappear behind hands – yet the brain modules that will

one day allow them to know why have not yet matured.

The frontal lobes first kick in at about six months, bringing the first glimmerings of cognition. By the age of one they are gaining control over the drives of the limbic system – if you offer two toys to a child of this age, they will make a choice rather than try to grab both. Up until the age of about a year babies are, in the words of one developmental psychologist, 'robotic looking machines' – their attention can be caught by more

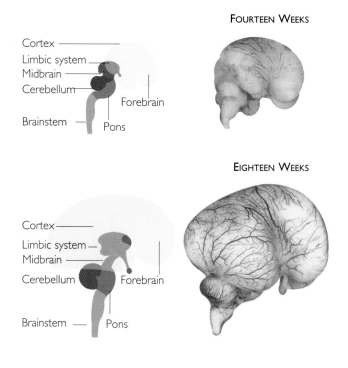

FOURTEEN WEEKS

Cortex
Limbic system
Midbrain
Cerebellum
Forebrain
Brainstem
Pons

EIGHTEEN WEEKS

Cortex
Limbic system
Midbrain
Cerebellum   Forebrain
Brainstem   Pons

SIX MONTHS

Parietal lobe   Frontal lobe
Occipital lobe   Limbic area

Parietal lobe
Occipital lobe
Temporal lobe

or less any visual stimulus. After that age they get an agenda of their own – not always one that fits in with other people's.

The language areas become active during the second year. The one that confers understanding (Wernicke's area) comes online at about 12 months, followed some 18 months later by the one that produces speech (Broca's area),[24] so there is a short time when toddlers understand more than they can say – a frustrating condition that probably does much to fuel the tantrums that typify the 'Terrible Twos'.

Around the same time as the language areas become active myelinization gets under way in the prefrontal lobes. Now children develop self-consciousness – they no longer point at their reflection in the mirror as though they see another child and if a dab of coloured powder is put on their face while they look at their reflection, they rub it off – they don't rub the mirror as younger children do. This self-consciousness suggests the emergence of an internal executor – the 'I' that most people say they feel exists inside their heads.

Certain brain areas take many years to mature. A nucleus called the reticular formation, for example, which plays a major role in maintaining attention, usually only becomes fully myelinated at or after puberty, which is why prepubescent children have a short attention span. The frontal lobes do not become fully myelinated until full adulthood. These parts of the brain are responsible for reasoning, judgement, and inhibiting emotion, and until they are mature people are driven more by emotion than sense. Hence young adults are more emotional and impulsive than those who are older, and more likely to take daft risks and commit crimes of 'passion'.[25]

Human brains are at their most plastic during infancy. You can take away an entire hemisphere from a child's brain and the other will rewire itself to take on the tasks of both. It will even manage to develop functions that are usually exclusive to its other half. As we age, however, brain functions become more rigid and more distinctive. By the time we are adults our mental landscapes are so individual that no two of us will see anything in quite the same way. A couple watching the same film, for example, would probably have entirely different patterns of neural activity because each would be cogitating on different aspects of the show and associating what they see with personal thoughts and memories. She might be wondering when the tiresome couple on screen will finally reach their feel-good ending so she can get some dinner; he might be thinking how the heroine's cute upper lip reminds him of his ex-girlfriend.

That is why experiments designed to reveal which brain areas are responsible for what have to involve artificially rigid and narrow tasks. The subjects who lay for more than two hours in a PET scanner doing nothing more than lifting a finger in response to a given signal, for example, must at times have wondered what possible insight could be gained from such a tedious manoeuvre.

In fact, wonderful discoveries are emerging from these unpromising exercises. The finger-lifting experiment, carried out by Chris Frith and colleagues at the Wellcome Department of Cognitive Neurology in London, revealed something that, not so long ago, would have been expected to remain one of life's eternal mysteries: the source of self-determination. They arrived at it by designing a procedure that first narrowed down what was going on in the participants' brains to a few things that they already knew from previous work would show up as particular patterns of activity in certain brain localities. In this case they got the subjects to move a specified finger on cue – a task that duly provoked activity in the somatosensory cortex (when the cue was a noise) and the motor cortex (the area that controls movement). They then added the element of the task for which they wanted to find a brain location: self-willed activity. Instead of telling the

The death mask of Phineas Gage showing the massive injury to the skull.

Reconstruction of the position of the rod which passed through the frontal lobe of Gage's brain.

This daguerreotype (an very early type of photograph) is thought to be of Phineas Gage. For years its owners, image librarians Jack and Beverly Wilgus, assumed it was a picture of a harpoon-bearing whaler who had survived a brush with an angry whale. In 2008, however, an historian spotted it on an internet site and suggested it might be the only surviving image of Gage. Subsequent research by the Wilgus' showed this is almost certainly the case.[28]

subjects which finger to lift they left it to them to decide which one to move. Then they watched to see how the brain activity involved in doing this differed from the brain activity involved in lifting an externally specified finger.

The difference was clear: as soon as the participants started to make their own decisions a previously 'dead' area of their brains sprang into life. The elegant and careful design of the experiment made sure that the bit of brain identified is almost certainly that which, quite specifically, allows people to do things of their own volition.[26]

Can identifying the brain activity involved in deciding which of two fingers to lift possibly shed any light on decision-making in the messy and infinitely more complicated world outside a brain research laboratory?

Indirectly, yes. The region of brain in which the self-will area was found is the prefrontal cortex, a region of the frontal cortex which lies mainly behind the forehead. Injuries to this area often produce a characteristic change in behaviour that includes loss of self-determination on a grand scale. The classic case is that of Phineas Gage, a nineteenth-century rail-worker who lost a large chunk of forebrain when a steel rod was blown through his skull by a mis-timed explosion. Gage survived, but from the time of the accident he changed from a purposeful, industrious worker into a drunken drifter. John Harlow, the doctor who treated him, described the new Gage as devising many plans of future operations which are no sooner arranged than they are abandoned... a child in his intellectual capacity and manifestations yet with the animal passions of a strong man.' Ladies were advised not to stay in his presence. The hallmark of Gage's new condition was his complete inability to direct or control himself.[27]

If self-determination lies in a specific bit of tissue, it follows that those who appear not to have it may simply be unlucky – victims of a sluggish brain module. So is it reasonable to blame the Phineas Gages of today for their ways? Should we be unsympathetic to addicts who fail to conquer their habit, or punish recidivist criminals?

The current discoveries about the brain are breathing new life into this ages-old debate. Some types of antisocial behaviour are clearly linked to brain damage or malfunction so perhaps we should accept the way forward is to manipulate the brains of troublesome individuals rather than, as now, punishing them or trying to change their behaviour by persuasion or coercion. If the idea sends shivers down your back, think of what we do to such people now. Is an artificially induced change of mind worse than a stretch in prison?

Windows on the Mind

The safety video that comes with one brand of MRI scanner shows a man walking up to the machine with a metal wrench in his hand. When he gets within a few feet the hand with the wrench in it suddenly shoots up and his arm locks into a rigid horizontal salute with the wrench pointing straight at the scanner. The next few seconds have a cartoon quality as the man engages in a tug-of-war with an unseen rival. As he inches nearer to the machine the wrench starts to quiver like a banner in a wind-tunnel, then slips through his clenched fingers towards the mouth of the scanner. The man clutches it with both hands and leans back, but he obviously cannot keep hold. Suddenly the tool jettisons forward into the tube, where it smashes into a strate-gically placed brick. The force of the impact is so great the brick is pulverized.

The scene is meant to show the dangers of taking metal near an MRI scanner. These machines are basically massive, circular magnets. Their gravitational pull is some 140,000 times greater than that of the earth — it is easy to see that the consequences of entering one with, say, a heart pacemaker in place, would be catastrophic. If you do not happen to have any metal about your person, however, fMRI scanning seems to be perfectly safe — no one has yet reported any detrimental biological effect from it.

Powerful scanning techniques like fMRI are opening the brain to scrutiny in a way undreamt of until a couple of decades ago. But brain mapping began long before fancy scanning machines were invented.

The two main language areas, which are still among the most important cortical landmarks on the map, were identified by Broca and Wernicke more than a hundred years ago. They did it by looking at the brains of people with speech

---

THE SEARCH FOR THE MIND

The first known brain map is found on an Egyptian papyrus thought to date from 3,000 to 2,500 BC.[29] In medieval times 'cell theory' placed various human attributes – spirit, thinking and so on – in the ventricles. Then, in the early seventeenth century the French philosopher René Descartes conceived the notion that mind existed in a separate sphere from the material universe. The brain was a sort of radio receiver that tapped into the dimension of mind via the pineal gland – the only brain component Descartes could find that was not replicated in each hemisphere.

Cartesian dualism was dominant for centuries.

But there were always scientists who held that mind and brain function were one and the same, and during the nineteenth and early twentieth centuries many of them worked feverishly hard to produce coherent brain maps. Brain mapping went out of favour, though, when the American neurologist Karl Lashley persuaded most of his colleagues that higher cognitive functions were the result of 'mass action' of neurons, and were therefore not susceptible to localization. But now brain scanning techniques are showing just how precisely it is possible to pin down even the most sophisticated and complex machinations of the human brain.

SCANNING THE BRAIN

The neuroscientific revolution has been driven by the development of increasingly sophisticated imaging technology, in particular the machines that show brain activity as well as anatomy. Each of the techniques below has its own advantages and drawbacks and it is becoming increasingly common for researchers to combine two or more techniques to give a more complete picture.

Diffusion Tensor Imaging is a form of MRI which measures the diffusion of water through fibrous tissue. It is particularly good at showing the connections between different areas of the brain and is therefore likely to shed ever greater light on how the brain's various modules interact.

Functional MRI (fMRI) elaborates this basic anatomical picture by adding to it the areas of greatest brain activity. Neuronal firing is fuelled by glucose and oxygen, which are carried in blood. When an area of the brain is fired up, these substances flow towards it, and fMRI shows up the areas where there is most oxygen. The latest scanners can produce four images every second. The brain takes about half a second to react to a stimulus, so this rapid scanning technique can clearly show the ebb and flow of activity in different parts of the brain as it reacts to various stimuli or undertakes different tasks. fMRI is proving to be the most rewarding of scanning techniques, but it is phenomenally expensive and brain mappers often have to share a machine with clinicians who have more pressing claims to it. For this reason a lot of experimental work is still done by the older technique of:

Positron Emission Topography (PET). PET achieves a similar end result to fMRI – it identifies the brain areas that are working hardest by measuring their fuel intake. The pictures produced by PET are very clear but they cannot achieve the same fine resolution as fMRI. The technique also has a serious drawback in that it requires an injection into the blood-

stream of a radioactive marker. The dose of radioactivity given in each scan is tiny but, for safety, no one person is generally allowed to have more than one scanning session a year.

Near-Infra-red Spectroscopy (NIRS) also produces an image based on the amount of fuel being gobbled at any moment by each part of the brain. It works by beaming low-level light waves into the brain and measuring the varying amount that is reflected from each area. NIRS is cheaper than fMRI and does not use radioactivity but it cannot (yet) give a clear picture of what happens in the deepest regions of the brain.

Electroencephalography (EEG) measures brainwaves – the electrical patterns created by the rhythmic oscillations of neurons. These waves show characteristic changes according to the type of brain activity that is going on. EEG measures these waves by picking up signals via electrodes placed in the skull. The latest version of EEG takes readings from dozens of different spots and compares them, building up a picture of varying activity across the brain. Brain mapping with EEG often uses Event-Related Potentials (ERPs), which simply means that an electrical peak (potential) is related to a particular stimulus like a word or a touch.

Magnetoencephalography (MEG) is similar to EEG in that it picks up signals from neuronal oscillation, but it does it by homing in on the tiny magnetic pulse they give off rather than the electric field. It still has teething problems: the signals, for example, are weak and easily masked by interference. Yet it has enormous potential because it is faster than other scanning techniques and can therefore chart changes in brain activity more accurately than fMRI or PET.

disorders and noting that those with the same problems all had damage in the same place. Broca located the area that allows us to articulate speech by post-mortem examination of the brains of people who were unable (usually as the result of a stroke) to get words out. His classic case was a man named Tan.

Tan was so-called because that was what he said when he was asked his name. It was also what he said when he was asked his date of birth, his address and what he wanted for dinner. 'Tan' was all that Tan could say, even though he understood speech perfectly well.

Broca had to wait until Tan was dead before he could look at his brain and see which bit was injured. Today, scanners allow neuroscientists to locate injured tissue in living patients, greatly speeding the process of working out what the injured bit does in a normal brain.

Another time-honoured technique is to stimulate different areas of the brain directly and see what effect it has. It was by doing this that the surgeons in California brought about so much amusement in their epilepsy patient and thus came across part of the circuitry which produces our sense of humour.

Direct stimulation was pioneered in the 1950s by the Canadian neurosurgeon Wilder Penfield, who charted large regions of the cerebral cortex by applying electrodes to different areas in the brains of hundreds of epilepsy patients. He demonstrated in this way that the entire body surface is represented on the brain's surface as though it had been drawn on: the bit that affects the arm lies next to the bit that affects the elbow, and the bit that affects the elbow is next to the bit that affects the upper arm and so on. More famously, he found that stimulating points in the temporal lobes produced what seemed to be vivid childhood memories, or snatches of long-forgotten tunes.

Most patients reported these recollections as dream-like, yet crystal clear. 'It was like …

Language

Movement, sensation

Visual processing

Thinking

Functional MRI has helped identify which bits of the brain are involved in specific mental tasks.

standing in the doorway at [my] high school,' reported a 21-year-old man. 'I heard my mother talking on the phone, telling my aunt to come over that night,' said another, '... my nephew and niece were visiting at my home ... they were getting ready to go home, putting on their coats and hats ... in the dining room ... my mother was talking to them. She was rushed – in a hurry.'[30]

RIVERS OF THE MIND

Different types of cells secrete different neurotransmitters. Information moves through the brain along neural pathways – tracts or chains of neurons which secrete the same chemicals and which spark one another off. Hence they link areas of the brain in much the same way as a train links stations along the line, causing them to flare up (or close down) in succession. Each brain chemical works in widely spread but fairly specific brain locations and may have a different effect according to where it is activated. Some neurotransmitters are excitatory – that is, they encourage the cells they come in contact with to fire. Others have the effect of shutting down neural activity. Hundreds of different neurotransmitters have been identified, but the most important seem to be:

Serotonin: the neurotransmitter that is enhanced by Prozac, and is sometimes referred to as the 'feel-good' chemical. Serotonin certainly has a profound effect on mood and anxiety – high levels of it (or sensitivity to it) are associated with serenity and optimism. However, it also has effects in many other areas, including sleep, pain, appetite and blood pressure.

Serotonin pathways

Acetylcholine (ACh): controls activity in brain areas connected with attention, learning and memory. People with Alzheimer's disease typically have low levels of ACh in the cerebral cortex, and drugs that boost its action may improve memory in such patients.

Noradrenaline: mainly an excitatory chemical that induces physical and mental arousal and heightens mood. Production is centred in an area of the brain called the locus coeruleus, which is one of several putative candidates for the brain's 'pleasure' centre.

Glutamate: the brain's major excitatory neurotransmitter, vital for forging the links between neurons that are the basis of learning and long-term memory.

Enkephalins and Endorphins: endogenous opioids that – like the drugs – modulate pain, reduce stress and promote a sensation of floaty, oceanic calm. They also depress physical functions like breathing and may produce physical dependence.

Oxytocin: helps 'melt the edges' of one's psyche, creating a sense of oneness with others and so creating bonds of warmth and trust between people, especially mothers and babies and lovers. It is produced in huge quantities by women during childbirth and by both sexes during orgasm.

THE DOPAMINE CONNECTION

Dopamine identifies potential rewards and sends us scurrying after them. In the process it generates desire, anticipation and excitement.

Dopamine pathways snake around the brain, doing different things in different places. Deep in the brain stem, dopamine-producing neurons in an area called the substantia nigra get and keep us going – physically as well as

mentally. When these cells degenerate, as happens in Parkinson's disease, a person loses their ability to stride out, both in thought and overt movement.

Another set of tracks is known as the brain's 'reward circuit'. They run from the Ventral Tegmental area to the amygdala, nucleus accumbens, septum and prefrontal cortex (known collectively as the medial forebrain bundle (MFB)). When stimulated by dopamine, the nucleus accumbens gets the body geared up to grab or chase the object of desire, while the amygdala registers its value and helps produce the conscious sensation of excitement and the prefrontal cortex and septum fixes the person's attention on the goal. Together these responses generate a pleasurable 'high'. However, they do not produce a sense of lasting satisfaction, so unless mediated by other neurotransmitters, a dopamine charge tends to be followed by the need for another, and another – the basis of psychological addiction. Dopamine is also involved in generating meaning – the feeling that the world 'hangs together'. Dopamine disturbances may therefore produce a sense of things 'falling apart', or, conversely, that everything is drenched in significance and connected in a wonderfully holistic way.

While such disturbances are dysfunctional there's nothing to say that the view of the world they afford is any less realistic than that delivered by normal dopamine function. This is set by evolution at an optimum level – high enough to keep us chasing those things we need such as food and reproductive opportunities, but not so high that we start to see our mortal enemies as part of a great, loving super-consciousness. This does not, however, mean that the 'optimal view' reflects the truth of the world.

Penfield's findings were widely interpreted at the time as showing that memories are stored in discreet packets ('engrams') just waiting to be revived. Since then, though a more complex arrangement has come to light. Long-term memories are distributed through the brain, encoded in the same parts of it that gave rise to the original experience. A childhood recollection of eating ice cream on a sunny day in the country with birds singing, for instance, would be stored in several sensory areas: the ice-cream taste in the 'taste' processing areas of the brain, the feeling of sun on your skin in the somatosensory cortex, the sound of the birds in the auditory cortex, the sight of trees in the visual brain and so on. Because they were originally experienced all together, when one part of the memory is triggered the other parts tend to be triggered too, reproducing a 'whole' memory from a bunch of separate bits. Penfield was probably stimulating just one sensory facet of the memory but eliciting a response in many.

The area stimulated in the laughing patient has similarly been found to be just one node of a much larger brain module — one which has its roots in the most primitive regions of our brains. The neat little 'spots' currently marking particular functions will almost certainly turn out to be the exposed peaks of mainly buried neural conglomerates — icebergs of the mind.

It is possible, too, that areas that light up when a certain mental task is performed are not themselves responsible for that task, but are simply registering it passing on a stimulus to the bit that is. There is an apocryphal story of a scientist who claimed to have discovered that frogs heard through their legs. When challenged to prove it he produced a frog that he had trained to jump on command. After demonstrating the frog's trick he picked the animal up and cut off its legs. Then he put it back on the table and told it, again, to jump. Naturally, it did not. 'There!' said the scientist, triumphantly. 'You see — it can no longer hear my voice!'

Another problem is that some of the apparent neural activity seen in brains may just be interference in the system – random blips. One researcher discovered this while working on the protocol of an fMRI study designed to examine the neural activity involved in social interaction. Rather than ask a human subject to sit in the scanner during the lengthy and tedious tests, the researcher used a passive 'test object' — a dead fish. The fish, a handsome Atlantic salmon, had been purchased in a state of unquestionable deadness from a local fish shop and, unsurprisingly, it showed no discernable reaction to the 'series of photographs depicting human individuals in social situations' that were presented to it. When the scans were examined, however, the area that matched the location of the fish's tiny brain appeared to show that the fish was *actually thinking* about the pictures it had been shown.

Brain mappers are trying hard to avoid falling into traps like these but sometimes, inevitably, they do. According to some there is still too much of the gold rush about this science — too many researchers trying to stake out new claims rather than replicating the findings of others. Yet the ground is firming up. Standard scanning protocols are being adopted that have drastically reduced the number of rogue results, and methodology — particularly the problems of designing experiments that give unambiguous results — is a constant concern. The New Phrenologists are determined that their discoveries — unlike those of Franz Gall — will stand the test of time.

DEVELOPMENT OF THE SOCIAL BRAIN IN ADOLESCENCE

SARAH-JAYNE BLAKEMORE
Royal Society University Research Fellow and UCL Reader in Cognitive Neuroscience.

Sarah-Jayne Blakemore's research focuses on the development of mentalising, action understanding and executive function during adolescence, using a variety of behavioural and neuroimaging methods.

Thanks to modern brain-imaging techniques, scientists are discovering that the human brain changes well beyond early childhood. Some brain regions – in particular, the prefrontal cortex (PFC) – continue to develop during adolescence and even beyond. The PFC is involved in a wide range of cognitive abilities, including planning and decision making. It is also part of the the network of brain regions involved in understanding other people.

At the beginning of adolescence, around the onset of puberty, there are dramatic changes in hormone levels and consequent alterations in physical appearance. This period of life is also characterised by psychological changes related to mood, self-consciousness, one's sense of identity, and one's relationships with others. The recent neuroscience studies suggest that hormones alone do not account for these psychological changes.

Understanding other people involves reading their behaviour in terms of their intentions and desires, a process called mentalising. A small number of recent brain-imaging studies have looked at the development of the functioning of the social brain during adolescence. There is now consistent evidence that activity in the medial prefrontal cortex during mentalising tasks decreases between the onset of adolescence and the beginning of adulthood. For example, a recent fMRI study by A.T. Wang investigated the development of communicative intent using an irony-comprehension task. Understanding irony requires separating the literal from the intended meaning of a comment. The medial PFC in children was more engaged than the medial PFC in adults during this task. The authors interpreted the increased medial PFC activity in children as reflecting the need to integrate several cues to resolve the discrepancy between the literal and intended meaning of an ironic remark.

A similar region of the medial prefrontal cortex was more highly activated by children than by adults in a recent fMRI study that involved thinking about one's own intentions. Thinking about your own (or someone else's) intentions to act requires mentalising. A group of adolescents and a group of female adults were presented with scenarios about intentions and actions (e.g. 'you want to find out what is on at the theatre. Do you look in a newspaper?'). The medial PFC was more active in the adolescents than in the adults when thinking about intentions.

The decrease in activity in the medial PFC during adolescence may happen because adolescence is a time when the prefrontal cortex is being fine-tuned by synaptic pruning, and a decreasing amount of activity is therefore necessary to carry out the task in question. An alternative (or additional) explanation is that there is a change in the cognitive strategy for mentalising that results in the recruitment of other brain regions.

This research shows that the human brain continues to be malleable for decades and that adolescence is a particularly important time in terms of neural change.

EVOLUTION

The human brain carries the story of its evolution in its anatomy. It began in water when fish developed a tube to carry nerves from the distant parts of their body to a central control point. First there was just a bulge on top of the spine, then the nerves started to sort themselves into specialized modules. Some became sensitive to molecules and formed what is now our smell brain. Others became light sensitive and formed eyes. These were connected to a clump that controlled movement – the cerebellum. This collection formed the reptilian brain, mechanical and unconscious. Its basic parts are still intact and form the lowest of the three-tier system that has developed since.

fish brain

On top of this, more modules developed: the thalamus, allowing sight, smell and hearing to be used together; the amygdala and hippocampus, creating a crude memory system; and the hypothalamus, making it possible for the organism to react to more stimuli. This is the mammalian brain, known as the limbic system. Emotions are generated here but their conscious acknowledgement – what we think of as 'anger' or 'fear' – occurs when the limbic system passes on the information to the more recently evolved cortex.

reptilian brain

mammalian brain

The cortex came into existence during mmalian evolution when the sense modules triggered the development of a thin matrix of cells, whose shape allowed for many neural connections to be formed between them with only a small increase in size. This skin became the cortex and it is from this that consciousness emerged. The mammals that were to evolve into humans developed an ever-larger cortex, pushing the cerebellum back to the position it now occupies. *Australopithecus Africanus* had a fairly human-shaped brain 3 million years ago, but it was only a third the size of a modern brain. One and a half million years ago the hominid brain underwent an explosive enlargement. So sudden was it that the bones of the skull were pushed outwards, creating the high, flat forehead and domed head that distinguish us from primates. The areas that expanded most are those concerned with thinking, planning, organizing and communicating.

human brain

Many theories have been put forward to account for mankind's 'great leap forward' and it is likely that it happened due to a combination of factors.

Bipedalism

Hominids were on their feet about 4 million years ago. It may have come about because they lived in swamps and along shores and needed to be able to wade. Or it may have happened when they were living in the Savannah and found that standing gave them the advantage of seeing further.

Bipedalism freed up the hands, which may have led to tool-making, which in turn encouraged finer and more sophisticated manual dexterity. It is also thought to have caused the larynx to descend, allowing breath to be controlled and thus for sounds to be articulated – a necessity for structured language.

Aquatic lifestyle

Early humans may have undergone a long aquatic or semi-aquatic period which led to them evolving hairless skin, hooded nose, sebaceous glands and other distinct physical features of modern humans. According to this theory, brain development was accelerated by the seafood diet, which contains large amounts of 'brain-building' fatty acids. It also led to bipedalism, in order to wade through swamps.

Tool use

Tool-making occurred more than 2.5 million years ago and the process of making tools may have enhanced hand/eye coordination. The manual dexterity required may also have primed the brain to make expressive gestures, allowing communication at a distance, which in turn facilitated hunting and helped to encourage communication and thus bonding in tribes. Gestures are thought to be the forerunners of language and the area in the left hemisphere which was originally given over to them has subsequently developed into the language area, which is unique to humans.

Hunting

Effective tools and better tribal communication led in turn to greater hunting success which gave access to an even more protein-rich diet capable of supporting the energy requirements of a bigger brain. Hence a positive feedback loop developed in which better tools and communication led to increased brain growth which further improved tool-making and communication.

Extended infancy

Brain growth plus bipedalism meant that infants had to be born at an earlier stage of maturity than most animals. Had gestation been longer the baby's head would be bigger, and the female pelvis would have had to become so wide to accommodate it that she would have been unable to run.

The helplessness of the human infant meant that mothers were increasingly dependent on the support of the group, and thus those who had brains best able to function socially would have had an evolutionary advantage and flourished. Extended childhood also gave humans extra time to learn and rehearse adult behaviours. The brain could remain plastic – and therefore open to change and development – for longer.

Language

Language is thought to be the springboard for the relatively sudden blossoming of culture that started about 80,000 years ago. Language creates a framework for abstract thought, which in turn facilitates the development of self-reflection and the ability to imagine future and distant worlds, and therefore to plan and innovate.

Social grouping

Humans lived in relatively large groups and the pressure therefore to understand, manipulate and communicate with others acted as an evolutionary pressure on the development of social skills, language and abstract thinking.

CHAPTER TWO
THE GREAT DIVIDE

The human brain is a marriage of two minds. Each of its twin hemispheres is a physical mirror image of the other, and if one hemisphere is lost early in life, the other may take over and fulfil the functions of both. Normally, though, the two are bound together by a band of fibre that conveys a continuous, intimate dialogue between them. Information arriving in one half is almost instantly available to the other and their responses are so closely harmonized that it produces an apparently seamless perception of the world and a single stream of consciousness.
Separate these hemispheres, however, and the differences between them become apparent. Each half of a mature brain has its own strengths and weaknesses; its own way of processing information and its own special skills. They might even exist in two distinct realms of consciousness: two individuals, effectively, in one skull.

A – vision

sinister *adj.* **1.** Threatening or suggesting evil or harm; ominous. **2.** Evil or treacherous. [C15: from Latin **sinister** – on left-hand side] – *Collins English Dictionary, third edition*

THE LEFT BRAIN IS WHAT HAS MADE *Homo sapiens* the spectacularly successful species it is. It is calculating, communicative and capable of conceiving and executing complicated plans. But it has always had a bad press. It is frequently held to represent the worst of the Western world: materialistic, controlling and unfeeling; while the right brain is seen as gentle, emotional and more at one with the natural world – a frame of mind commonly associated with the East.

B – touch

This notion has spawned a small industry of specialized self-help books and training courses that claim to encourage right-brain thinking. There are books that show you how to draw with your right brain, ride horses with your right brain, even make love with your right brain. You can take all manner of courses to put you back in touch with your right half, and big businesses hire consultants to test their employees for left/right dominance and slot them into appropriate jobs.

Is it all nonsense? Brain scientists will tell you the idea of a rigid divide is a popular myth. They even have a word for the public's enthusiasm for the subject: 'dichotomania'. Like 'modern phrenology' the word is a put-down, intended to imply that the real situation is far too complex for simple conclusions to be drawn.

C – hearing

It is true that the brain is marvellously complicated, and the constant interaction of its two hemispheres makes it extremely difficult to pinpoint what is happening where. Even the most obviously lateralized of skills – language – is atypically organized in about 5 per cent of people and tends to shift rightwards (typically) in the course of a person's lifetime.[1] The brain is also very malleable and its wiring can be influenced by all sorts of environmental factors. Given extraordinary circumstances a genetically typical brain may end up organized in a very odd way indeed. Nevertheless, brain imaging studies confirm that the two hemispheres really do have quite distinctive ways of operating, and they seem to be 'hard-wired' to the extent that, in normal

D – smell

Most sensory input to the brain crosses over from the incoming side to the opposite hemisphere for processing. Once the information enters one hemisphere it is swiftly sent on to the other via the corpus callosum. A. Visual input from the left half of each eye goes to the right hemisphere and vice versa. B. Apart from certain facial nerves, the neural pathways from the body also end up in the opposite side of the brain. C. Most auditory input is processed on the opposite side of the brain to the ear through which it enters. D. Smell is the exception to the cross-over rule – odours are processed on the same side as the nostril that senses them.

circumstances, certain skills will always develop on a particular side.

The layout, furthermore, is more or less as is popularly conceived. The left brain is analytical, logical, precise and time-sensitive. The right brain is dreamier, it processes things in a holistic way rather than breaking them down and it is more involved with sensory perception than abstract cognition.[2]

In working out the meaning of a verbal message, for instance, the left hemisphere tends to root around in memory to see what the words are likely to signify, and then come up with what the person expects to hear. The right hemisphere, by contrast, is inclined to interpret the message in the context of the information that is coming in right then and there rather than pre-judging what it means.[3] This makes the left hemisphere very *efficient* at understanding messages – but not very smart; subtle discrepancies between the context in which something is said and its literal translation (the person who smirks as they say sorry, for instance) are lost on it. The right hemisphere, by contrast, might understand the whole message very clearly but be unable to describe how it knows it. The right hemisphere's relative inability to articulate its knowledge means that they are experienced as 'hunches' or intuitions rather than as clear thoughts.

There is truth, too, in the idea that the right brain is more emotional than the left. In particular it is responsible for fearful and mournful feelings and for general pessimism. This is why people who suffer severe left-brain strokes quite commonly behave as though what has happened is a catastrophe, even if the disabilities they suffer as a result are relatively mild. What seems to happen in these cases is that the damaged left brain can no longer keep the right brain subjugated, so the right hemisphere floods consciousness with its own intensely emotional reactions.

Patients with bad right-brain damage, by contrast, sometimes appear to be entirely unmoved by it, maintaining an optimistic, what-the-hell sanguinity in the face of what might otherwise be quite dreadful suffering. In the most extreme cases they refuse to recognize their shortcomings at all. A very senior American judge is said to have caused huge embarrassment after a severe right-brain stroke because he insisted on continuing at the bench despite having lost his ability to weigh evidence in anything like a sensible way. He maintained an exceptionally jolly courtroom, happily allowing serious criminals to go free while occasionally dispatching minor offenders to lifelong prison sentences. He resisted his colleagues' attempts to persuade him to retire and was finally sacked. He seemed perfectly content – if puzzled – by this turn of events, and subsequently enjoyed a long and happy retirement.

Sometimes this sublime disregard for their condition is taken to such extremes that people with right-hemisphere injuries fail to notice frankly disabling conditions like paralysis or even blindness – a condition known as anosognosia.

Despite the angst-defying perspective of an unopposed left brain it takes the combination of both hemispheres to produce a fully rounded sense of humour. Consider a fairly standard joke: a kangaroo walks into a bar, sits down and asks for a pint of beer. The barman, astonished, gives the kangaroo his drink. 'How much?' asks the animal. The barman, recovering his composure, decides to see if the kangaroo is really as clever as it seems. Winking knowingly at his human customers, he names an exorbitantly high price. The kangaroo duly pays it, and the barman, reassured of the continuing superiority of his own species, relaxes. 'Don't get many kangaroos in here,' he remarks casually ...

Now, here are three possible punchlines: (a) Then the kangaroo gets out a gun and shoots the barman. (b) Then the man on the next stool admits that he is a ventriloquist who has trained the kangaroo to drink beer. (c) 'I'm not surprised,' replies the kangaroo, 'with beer at that price.'

(A) *Patients with single hemisphere brain damage were asked to look at this figure, then copy it.*

(B) *This is typical of an attempt by a patient with left hemisphere damage: the outline is fine but details are neglected.*

(C) *While a patient with right hemisphere damage draws only the details.*

Punchline (c) might seem the obvious choice – but a person with a right-brain lesion would be quite likely to pick the literal and – to most people humourless – option of (b). Left-brain-damaged patients, on the other hand, may choose (a) – a seemingly arbitrary surprise ending.

The difference is probably because the left brain creates the feeling of amusement and so is quite happy to laugh at more or less anything when prompted – rather like the epileptic girl who laughed at the surgeons when part of her left hemisphere was stimulated on the operating table. Hence ordinary situations, with no 'twist', may be seen as jokes if presented as such. The right hemisphere is the one that 'gets' the joke, in that it registers the dislocation in logic that is a hallmark of most formal humour. This is a mild form of alert – a 'something not quite right here!' effect that, on its own, is not funny at all. In fact, it is a mild form of fear. Someone equipped only with this right-brain ability might well think that any surprise ending makes a joke.

The combination of (right-brain) alert and (left-brain) jollity is still not enough to make something funny – humour also needs meaning in order to work. This is why seeing a nice-looking person slipping on a banana skin is not funny but watching a pompous bully come a cropper is. Meaning emerges from the pulling together of all the threads of the joke, including context, assumptions and knowledge of our own prejudices.

Humour is a diffuse, fuzzy sort of thing – a matter of taste, often, and something you don't expect to find in even the most sophisticated computer unless it has been programmed in by a human. In this it is typical of the type of functions that engage both hemispheres. Specialized functions tend, by contrast, to be lateralized. Finding your way around in space, for example, is very much a right-brained activity, and if the parts of the brain that do it (right hippocampus and right parietal cortex) are damaged, a person may find they get lost in what were once the most familiar places. One such patient could not even find his own front door. Whenever he wanted to go out he would spend up to five minutes blundering around his (relatively small) bungalow searching for the exit.[4]

In time most people who suffer one-sided brain damage find that their condition improves. Sometimes this is because the undamaged hemisphere learns to do tasks usually left to the other. It probably does not do them in the same way, though, nor so efficiently. If the ability to negotiate from place to place is lost, for example, the left brain may take on the job, using its own special skills of sequential memory and deduction. So, instead of just 'knowing' (as the right brain did) that the front door is the third door along from the kitchen, the left hemisphere remembers that as a fact and arrives there by counting the intervening doors. Similarly, recognizing familiar faces is a right-hemisphere activity that is sometimes lost after brain injury.

Face recognition does not require thought – again, like all right-brain activity, it just happens. If the right-brain area responsible for this skill is lost, the only way a person can recognize those they know is by deliberately taking note of their distinguishing features, then matching their mental notes to each face they see. This imperfect technique often fails, making social gatherings a nightmare. One man, after a particularly embarrassing incident at a dinner party, insisted his wife wore a red ribbon in her hair when they went out to prevent him again trying to go home with the wrong woman.

The right hemisphere is also good at grasping wholes, while the left brain likes detail. Other right-brain strengths include the ability to make out camouflaged images against a complex background and to see patterns at a glance. This could well have had important survival benefits when our ancestors needed to watch for predators. The left, by contrast, is good at breaking down complicated patterns into their component parts. This might have survival value in a large corporation where you have to pursue a plan, step by step, through a jungle of bureaucracy, but a left brain alone in the wild would be unable to see the wood for the trees, let alone a half-hidden bear in search of dinner.

Almost every mental function you can think of is to some extent lateralized. Precisely how it happens is not fully understood, but it seems that incoming information is split into several parallel paths within the brain, each of which is given a slightly different treatment according to the route it takes. Information that is of particular 'interest' to one side will activate that side more strongly than the other. You can see this happen in a brain scan – the side that is 'in charge' of a particular task will light up while the matching area on the other side will glow far more dully.

Generally the tasks that each hemisphere takes

on are those that fit its style of working: holistic or analytical. The key to the differences in left- and right-brain style may in part be found in a curious physical difference that exists between them. If you were to cut the hemispheres open you would find they are made up of a mixture of grey and white matter. The grey matter consists of the central bodies of brain cells and is found mainly in the cortex, which is a couple of millimetres thick. The white matter lies beneath this. It is made up of dense bundles of axons – the threads that project from the cell bodies and carry messages between them.

The distribution of white matter to grey is not even throughout the brain – the right hemisphere has relatively more white matter, while the left has more grey.[5] This microscopic distinction is significant because it means that the axons in the right brain are longer than in the left and this means they connect neurons that are, on average, further away from one another. Given that neurons that do

Very rarely, the corpus callosum fails to develop, so the two brain halves can't communicate normally. Recent work from the Center of Biopsychosocial Research, Travis Research Institute, Pasadena, CA shows that such people typically display Asperger's-like symptoms: social difficulties, literal-mindedness and problems understanding subtle, complex situations. They also tend to have poor co-ordination and recognition problems. Above, left: the red area in the upper picture shows densely packed information-carrying tracts between two hemispheres of a normal brain. Above, right: in this person just a tiny thread of tissue – capable of carrying only a trickle of information – links the two sides. Such information exchange as there is occurs lower in the brain (green/yellow tracts).

D
D
D
D
D
DDDDD

Concentrating on the 'L' (left) creates activity in the right hemisphere (A) while attending to the 'Ds' causes activity in the left (B). These scans demonstrate how the two sides of the brain deal with different aspects of a single stimulus.

similar things or process particular types of input tend to be clustered together, this suggests that the right brain is better equipped than the left to draw on several different brain modules at the same time. The long-range neural wiring might explain why that hemisphere is inclined to come up with broad, many-faceted, but rather vague concepts. It might also help the right brain to integrate sensory and emotional stimuli (as is required to apprehend art) and to make the sort of unlikely connections that provide the basis of much humour and creativity. 'Lateral thinking' would be helped, too, by the neural arrangement in the right brain – the sideways extension of axons even makes the phrase literal rather than figurative. The left brain, by contrast, is more densely woven. The close-packed, tightly connected neurons are better equipped to do intense, detailed work that depends on close and quick co-operation between similarly dedicated brain cells.

Some studies also show that the left hemisphere produces (or responds) more to dopamine, while the right is more sensitive to noradrenalin. Dopamine is the 'driver' neurotransmitter, pushing people towards goals regardless of obstacles, while noradrenalin produces heightened arousal and greater sensitivity to environmental perils. Heightened left-brain activity might therefore be what produces dominating, power-seeking behaviour, while those whose right brains are more turned on tend towards back-shrinking and fearful. In one experiment a group of volunteers were split into two groups, one of which was manipulated by the researchers to feel socially superior and capable while the other was made to feel that they were at bottom of the heap. The volunteers' brain activity was monitored by EEG while this was done, and the results suggested that the experimentally-elevated top dogs had significantly higher activation in the left hemisphere than the downtrodden group.[6] Each hemisphere, then, plays a slightly different role.

To draw a fanciful (and very right-brain) analogy: imagine the two hemispheres as two halves of a flat black screen. A film is to be projected, in duplicate, on both halves of the screen concurrently, and you need to extract as much information from this film as you can. The screen needs to be white to reflect the picture, and you have one pot of white paint with which to transform it. Unfortunately, you need double that amount to cover the whole area, and you can't just whiten one half and forget the other – you have to use half the paint on one half of the screen and half on the other. What to do? You cannot afford to risk missing either the outline of the film you are to watch, nor certain details.

One solution would be to spread your paint thinly but completely over one side, and on the other to create islands of dense white where you think the main action of the film is likely to take place, leaving less important areas uncovered. Now, when the film is projected the right half of the screen will show a shadowy but complete outline, while the left half will show patches of sharp, detailed imagery but no overall shape.

With this arrangement you can get the full

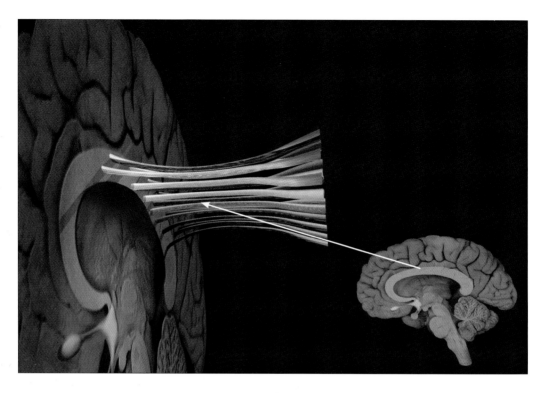

picture providing you constantly scan both halves of the screen, looking to the left for details and to the right for an overall impression of what is going on.

This seems to be how the two hemispheres work. They each process their 'halves' of the big picture, and then pool their information by sending signals back and forth via the corpus callosum. The side that sends the loudest signals is the 'winner' in that it provides the conscious content of our thoughts although it doesn't always succeed in dictating our behaviour.

To use another simile: overall the two sides of the brain are like an old married couple who long ago fell into doing things according to a 'his 'n' hers' division of labour. The partner that can communicate takes the dominant role, speaking and acting, most of the time, for both and doing much of the day-to-day business of thinking, calculating, and dealing with the outside world. The other stays largely in the background, quietly doing its moment-by-moment chores and constantly using its singular talents to sniff and taste the social environment for signs of anything that may be a threat

The corpus callosum is a thick band of axons – 80 million or so – which connect the brain cells in one hemisphere to those in the other. The two sides keep up a continuous conversation via this neural bridge.

or of benefit. They keep each other perfectly informed of what is going on in their own spheres through a continuous, intimate conversation. So natural to them is this pattern of working that they can carry out the most complex tasks together in a perfectly integrated way.

Most of the time the marriage of our two brains is pretty harmonious and conscious decisions, although they may seem to be made by the dominant partner alone, are in fact informed by the findings of both hemispheres. Sometimes, though, the conversation between them falters. The dominant hemisphere may ignore the information supplied by its partner and make a decision based purely on what it alone thinks. The result may be an emotional disquiet that is difficult to explain. Conversely, the non-dominant partner sometimes bypasses the executive control of the other side and triggers an action which the person is at a loss to explain. These are the sort of things we look back on (usually with embarrassment) and say: 'I didn't mean to do it – I just couldn't help myself.'

Sometimes, too, a hemisphere acts unilaterally because it does not receive all the incoming information. The corpus callosum can carry enormous amounts of information from one side of the brain to the other in milliseconds, but sometimes there is a split second during which incoming data lingers in one hemisphere only. And some information – the sort for which one or the other hemisphere has a very strong preference – may be registered only dimly by the other.

We all experience this half-knowledge in subtle ways. Odd remarks that just slip out, feelings we can't explain, silly errors like mistaking one object for another, are traditionally seen as evidence of deep inner conflicts. In fact, many of these may be caused by faulty or incomplete inter-hemispheric communication. The giveaway signs are comments like: 'There's something about her/him/the décor I don't like but I can't put my finger on it', or 'I know something awful has happened but it hasn't hit me yet.' In the first situation the person's right brain may have grasped something of which their left brain is only faintly aware, and in the second the left brain has acknowledged something but the right brain has not yet taken it in.

Not understanding a feeling does not stop us from acting on it. Much human behaviour is based on right-brain hunches. We see millions of things happening around us from minute to minute and only a tiny percentage of them is consciously registered. The rest enter the brain fleetingly as momentary blips of energy, leaving no impression. Some of them are probably just noticeable enough to create a momentary emotional response in the right brain, but not significant enough to create conscious awareness in the left. Such half-seen stimuli may account for the odd, uncalled-for flicker of irritation or the little cloud of inexplica-

ble melancholy that most people experience from time to time.

These subtle shifts of feeling are more likely when the left brain is relatively idle and therefore sending fewer than normal inhibitory signals to its moody twin. This may be one reason why throwing yourself into some left-brain activity like reading, talking, or even doing your tax return often brings relief from mild anxiety or depression. Similarly, feelings of grief may be lessened by frenetic left-brain activity, which inhibits the emotional response of the right. Conventional wisdom has it that the brisk 'get on with it' school of therapy is ultimately damaging – rather like putting a tight lid on a fermenting pot. Hence until quite recently people were frequently encouraged to talk about their negative emotions, in order to 'get it out'.

'Talking therapy' does, in some circumstances, work. But this is probably not because it allows emotions free rein, rather that it helps us to elevate them to cortical level where they can be consciously processed. One of the most successful types of psychological treatment is cognitive behavioural therapy (CBT), which, by definition, involves left-brain activity. Talking and thinking

A meaningless collection of blobs, or a Dalmatian sniffing at something on the ground? The left hemisphere sees only the lines – the right sees the dog.

about emotions gives us control over them, so they cease to overwhelm us. Simply allowing emotions to well up until we are engulfed by them is, on the other hand, likely to make them more painful, if they are painful to begin with. This sort of post-traumatic counselling that involves getting someone simply to talk about the original experience, for example, can make people feel worse rather than better because it simply reinforces the horrible memories and, with them, the frightening emotions.[7,8] If people are encouraged to replace such negative memories with positive thoughts, however, they can transform them.

The left/right hemisphere split often shows up in our reactions to art: 'I like it but I don't know why' is not necessarily a philistine reaction – it demonstrates only that the work is being appreciated by the right brain rather than analysed by the left. Artistic 'experts', of one sort or another, tend to use the two hemispheres more equally than others when assessing works that fall within their field of expertise. Most people listen to music predominantly with their right hemisphere, for example, but professional musicians process the sound in their left hemisphere too, reflecting a critical, analytical response in addition to the emotional affect.[9] Much advertising is designed to exploit the gap between the impressionable right brain and the critical left. Those adverts that use visual images rather than words to convey messages are particularly likely to impinge on the right hemisphere without necessarily being registered by the left. The purpose of such communication is, of course, to make us buy whatever is being advertised. We may like to think of that action as the result of a rational decision, but a lot of the time the 'decision' is just an impulse.

Not that we like to admit this. The idea that our actions may be irrational is peculiarly unacceptable to the left hemisphere. A series of famous experiments[10] showed that people hardly ever admit to making arbitrary decisions. In one of the experiments, for example, a selection of nylon stockings was laid out and a group of women were invited to choose a pair. When they were asked why they had made their particular choice all the women were able to give detailed and sensible reasons, citing slight differences in colour, texture or quality. In fact, all the stockings were identical – the women's 'reasons' for choosing them were actually rationalizations constructed to explain an essentially inexplicable piece of behaviour.

You do not have to use much imagination to realize how such a process may be used to dignify emotional or arbitrary acts in ordinary life: choosing to employ a person of one colour, for example, over that of another. It is also easy to see why so many of us are continuously and compulsively drawn to analyse and explain our own and others' behaviour – spinning elaborate explanations for the way we behave is a built-in hobby. It may also go some way towards explaining why Freudian psychoanalysis – despite an almost complete lack of evidence for its efficacy as therapy – became a near century-long obsession in those societies that could afford it.

Our urge to rationalize behaviour probably has considerable survival value. The human species got where it is largely by forming complex social constructs – from the hunting party to the political party – and making them work. To work they require that we have confidence in them and to have confidence we need to believe that the actions of these organizations are based on sound, rational judgements. At one level, of course, we know we are kidding ourselves. For example, all governments, in all societies, have some policies that are demonstrably irrational. However, no government member, anywhere, ever admits this – not at the time, anyway. Instead they rationalize their policy-making. We may see through it, but basically we like things this way – it makes us feel safe.

Similarly, rationalizing our own actions gives us confidence in our sanity. You can see it happening all around you: watch some harassed mother trying to cope with a lively toddler, for example.

Visual information flows back and forth between the hemispheres, so each side of the brain has the full picture.

In a split-brain visual information is trapped in each hemisphere. Providing the eyes are kept still, this means that each side of the brain receives information from the opposite half of the visual field only. Below: *The brain is split by severing part of the corpus callosum.*

Sooner or later she is likely to snap at the child, or slap it, or just withdraw her attention. She does this because she feels irritated, worried or tired. The feelings may be generated by circumstances that are, at that moment, quite out of mind, and nothing to do with the child. Yet the child feels the brunt of it. Can that mother admit this? Later on, perhaps, when she is at home, relaxed, and the child is sleeping she may reflect that she was rather unfair. But at the time, when the child wails: 'Why did you do tha-a-at?' she will rationalize: 'Because you were rude/naughty/disobedient.' If she didn't do this, her confidence in her ability to cope would be dented. Better have a reason for doing things – any reason – than no reason at all.

Splitting the brain
'I don't know why, but I feel scared,' said the woman. 'I feel kind of jumpy … I know I like Dr Gazzaniga, but right now I'm kind of scared of him' – *split-brain patient to researcher.*[11]

The patient, V.P., had good reason to feel jumpy. She had just seen a particularly violent murder and it had clearly affected her mood. The murder was merely on film, and the neurologist who was investigating her, Michael Gazzaniga, was not the culprit. But his patient did not know these things. Although she had been fully awake and alert throughout the film-show she was now apparently unconscious of having seen anything but a flash of light. She was therefore ascribing the

The image of the cup goes to the left hemisphere only and — because the brain is split — it cannot travel to the right hemisphere.

The spoon image went only to the right hemisphere — and because this side does not have speech the subject could not report seeing it. Her left hand 'knew' what was on the screen, however, because it, too, is wired to the right hemisphere.

emotions roused by the images to anything in the vicinity — including the man in charge of the experiment.

V.P.'s curious half-knowledge of the trauma she had just been through was caused by a weird and rare condition: her brain had effectively been sawn in half. This drastic operation was carried out to control what had been very severe epilepsy. Cutting the neural connections between one hemisphere and the other stopped the flurries of random electrical activity — her fits — from travelling along them and engulfing her whole brain. Once it had been done the seizures remained localized in the side in which they arose and were far less troublesome. It left her — and similar patients — with some of the most bizarre neurological side-effects ever reported.

V.P. was part of the second cohort of split-brain patients to offer themselves for psychological testing. The first were investigated by the psychobiologist Roger Sperry, who, in 1981, won the Nobel Prize for his work. Sperry had already

done much to demonstrate that the brain was a modular system rather than some homogenous black box. Much of his work was based on cutting connections between various parts of animals' brains and seeing what effect it had. The split-brain technique had already proved particularly revealing. Together with Ronald Myers he had shown, for example, that if you divide a cat's brain you can teach one hemisphere to do a task — pressing a lever for food, say — but leave the other ignorant.

Would human consciousness prove to be similarly divisible? The human split-brain patients provided the perfect means to find out because their hemispheres were already separated. They also held out the wonderful promise of being able to report directly, from inside, on the curious state of half-knowledge that had been observed in the split-brain cat. Sperry duly designed a series of experiments to show how each brain hemisphere worked in isolation, and the two hemispheres pass information across the corpus callosum

anterior commissure

emotional information passing across the two hemispheres

to tease out the functional differences between them.

A typical experiment involved N.G., a Californian housewife.

The woman was placed in front of a screen that had a small black dot in the centre. She was asked to fix her eyes on this dot, thus ensuring that images entering her eyes from the side were sent to one hemisphere only. The experimenter then briefly flashed a picture of a cup to the right of the dot. The image stayed on the screen for a very short while – about a twentieth of a second. This is just long enough for an image to be registered, but not long enough for a person to shift their eyes to bring it into focus and thus send it to both hemispheres. So the image on the screen went to N.G.'s left hemisphere only and there it stopped, because the normal route to her other hemisphere – the corpus callosum – was cut. Asked what she saw, N.G. replied, quite normally: 'A cup.'

Next, a picture of a spoon was flashed on the left side of the screen so that it entered N.G.'s

The anterior commissure lies below the corpus callosum. It connects the unconscious limbic structures in both hemispheres and carries emotional information between them. It does not connect the conscious areas of the brain, though, so words and thoughts cannot be exchanged.

right hemisphere. This time, when she was asked what she had seen, she said: 'Nothing.' The experimenter then asked N.G. to reach under the screen with her left hand and select, by touch only, from among a group of concealed items the one that was the same as the one she had just seen. She felt around, pausing briefly at a cup, a knife, a pen, a comb – then settled firmly on a spoon. While her hand continued to hold it behind the screen, the experimenter asked her what she was holding. 'A pencil,' she said. These responses, though inexplicable at first sight, actually gave Sperry and his colleagues a uniquely clear picture of what was going on in N.G.'s brain. N.G. was right-handed, and it was already known that speech, in most right-handed people, is located in

THE PUZZLE OF THE LEFT-HANDER

More than 90 per cent of people in the world are right-handed. It has been the same throughout the history of man — studies of tools used since the Stone Age, pictures drawn by ancient man on cave walls and analysis of the fractures on baboons' heads presumed to have been made by human hunters all show that the vast majority of people use their right hands in preference to their left for skilled single-handed tasks.

Right-handedness is strongly associated with left-brain dominance. But what of the 5 to 8 per cent of people who use their left hands? Are they cerebral mirror-images of the norm?

Not quite, is the answer. Whereas 95 per cent of right-handers have language firmly lodged only in their left hemispheres, left-handed people vary much more in the way their brains are organized.

About 70 per cent of them have language in the left hemisphere only. Of the other 30 per cent, most of them seem to have language in both hemispheres.[12]

Is left-handedness pathological? Culturally, it has always been treated as such and almost every language has some derogatory term derived from the word for left. 'Gauche' — French for left — is used in English to mean awkward, and 'Amancino' in Italian means deceitful as well as left. The Bible offers one of the most striking indictments: in Matthew's vision of the Judgement it states that God will set the sheep on the right, the goats on the left, and then dispatch the former to life eternal while consigning the latter to everlasting fire.[13]

Not surprisingly, given this authoritative prejudice, parents of left-handed children often went to great lengths to encourage their offspring to use their right hands. The fact that many succeeded — and now appear to be right-handed despite having cerebral arrangements that predispose them otherwise — has confounded subsequent research on the subject.

Handedness is well established by the time a baby is born — in fact, the first signs of it can be seen at just fifteen weeks' gestation[14] when most babies start to show a distinct preference for sucking their right thumbs.

The current consensus about left-handedness is that some of it is simply genetically determined and of no particular significance, while in others it is because of some pre- or perinatal disturbance that arrests the normal development of left-brain/right-hand dominance. It might be something like mild brain injury, which affects left hemisphere growth at a crucial time; or it might result from the failure of neuronal apoptosis, or of some neurons to navigate to their proper place. About 20 per cent of twins are left-handed — a far greater proportion than among the general population — and some researchers have speculated that some singleton left-handers — perhaps all of them — are the sole survivors of what started out as a twin pair.[15] The shift in cerebral dominance may have been caused by mild damage sustained when competing with the twin for limited resources in the uterus, or the result of whatever trauma or uterine deficit it was that killed the other twin. There is also some genetic influence on handedness — one particular gene variation, catchily known as LRRTM1 (Leucine-rich repeat transmembrane neuronal 1) has been positively associated with left-handedness, and also with a slightly increased likelihood of developing certain neurological disorders, including schizophrenia.[16]

One intriguing theory holds that left-handedness

certainly has consequences way beyond the simple business of which hand you use to sign your name. Stanley Coren, Professor of Psychology at the University of British Columbia, claims to have shown that left-handers die, on average, some nine years before right-handers.[17] This finding, if correct, ties in with findings that link left-handedness to a variety of physical abnormalities, most of which can be traced to developmental or immune system dysfunction. They include asthma, bowel and thyroid complaints, myopia, dyslexia, migraine, stuttering and allergies.

On the bright side, left-handedness is associated positively with various types of creativity, and one study found that that left-handed men are 15 per cent richer than right-handed men for those who attended college, and 26 percent richer if they graduated.[18]

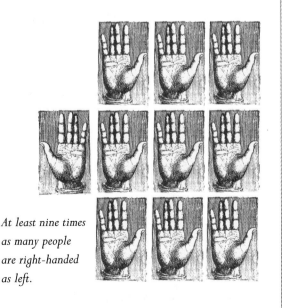

At least nine times as many people are right-handed as left.

the left hemisphere. Thus, when the cup image was sent to the left hemisphere she saw it and named it in the usual way. When the spoon image was fed to her right hemisphere, however, she could not tell the experimenter about it because her right hemisphere was unable to speak. The words that came out of her mouth, 'I see nothing', were uttered by the left hemisphere – the only one that could reply. And, because the left hemisphere is isolated from the right, it was speaking quite truthfully – it had no knowledge of the spoon picture because, without the usual passage of information across the corpus callosum, the image never reached it.[19]

That does not mean that the spoon image did not go in, however. When the subject was asked to use her left hand to select an item it was the knowledge in the right hemisphere (which is wired, remember, to the left hand) that was brought to bear on the task. Thus she selected the spoon. But when the experimenter asked her to name it she was up against the same problem she encountered when asked to name the image of the spoon – the right hemisphere could not tell of it. Instead the left hemisphere kicked in and did the logical thing. Because it was unaware of the spoon image, it had no way of knowing that the left hand had selected a spoon rather than any other item. It could not see the spoon because the hand that grasped it was under the screen. And it couldn't feel it because the sensory stimuli from the left hand were going, as normal, to the right hemisphere, where – in the absence of the corpus callosum – it stayed. The left hemisphere knew that something was in the left hand, but it had to identify it by guesswork or deduction. As it happens the left hemisphere is pretty good at deduction, and it calculated that of all the objects that might be tucked away behind the screen a pencil seemed like a good bet. So 'pencil' it said.

The spoon and cup exercises demonstrated that straightforward factual knowledge does not travel between hemispheres in a split-brain patient. But what about emotional stimuli? The corpus callosum is the only information conduit to link the cortical areas – the thinking part – of the two hemispheres. But beneath the corpus callosum there is an older pathway between the hemispheres, the anterior commissure. It connects the deep, subcortical regions of the brain commonly known as the limbic system. Here, in this cerebral underworld, raw emotion is generated: alarm bells are set off in response to threat; false smiles are registered; and lust first twitches at the sight of an attractive other.

All of this happens unconsciously, but the limbic system is firmly and broadly connected by millions of two-way neural connections to the conscious, cortical areas of the hemispheres. Everything that the conscious brain takes in is sent down from the cortex to the limbic system where – if it is emotionally significant – a basic response to it is made. That response is then fed back to the cerebral hemispheres where it is processed into the complex, context-sensitive feelings we think of when we speak of fear, anger, embarrassment or love.

These sophisticated expressions of emotion cannot pass from one hemisphere to another in a split-brain patient, but the basic emotional responses generated at subcortical level can, via the anterior commissure. The arrangement is rather like a pair of lifts in a twin-towered building that is connected only by a walk-through basement.

Michael Gazzaniga, of the University of California, together with Joseph LeDoux of New

York University, demonstrated this in a series of experiments carried out on a second set of split-brain patients. They were helped by the development by another split-brain researcher, Eran Zaidel, of a special contact lens that refracted the light falling on the eye in such a way that any image presented to it entered only one side of the retina. With the lens in place the subjects could no longer see both fields of vision just by turning their eyes, so much lengthier and more detailed information could be presented to each hemisphere.

In one experiment Gazzaniga and LeDoux showed the right hemisphere of one of their female subjects a series of film vignettes that included a person throwing another into a fire. The patient, V.P., did not consciously know what she had seen, just as N.G. had not been conscious, when asked, of seeing the spoon in Sperry's earlier experiment. 'I think I just saw a white flash – maybe some trees, red trees like in the fall,' she told the researcher who was with her. 'I don't know why, but I feel scared … I feel kind of jumpy. I don't like this room … or maybe it's you who's making me nervous.' Dropping her voice, she then said to the researcher: 'I know I like Dr Gazzaniga, but right now I'm scared of him for some reason.' The same sort of unconscious emotional reaction was found when the images presented to the right brain were pleasant: Gazzaniga and LeDoux found that showing scenes of ocean surf, leafy woodland and so on produced feelings of calmness and serenity in their subjects.

Clearly, the right brain, for all its muteness, is capable of making itself felt by the conscious mind. But what actually happens within that hemisphere? Is it possible that it has its own way of seeing things, its own opinions, its own personality, even? What would it say if it could speak?

Sperry's split-brain patients appeared to be almost entirely bereft of language in their right hemispheres, but among the patients who worked with Gazzaniga and LeDoux were two who, unusually, had language ability in the right as well as the left sides of their brains. These patients helped

If serene images are fed to the right hemisphere of a split brain they will produce a conscious emotional reaction even though the subject will be unconscious of the actual images.

illuminate the wide range of differences between the two hemispheres, and one of them provided the first verbal message known to emanate exclusively from the right side of the brain. It consisted of just two words – but – as we shall see – they demonstrate, beyond doubt, that being 'in two minds' can be more than a figure of speech.

In two minds

'In living skills M.P. was making good progress with an omelette when the left hand "helped out" by throwing in, first, a couple of additional, uncracked eggs, then an unpeeled onion and a salt cellar into the frying pan. There were also times when the left hand deliberately stopped the right hand carrying out a task. In one instance I asked her to put her right hand through a small hole. "I can't – the other one's holding it," she said. I looked over and saw her left hand firmly gripping the right at the wrist' – *Patient study*[20]

Can you imagine how it would feel to be out of control of one of your hands? To watch, helplessly, as it undid your shirt buttons seconds after your other hand had done them up, or pluck goods you didn't want from supermarket shelves and place them in your pocket? Worse – think of reaching out with one hand to give your lover a gentle caress, only to see the other hand come up and deliver a right hook instead. All of these things have happened to sane and otherwise quite normal-seeming people. Such events are described in the dry jargon of medical reportage, as 'inter-manual conflict'. Between themselves researchers call it the Dr Strangelove Syndrome.

Alien hands arise in people who have suffered brain injuries which disconnect parts of the brain which generate hand movements from the parts which ordinarily direct or inhibit them. In some cases it is the result of a blockage or severing of the tracts which run between the two hemispheres. Some people with alien hands, like the woman with the culinary problems above, have had a haemorrhage or stroke while others involve people who have undergone split-brain surgery.

Each hemisphere has local control over its own physical realm – mainly the longitudinal half of the body on the opposite side to itself (some facial nerves have a slightly different arrangement). So if the right leg is to be extended, it is the left hemisphere that instigates the movement, and vice versa. Overall control, however, is vested in the dominant (usually left) hemisphere. It is here that the decision to extend the leg is made in the first place. The left brain exercises control by sending commands, mainly inhibitory ones, to the right hemisphere via the corpus callosum. The system makes for smooth running – there is only room for one boss in a single skull.

Sever the connection between the hemispheres, however, and in certain circumstances the command system breaks down. In split-brain patients the inhibitory messages cannot pass from hemisphere to hemisphere, but most of the time this doesn't matter because the two hemispheres are so well versed in their respective roles that things just carry on as normal. Occasionally, though, the non-dominant hemisphere seems to decide that it should be involved in something that is already being handled quite satisfactorily by the left hemisphere, and without its usual line of communication the left brain has no way of stopping it from acting. The two sides can therefore find themselves fighting – literally – for control.

One woman whose brain had been surgically

split found, for example, that it often took her hours to get dressed in the morning because her alien hand kept trying to dictate what she should wear. Time and again she would reach out with her right hand and select an item from the wardrobe, only to see her left hand whip up and grab something else. Once her left hand had got hold of something it would not let go, and she, of course, had no way of making it obey her conscious will. Either she had to put on the clothes she was clutching or call someone to help her prise her fingers open. Interestingly, the clothes selected by this woman's alien hand were usually rather more colourful and flamboyant than those the woman had consciously intended to wear.

Another patient had a hand that insisted on pulling down his trousers immediately after his other hand had pulled them up. A third found his alien hand unbuttoned his shirt as fast as his other hand could fasten it. M.P., the woman whose hand chucked uncracked eggs into her omelette, had to put half a day aside to pack when she went away because her alien hand would systematically remove each item from her suitcase just after she had put it in.[21]

Most alien hands are merely irritating or comical. 'It feels like having two naughty children inside my head who are always arguing,' said M.P. Occasionally, though, alien hands seem to be intent on more than mischief. One man reported reaching out with his right hand to give his wife a hug, only to see his left hand fly up and punch her instead. M.P., too, sometimes found her alien hand would prevent her other hand from making affectionate gestures – her husband was often subjected to a tug-of-war as one hand reached out to embrace him while the other pushed him away.[22]

Despite this alien hands rarely do anything seriously violent and the world still awaits the first case of murder to be defended on the grounds that 'it wasn't me who did it – it was my hand'. Some people with alien hands have nevertheless become terrified that they might unwittingly do something catastrophic. One poor man, for instance, was frightened of going to sleep in case his hand strangled him in the night.[23]

The contradictory nature of alien hand behaviour reflects the dichotomous nature of our brains: forward/back; grasp/reject; hit/flee. Which of these wins from moment to moment is usually decided by the dominant hemisphere – alien hand movements just show what would happen if our inner conflicts were not continuously controlled. This doesn't mean that we harbour deep contradictory intentions – the actions we normally inhibit are simply reflexes. Nevertheless the idea of an alien hand as an emissary from some deeper level of the psyche has a compelling attraction.

There is anyway a sort of truth in the notion of a cantankerous alter ego at work. Alien hands are nearly always on the left, so their actions are triggered by the right hemisphere. This, as we have seen, is usually the mute half of the brain and its inability to communicate has led many researchers to conclude that it must merely be an unconscious servant of its dominant partner, with no ability to form intentions or concepts of its own.

This may not be so. Among the split-brain patients that Gazzaniga worked with at the University of California was one, identified as P.S., who had enough language ability in his right hemisphere for it to be able to understand short phrases as well as individual words. Even more unusually – it could use words to communicate back.

To make contact verbally and exclusively with his right hemisphere nevertheless required an elaborate experimental set-up. Spoken questions, unlike images, cannot be sent to one hemisphere or the other, even in split-brain patients. If a question is spoken in the normal way, the left brain 'grabs' and answers it, and words cannot easily be presented to the right hemisphere only because ear-to-brain wiring is not conveniently separable in the way that eye-to-brain wiring is.

LeDoux and Gazzaniga got around this problem by presenting P.S. with spoken phrases and questions minus the keywords that would make

The difference between the two brain hemispheres is reflected in the face. The self-portrait of Durer above (centre) has been split and the two halves matched with mirror images of themselves. The resulting two portraits show distinctly different characters.

them answerable. This essential information was then sent to the right hemisphere only by presenting the keywords visually. Thus they might say: 'Please would you spell out …' and then flash the word 'hobby' in his left visual field. This convoluted exercise ensured that the right hemisphere was the only half with all the information required to formulate a reply. P.S.'s right hemisphere could not generate speech, but it was able to write. It therefore spelt out its answers, using P.S.'s left hand (the one under right-brain control) to organize Scrabble letters into words. The resulting conversation was stilted, to say the least. But it was also revealing.

Most of the responses from P.S.'s right hemisphere were similar to those given when the same questions were asked of his left. But the right hemisphere showed distinctive likes and dislikes. When both hemispheres were asked, separately, to evaluate a long string of things – foods, colours and personal things like his and his girlfriend's names – the right hemisphere consistently rated them less highly than the left. More startling than

this was the difference that emerged when the investigators asked the two hemispheres about their ambitions.

'What do you want to do when you graduate?' they asked one day. The question was addressed, first, to the boy's left (dominant) hemisphere. 'I want to be a draftsman,' he said. 'I'm already training for it.'

'What do you want to do when you …?' – this time the word 'graduate' was flashed on a screen to P.S.'s left. The boy's left hand reached for the Scrabble letters. To the amazement of all in the laboratory, including, presumably, P.S. himself, the hand arranged the letters to form the words 'A-U-T-O-M-O-B-I-L-E R-A-C-E-[R]'[24]

These two words constitute about the longest and most complex verbal message ever to emanate from a non-dominant hemisphere. The fact that it was so clearly in conflict with the boy's declared ambition suggests that it was not just conveying a concept that had been constructed by the dominant hemisphere and somehow 'leaked' to it. It was its very own idea – one that had hitherto been hidden from its twin and from the outside world to whom, until that sophisticated laboratory set-up was in place, the right hemisphere had been unable to speak.

The possible implications of this are mind- boggling. It suggests that we might all be carrying

CONSERVATIVE LEFT BRAIN, LIBERAL RIGHT BRAIN?

 CHARLES BRACK
Founder, Neuropolitics.org

The divergent politics of the left and right hemispheres have been hinted at in a number of studies. In one split-brain patient, for instance, the left hemisphere reported liking Richard Nixon, while the right indicated that it didn't.[i]

Conservatives tend towards black and white thinking while liberals tolerate greater ambiguity, reflecting the 'step-by-step' cognitive style of the left hemisphere versus the 'fuzziness' of the right.[ii] In contrast to liberals, Conservatives opt for freedom over equality, perhaps because they are more 'driven' due to higher dopamine expression. Some studies suggest that dopamine function is higher in the left hemisphere than the right.[iii] It may also be due to a left-hemisphere tendency to rank individuals into pecking orders.[iv]

Conservatives, more than liberals, react strongly to verbal threats which are known to activate the left amygdala preferentially[v]. Liberals report lower levels of racial prejudice and the inhibition of racial prejudice is handled mainly by a right-lateralized network.[vi]

Conservatives, over time, have fewer sex partners than liberals, while their relationships last longer and are more likely to produce offspring. Romantic bonding seems to be facilitated by activity in the dopamine system and there is some evidence that the right hemisphere is more deactivated than the left with romantic love.[vii-viii]

[i] M. Gazzaniga and J. LeDoux. *The Integrated Mind*. Plenum Press, New York and London, (1978) p153.

[ii] J. Coney and K. Evans. *Hemispheric asymmetries in the resolution of lexical ambiguity*. Neuropsychologia. Vol. 38, No. 3, (2000) pp. 272–282.

[iii] H. Demaree, E. Everhart, E. Youngstrom, and D. Harrison. *Brain Lateralization of Emotional Processing: Historical Roots and a Future Incorporating 'Dominance'*. Behavioral and Cognitive Neuroscience Review. (2005);4;3

[iv] K. Knutson, J. Wood, M. Spampinato, and J. Grafman. *Politics on the Brain: An fMRI Investigation*. Social Neuroscience. March 2006; 1(1): 25–40.

[v] M. Gazzaniga ed. *The Cognitive Neurosciences*, MIT Press. (2004) p1006.

[vi] J. Richeson, A. Baird, H. Gordon, T. Heatherton, C. Wyland, S. Trawalter, J. Shelton. *An fMRI investigation of the impact of interracial contact on executive function*. Nature Neuroscience. Nov 2003.

[vii] A. Bartels and S. Zeki. *The neural correlates of maternal and romantic love*. Neuroimage 21 (2004) 1155–1166.

[viii] A. Bartels and S. Zeki. *The neural basis of romantic love*. NeuroReport. 11:3829-3834 (2000)

around in our skulls a mute prisoner with a personality, ambition and self-awareness quite distinct from the day-to-day entity we believe ourselves to be. Our consciousness may be a single stream because it is the consciousness of our dominant hemisphere only. And if this is so, where is the other entity actually doing its experiencing?

There are other interpretations: the apparent bifurcation of consciousness observed in split-brain patients and occasionally in ourselves may simply reflect a repeated alternation of consciousness from one hemisphere to the other — the meandering of a single stream rather than two separate flows. Or it could be that there are many streams of consciousness in each of us, and that the split personality observed in P.S. was simply the result of his being able to bind them altogether because of his condition.

The notion of some parallel universe peopled by our other halves — each watching helplessly as we hurtle through life oblivious to their cries — is the most sensational of all the explanations, but it was one that Roger Sperry came to believe in after observing split-brain patients at close quarters for months on end. 'Everything we have seen indicates

Alien hands spring into action when the non-dominant side of the brain gains momentary control.

that the surgery has left these people with two separate minds,' he wrote. 'That is, two separate spheres of consciousness.'[25]

Homosexual people of both sexes differ from heterosexuals in certain cognitive abilities, suggesting there may be subtle differences in their brain structure. Brain imaging studies have now demonstrated that this is so.[26]

The brains of 90 healthy gay and heterosexual adults, both men and women, were scanned to measure the volume of the two hemispheres. The results showed that lesbians and heterosexual men shared a particular 'asymmetry' in their hemisphere size, while heterosexual women and gay men had no difference between the size of the different halves of their brain.

In other words, structurally, at least, the brains of gay men were more like heterosexual women, and gay women more like heterosexual men.

A further experiment found that in one particular area of the brain, the amygdala, there were other significant differences. In heterosexual men and gay women, there were more nerve connections in the right side of the amygdala, compared with the left. The reverse, with more neural connections in the left amygdala, was the case in homosexual men and heterosexual women.

The physiological differences are too great to be due to environmental factors, and it seems likely that they were laid down quite early in fetal development.

CHAPTER THREE
BENEATH THE SURFACE

The architecture of the brain is more complex than the familiar wrinkled cortex suggests. At its centre lies a cluster of strange-shaped modules that together are known as the limbic system. This is the powerhouse of the brain — generator of the appetites, urges, emotions and moods that drive our behaviour. Our conscious thoughts are mere interpreters and moderators of the biologically necessary forces that emerge from this unconscious underworld; where conscious processes pull in an opposite direction to emotion, the latter is designed by the neural circuitry in our brains to exert the stronger force.

'The heavings … began in my tummy and over the course of a second or two rose up within my body past my chest eventually to my mouth, throat and vocal chords as if I was being "verbally sick". I … suggested [to hospital staff] that the impulse [to shout obscenities] might make partial use of the same circuitry as that in the sneeze mechanism, as the heavings, and even the thoughts accompanying them were totally eliminated when I deliberately held my nose. This was treated as completely irrelevant … what I was suffering from was a motivational problem and all I had to do was get my anger out and the problem would disappear.' – *Peter Chadwick, psychologist and one-time Touretter*[1]

PEOPLE WITH SEVERE TOURETTE's syndrome can cut a clean swathe through the most crowded pavement. They lurch along, their faces a-twitch and with a stream of weird noises – barks, disjointed phrases or obscenities – issuing from their mouths. Some people glare at them; children giggle; occasionally, someone swears back. Most people adopt a preoccupied expression and scuttle out of their way.

If you find these passing encounters embarrassing, try to imagine what it must be like for the Touretters themselves. Most are of normal or above-average intelligence and they are often painfully aware of how ridiculous or offensive they appear to others. Coprolalia – the uttering of foul language – is particularly distressing because, more than anything else, it causes people to shun them. Some can control their symptoms by concentrating very hard on some cerebral activity (a dozen or so Touretters work, quite safely, as surgeons). When they cease to make an intense, conscious effort, however, or if they become emotionally aroused, their jerks and tics, animal noises and spat curses well up from the unconscious underworld of their brains and emerge with explosive force.

Tourette's syndrome was around long before the French physician Georges Gilles de la Tourette lent it his name in the late nineteenth century. Several medieval reports of people supposedly possessed by devils clearly describe its symptoms. More recently, Freudian psychoanalysts seized on the condition as a perfect demonstration of what happens when anger is repressed: 'Look! The anger must out!' Treatment was therefore directed towards revealing the 'root causes' of the supposed anger, or encouraging the patient to express it more openly. This approach didn't work and often made things worse but that did not lead to its abandonment (in fact, it is still handed out even today – as Peter Chadwick discovered).

The theoretical underpinning of the suppressed anger approach to Tourette's syndrome was irretrievably undermined by the discovery, in the 1960s, of a drug that drastically reduced its symptoms and in some cases took them away altogether. The drug – it transpired – fitted into the receptors designed to take the neurotransmitter dopamine. By filling these chemical 'locks' on the surfaces of cells it prevented dopamine from activating them and once these neurons were quietened the tics stopped. Today Tourette's syndrome is coming to be recognized as one of a wide range of mental disorders associated with malfunctions in the elaborate chemically modified system that ensures that necessary urges – the ones that keep us going – are properly attended to.

The brain's main function is to keep the organism of which it is part alive and reproducing. All its other tricks – the ability to appreciate music, to fall in love, to create a unified theory of the Universe – arise out of that single overriding ambition. So it shouldn't be too surprising to find that a huge part of brain structure and function is given over to making sure its neighbouring body parts do whatever is required to find food, sex, security and other vital requirements.

It does it by means of an elaborate carrot-and-stick control system. There are three basic steps. First, in response to the appropriate stimuli the brain creates an urge that demands to be satisfied. If the stimulus is, say, falling blood glucose, the urge will be hunger, and if the stimulus is sexual, the urge will be lust. More complicated stimuli like social isolation or separation from familiar surroundings may produce less easily identifiable drives – a desire to socialize, or a hankering to return home. Whatever form it takes, urges are often accompanied by a feeling of 'emptiness'. This may resemble a literal emptiness like an empty stomach. Or it may be something more vague – an emptiness of spirit. Whatever the feeling its purpose is the same: to trigger action.

Second, the action brought about by step one – eating, sex, homecoming, socializing – is rewarded with positive feelings of pleasure. Note – the *action* is the thing. Not just the food, or the sex, or the being at home. Having nutrients pumped into the blood keeps you alive but it does not give the same pleasure as a meal that has to be prepared, served, chewed and swallowed. This is why so many essential functions are elaborated with rituals. The preparation of a feast, the courtship that precedes sex, the journey home – these are not just necessary peripherals; they are the very things that make life enjoyable.

Third, when the action is complete the rush of pleasure is replaced by a sense of contentment and – note the word – fulfilment.

Most of the time, this system works away quietly and efficiently, creating cycles of 'desire – action – satisfaction' that mould our behaviour and provide the background rhythm of our daily lives. We feel hungry when our bodies are short of fuel; we eat, which is pleasurable; then we feel satiated – a serene feeling that lasts until our bodies again need fuel. Yet sometimes – indeed, quite often – the system breaks down. Either our urges cease to prompt appropriate action, or normal actions cease to be enough to satisfy them.

The first type of breakdown may be catastrophic. At its most mechanical, the ability to make purposeful movements may be lost, resulting in the physical stasis seen in Parkinson's disease and similar movement disorders. When higher brain areas are affected the result may be more subtle but just as disruptive to normal life. If a person loses the urge for self-protection, for example, or if their natural drives are sublimated to an overriding ambition – to climb a mountain, perhaps, or win a sporting contest – they appear reckless and may well injure themselves. If they lose the urge to keep clean, their health will suffer. If hunger fails to make itself felt or is overruled by conscious self-denial, they may die of starvation.

Conversely, if a person's urges become insatiable, they cease to behave normally. The insistent demands of the body force them to repeat and repeat the actions that once gave them relief: food is stuffed, sex is taken wherever it can be found; self-comforting rituals like hand-washing, door-checking or talk-talk-talking are indulged in to the point of exhaustion. Yet still the nagging hunger, lust or anxiety continues.

Physical Tourette-type tics are an example of this. The twitches are fragments of skills – each a tiny, degraded echo of some once-purposeful movement — that are triggered into existence by bursts of activity in an area of the unconscious brain called the putamen. The putamen is one part of the complex intertwined knot of nuclei that makes up the basal ganglia, deep in the centre of the brain. Its function is to look after automatic movements — those that have been learned by repetition — and to keep them flowing smoothly so the conscious brain can get on with the grander business of deciding how to direct those movements and learning new ones. Pedalling a bike (providing the rider is experienced), for example, is controlled by the putamen, while the movements needed to execute a new and complicated dance, say, would be controlled by different brain areas.

In normal people these little spasms of motor activity are inhibited before they become evident by neurons in adjacent areas which damp down the errant sparks. In those with Tourette's syndrome the inhibition fails, and the actions carry through.

In some children Tourette-type symptoms have been found to start, or become worse, after an infectious illness. One theory is that certain bacteria create an autoimmune condition in which the inhibitory cells in the striatum are selectively killed off. The condition has been dubbed PANDAS (Paediatric autoimmune neuropsychiatric disorders associated with streptococcal infection) but, despite more than a decade of research, it remains unclear whether the infection really causes Tourette's syndrome, or whether it is just one of a cocktail of causes.[3] Most people with Tourette's syndrome can identify 'premonitory urges' and — by making a conscious effort — suppress the movement that would normally follow.[4] Blocking tics like this does not, however, stop them. Until the urge has been translated into movement it continues to beat up against the walls of consciousness like an ever-intensifying itch demanding to be satisfied.

Brain scans of people with Tourette's syndrome typically show significant lack of activity in three brain areas: 'A' is the dorsolateral prefrontal cortex, an area which is concerned with generating appropriate actions. 'B' is the left basal ganglia which is concerned with the control of automatic movements. 'C' is the anterior cingulate cortex, an area which is concerned with focussing attention on actions. The lack of activity in these areas allows inappropriate fragments of actions — tics — to 'burst through'. [Ref: J. Moriarty et al. Brain Perfusion abnormalities in Gilles de la Tourette's syndrome, British Journal of Psychiatry 167 (2): 249–254 (August 1995)] People with Tourette's syndrome have also been found to have reduced tissue volume in these and other areas of the brain, which may be the result of the failure of certain nervous tracts to develop properly.[2]

One man, who has an elaborate combined shoulder-jerk and jaw-thrusting routine that he generally does about five times a minute, says:

'I can hold it off for a few minutes or even for an hour or so if I have to. When I meet someone new, or if I am doing something important I can appear quite normal for the duration. But when the pressure is off I have to catch up by ticcing some extra — I usually lock myself in the bathroom

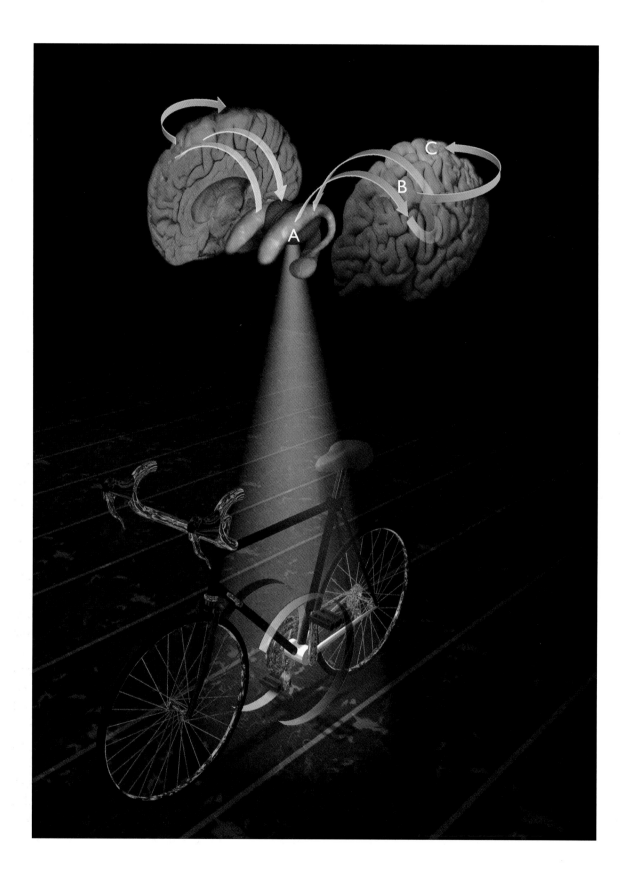

for ten minutes to do it. People say to me then: "If you can control it, why do you do it at all?" I explain to them: it's like holding your breath – you can do it for so long, but eventually you have to let go. And when you do, you pant for a while.'[5]

The shouts and curious vocal habits of Tourette's come from overactivity in another part of the dopamine-fuelled pathway that links the unconscious brain to the conscious. Here the pathways that are affected touch on the language areas in the temporal zone. The words seem to be tiny residual fragments of otherwise long-forgotten phrases. Tourette's syndrome, with its obvious physical manifestations and sometimes extravagant behaviour, seems on the face of it to be light years removed from the quiet mental anguish felt by people with obsessive–compulsive disorder (OCD). Recently, however, the two conditions have come to be recognized as different manifestations of the same underlying biological disturbance.

In OCD the urges are more complicated than in Tourette's. Instead of being compelled to, say, shout a word or move a limb in a particular way, people with OCD are driven to carry out complicated routines to still an ever-present feeling of unsettlement or doubt.

The routines may be purely mental or they may involve elaborate behavioural rituals. Counting is common. One woman says:

'I have to count to seven between each mouthful of food. If someone asks me a question while I

Above: *When people with obsessive-compulsive disorder (OCD) are put in situations where they feel uneasy a loop of neural activity sparks up in their brains. It runs between the caudate (A), which triggers the urge to 'do something', through the orbital prefrontal cortex (B), which gives the feeling that 'something is wrong', and back through the cingulate cortex (C) which keeps attention fixed on the feeling of unease.*

have food in my mouth I have to finish the counting before I can swallow to reply. If I try to swallow without completing the sequence, I gag. And if for some reason I lose count, I have to spit the food out, count seven again and take a new mouthful.'[6]

Another OCD patient has a fixation with the number four. Everything has to be done four times: four foldings back of the duvet in the morning before getting out of bed; four steps to the door, teeth-scrubbing movements in groups of four and so on. He has a particular horror of being left on an uneven number. Once his girlfriend told him that she loved him. He wasn't too sure if he reciprocated this feeling but the words 'sort of hung about in the air...like a big number one', so he told her he loved her, too. His tone of voice was not, perhaps, convincing enough for the girl to feel satisfied with this exchange, and she said it again: 'I love you.' Now, of course, the words hung like a huge number three, so he had to

Left: *Familiar motor skills, like riding a bicycle, are controlled by the putamen (A), which is part of the unconscious limbic system. The putamen is connected via a complex loop of nerves to the premotor cortex (B) – the part of the conscious brain which creates the urge to move. If the putamen is stimulated it passes the message on to the premotor cortex which, in turn, passes a 'move it' message to the adjoining cortex (C). The motor cortex then instructs the appropriate muscles to contract. In Tourette's syndrome the putamen is overactive, and triggers the acting out of fragments of old learned skills at inappropriate moments.*

repeat them again, to make it up to four. Satisfied by this, the girl then said she wanted to marry him – a proposition that brought about a further cascade of reciprocal pledges.[7]

Other internal compulsions may include thinking about a subject to the exclusion of almost everything else; going over and over past conversations; or being plagued by the need to imagine doing something terrible – killing someone, for example. People with OCD tend to be exceptionally good, in that they go to extreme lengths to avoid doing anything wrong. They are often obsessed with morality and are scrupulously honest. The need to be truthful may be taken to absurd lengths, as with this patient:

'If I was talking to you and I mentioned that I had seen someone in a red dress, as soon as I said it I would start to think: "Was it really red? Or could it have been another colour?" Once the idea had got into my head that I might have misled you – even if it didn't matter one bit what colour the dress was – I would start thinking: "Should I confess that I said the wrong colour or should I make myself live with the guilt?" So I try to avoid saying anything that could be wrong. I put "I think" or "I'm pretty sure" or "it could have been" in front of everything. It is a sort of ritual – a way of making sure I can never tell a lie.[8]

The behaviours associated with OCD tend to be the same the world over. The two most common are washing and checking. People who need to wash themselves may actually wear away the skin of their hands by constantly scrubbing them with soap and water. People who need to check things may find the activity takes up nearly all their time. A man who was compelled to check every car journey he made to make sure he had not knocked someone down had to get up at dawn to leave time to go over his journey to work two or three times to check for signs of an accident. The journey home was similarly repeated. And still he wondered, all day and all night, if in his minute scouring of the route he might somehow have overlooked a crushed corpse in the gutter.[9] Hypochondria (the need to check constantly for signs of bodily illness) and body dysmorphic disorder (the conviction that something is wrong with the way one looks) are variations on the theme. OCD is also thought to be the cause of about half the reported cases of compulsive hair-pulling.

These mental and behavioural tics are, like the physical jerks of the Touretter, fragments of pre-programmed skills. But in this case the memories are not personal ones picked up during the person's lifetime but those that are built into the species as instincts. The instinct to keep clean; to check the environment constantly for signs of anything untoward; the need to keep order and balance – all these things have a basis in survival. In OCD they have simply come adrift from the survival superstructure and appear as isolated, inappropriate and exaggerated habits.

As with Tourette's, what seems to be happening in OCD is that a particular neural pathway is overactive. This time it is one that runs between the frontal lobe (including the premotor area) to another part of the basal ganglia – the caudate nucleus. The caudate nucleus is joined to the putamen and they develop in the embryo as a single structure. The main difference between them is that, while the putamen is mainly connected to the premotor cortex, the caudate nucleus is in touch with the frontal lobes where thinking, assessing and planning – the highest forms of cognition – take place. In a normal brain the caudate nucleus looks after certain aspects of automatic thinking just as the putamen looks after automatic movements. The caudate nucleus is the part of the brain that automatically prompts you to wash when you are dirty; that reminds you to check the doors before you leave the house; and that alerts you to and focuses your attention on anything that is out of order.

It does all this by activating one particular area of the frontal lobe – a spot in the orbital cortex, the area of the frontal lobe just above the eyes. This is the area that lights up when something caudate nucleus   basal ganglia

putamen   amygdala

The caudate nucleus is closely connected to the amygdala,
which gives rise to feelings of fear. The knock-on effect of
caudate activity in OCD may partly explain why people with
the disorder suffer such anxiety.

unexpected happens. It was first identified during
monkey studies done by Professor E. T. Rolls at
Oxford University. The animals were shown
green and blue lights and trained to associate the
blue light with a reward of fruit juice, and the
green light with a salt drink. Once they had
grasped the link between blue = juice and green
= salt the drinks were switched. Suddenly the
monkeys got a salt drink when they saw the blue
light. When this happened an area of the brain that
had been quiet until then leapt into life. The neurons in the orbital cortex that lit up were not
simply responding to the saltiness of the drink –
taste discrimination and the simple 'ugh!' reaction
happen elsewhere in the brain. This particular
area was clearly activated by the discovery that
something in the world was not quite right – it
was a 'hey! something is wrong here' reaction – a
built-in error-detection device. Once the monkeys got used to getting salty drink occasionally,
instead of the usual juice, the reaction disappeared.

Since then brain scans on humans have shown
that this area is particularly lively in people with

OCD. When a person with a hand-washing compulsion is told to imagine themselves in some
filthy place their caudate nucleus and orbital frontal cortex fire away like mad. An area in the middle of the brain – the cingulate cortex – also
responds strongly. This is the part of the brain that
registers conscious emotion, and its involvement
demonstrates the emotional discomfort generated
by OCD.

A similar brain pattern can only be produced in
a normal person by persuading them to think very
hard about some major catastrophe like watching
their home burn down with their family inside.
After these imaginings have been engineered in
the subjects' minds and when the researchers tell
them they can relax and forget their terrible
thoughts, the person with OCD continues to
show a lit-up caudate nucleus and orbital frontal
cortex. It doesn't matter to them that the laboratory and their hands are obviously shiny clean,
the thought that they are contaminated by dirt just
won't go away. Once they have left the scanner
and slipped off to wash, the feeling may be
reduced. A scan at that moment might show little
caudate or orbital frontal activity. But soon the
circuit will glow again, and the urge to wash will
be rekindled. Their error-detection mechanism
has somehow become stuck on alert, and no matter how often the appropriate turn-off action is
carried out it continues to shriek its warning.

OCD is diagnosed when obsessions and compulsions are so severe that they disrupt normal
life. Depending on local diagnostic criteria
between one–three people in every hundred
come into this category, a proportion that appears
to be more or less the same wherever statistics are
available.[10] But you do not have to have OCD to
be nagged by that feeling that everything in the
world is not quite right. People who are forever
cleaning and ordering their homes; people who
can never relax unless they have double- and
treble-checked that the doors are locked before
they go to bed; people who insist on having twice

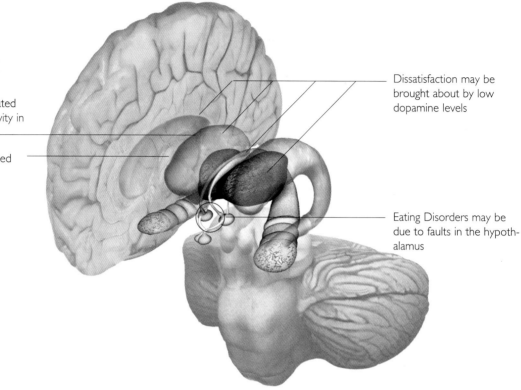

OCD: associated with overactivity in caudate

Tics are created by flurries of activity in the putamen

Dissatisfaction may be brought about by low dopamine levels

Eating Disorders may be due to faults in the hypoth-alamus

the usual number of health checks and still worry they might have a terminal disease – these may all be cursed with an overactive error-detection system, a neural circuit that lights up too readily and stays lit up too long.

The same may be true of people who worry overly about the effect they are having on other people. Just as washing and checking doors stems from the need to ensure physical safety, so fretting about social behaviour may stem from a need to be secure within the group. This form of obsessiveness might involve, for example, going over and over each conversation, analysing what you said, or didn't say, and worrying about every unintended or imagined slight.

The drive to be 'good' and the need to follow rituals may encourage many people with OCD to embrace formal religion or to enter sects where their need for security is satisfied by group adherence to a strict set of values that allows little

room for doubt. Even Tourette's syndrome may have its mild echoes in normal people. The sniffers, the blinkers, the girls who repeatedly brush imaginery hair from their eyes – are these actions driven by the spasms of neural activity from the putamen?

Similarly, some people seem to live permanently in the grip of some seemingly unassuageable appetite. They can never get enough of whatever it is they are hooked on: sex, food, risk or drugs. US geneticists Kenneth Blum and David Comings have labelled this type of discontent reward deficiency syndrome, and they propose that an extraordinarily wide range of disorders can be clustered under its umbrella. Depending on which part of the reward system (and thus which part of the brain) is most affected, a person may display anything from mild anxiety, irritability or risk-taking to eating disorders, compulsive shopping and gambling, drug addiction and alcoholism.[11] As the name suggests, people with reward deficiency syndrome are unable to get satisfaction from life. Something in the way their brain works makes it impossible for them to turn off their appetites.

This type of discontent is very widespread: some surveys have concluded that one in four people suffer from one of the conditions included by Blum and Comings in reward deficiency disorder.[12] Many of these conditions are hard to treat because they engage the brain at all levels. Although all urges are ultimately connected to bodily needs, some of them bring about very complex behaviour that can become an end in itself. The urge to eat, for example, may set off an extraordinarily sophisticated train of behaviour: not just seeking food, but selecting it carefully and making it into a complicated dish. Once you have sampled the joys of double chocolate chip cookie and yoghurt ice cream it requires a very faint urge, in this author's experience, to prompt a visit to the freezer. Therefore, urges involve both the most mechanical of brain functions – monitoring glucose levels, for example, in the case of hunger – and the most advanced. In physical terms this means everything from the brainstem to the frontal cortex.

This complicated system has evolved over millions of years and until recently it has worked for us pretty well. In a world of sparse resources the reward it delivers for the *act* of pleasure-seeking, as well as the goal, ensures that people will chase their supper or toil long and hard to gather sufficient food for survival. The trouble with evolution, however, is that it cannot keep pace with human ingenuity. Today we can get our dinner by pulling the plastic covering off an oven-ready pork chop rather than by chasing a wild boar to its death. No wonder our puny achievements give us so little satisfaction.

As the map of the brain takes shape, it is becoming possible to see where and how it might be possible to alter its architecture and function in a way that might cause it to serve us better than the design currently arrived at by evolution.

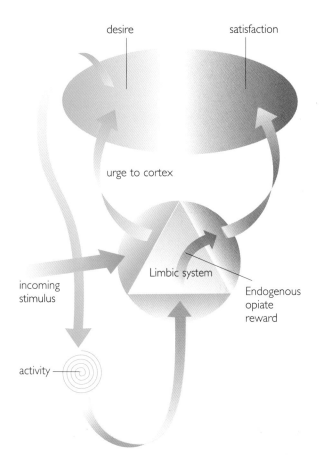

The brain uses a carrot-and-stick system to ensure that we pursue and achieve the things we need to survive. A stimulus from outside (the sight of food, say) or from the body (falling glucose levels) is registered by the limbic system which creates an urge which registers consciously as desire. The cortex then instructs the body to act in whatever way is necessary to achieve its desire. The activity sends messages back to the limbic system which releases opioid-like neurotransmitters which raise circulating dopamine levels and create a feeling of satisfaction.

Pharmaceutical companies are already investing vast sums of money in developing drugs to moderate urge-driven behaviour by affecting levels of the various neurotransmitters – 'behavioural pharmacology' is now a recognized vocational category.

After drugs comes genetic engineering. The

system that once served us so well is encoded in our genes and by the middle of the twenty-first century we will probably have the knowledge and techniques to tweak those genes to produce a brain that is better suited to its time.

The genetic foundations of our elaborate seek-and-reward system are complex. Researchers have already identified no fewer than 1,500 human gene mutations which appear to contribute to the growing, global-wide problem of addiction. All these genes seem to affect a handful of neural pathways, which are driven by dopamine (see pp 104–105).[13]

Many people recoil instinctively from the idea of reinventing the species – it reeks to them of cheating nature or playing God. Certainly, there are dangers – from the story of Frankenstein's monster to the development of antibiotic resistance, the consequences of scientific hubris are spelt out in neon.

Yet there are dangers, too, in ploughing on with what is in some ways outdated equipment. Evolution has produced marvellous mechanisms to aid our survival, but it cannot change us as fast as we can change our world. Perhaps the time has come to use the ingenuity with which aeons of natural selection have endowed us, to make ourselves more fit for the environment that we have created.

Hunger

People are getting fatter, and fatter, and fatter. In the US and Western Europe 30–40 per cent of people are overweight and The World Health Organisation predicts that by 2015 700 million will be obese.[14] Millions of us die early each year from clogged arteries and other complications of obesity. Our drive to pleasure is killing us.

As with all our urges and appetites, the mechanism by which simple, physical hunger is generated and satisfied centres on the hypothalamus. Information about the state of the body is constantly fed to the hypothalamus through a complex interplay of hormones, neuropeptides and neurotransmitters. If glucose, mineral or fat levels

drop, the information is signalled from the blood, stomach, intestines and fat cells. The hypothalamus then feeds these signals up to the cortex where they excite the many areas that consciously register hunger and organize the finding, preparing and eating of food. As the meal is eaten the system goes into reverse: the body signals its satisfaction back to the hypothalamus, which passes the message on to the cortex, which then creates a conscious desire to stop eating.

This all sounds very straightforward and efficient. Yet clearly it is not fail-safe enough to prevent what amounts to a global epidemic of over- (and occasionally under-) eating.

One cause of eating disorder may lie in the hypothalamus itself. Two hypothalamic nuclei – the lateral and the ventromedial – play a central role in controlling appetite. The lateral nucleus senses falling blood glucose and signals hunger while the ventromedial responds to rising glucose levels and signals satiety. Animals with damage to the lateral nucleus thus eat very little while those with damage to the ventromedial nucleus gorge.

This dual-lobed mechanism is not a simple off/on appetite switch, however. Rats with ventromedial nucleus damage may overeat – but only if eating is made easy. If they have to press a lever to get food, they will do so less often than normal rats. An interesting experiment suggests that the same may be true of people. Two groups of obese subjects were each a given a dish of nuts and invited to nibble freely at them while they did some dull task. The nuts in one dish were pre-shelled while the others were in their shells and accompanied by a nutcracker. The subjects ate large quantities of the pre-shelled nuts but very few of those that had first to be shelled. This curious finding may, in part, explain why obesity is strongly correlated with consumption of processed, heat-and-eat meals and junk food.

Anorexics, like those who are obese, may also have impaired hypothalamic function. Brain imaging studies[15] show that activity in the limbic system does not seem to be transferred in the normal way to the cortex – for some reason the neural

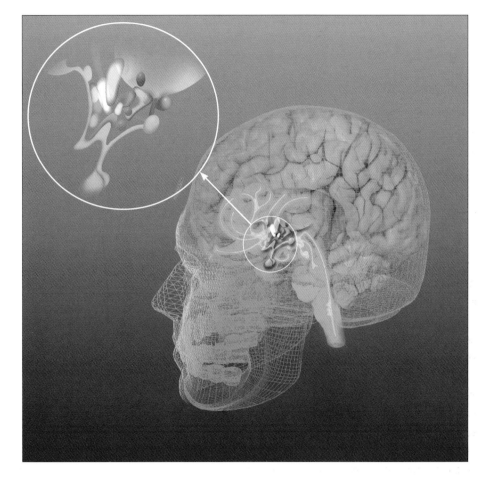

The hypothalamus is a cluster of nuclei, each of which helps to control our bodily urges and appetites. It is part of the diencephalon which means, literally 'in between brain', and acts like a bridge between the body and the brain. The hypothalamus is tiny — it weighs just one three hundredth of the total brain mass — but it has an enormous effect and even small dysfunctions in a single one of its nuclei can create serious physical and mental problems.

connections between the appetite sensors in the hypothalamus and the areas that register conscious hunger are not carrying signals effectively.

The failure to convey the full impact of bodily changes to the conscious brain may explain a curious difference between people subject to anorexia and normal eaters. Researchers at the University of Pittsburgh gave two such groups a game to play while looking at the activation in a part of their brains concerned with immediate emotional response, the anterior ventral striatum. The game was a simple win/lose set-up, in which winning gained the participant a monetary reward. The brain scans showed that in the normal group the emotional areas of the brain showed clearly different responses according to the win or lose situation. Those of recently-recovered anorexics, however, showed very little variation — it was as though their capacity for feeling was reduced to a

narrower spectrum. Hence, possibly, the reward gained from a nice meal, and the punishment of starvation, had less emotional effect on them.[16]

Damage to deep limbic structures like the hypothalamus is relatively rare, so it seems likely that most hypothalamic dysfunction stems from a disturbance of the neurotransmitters that carry messages to and from it. Serotonin, for example, damps down activity in the lateral hypothalamus, so a high level of it is likely to reduce appetite, while a low level is likely to increase it. This is borne out by studies that show that anorexics do indeed tend to show abnormally raised serotonin, while people with bulimia have unusually low levels.[17] This may eventually translate into actual damage because, if a brain area is not fully stimulated, it may wither and shrink.

Although limbic area dysfunction is increasingly seen to play a part in eating disorders, it is clearly only part of their underlying cause. Cultural influ-

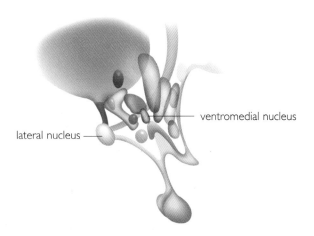

The lateral and ventromedial nuclei of the hypothalamus act like 'on' and 'off' switches for the appetite.

ences are at work, too. An anorexic's ambition to be thinner-than-thin, or the bulimic's determination to prevent their body absorbing what they have eaten, is conceived in the conscious part of the brain and clearly has a lot to do with the way that a person thinks. Anorexics, for example, tend to be disciplined, persevering and introvert, while bulimics are more inclined to be extravert, distractable and impulsive.[18] This makes these disorders open to treatment by psychological methods, and – although there are now several fairly effective drugs that work directly on the brain – most therapies are currently based on altering consciousness rather than altering physiology.

One day brain mappers may deliver a detailed enough blueprint of the food appetite system to allow direct modification, rather as is being tried now for people with OCD. For the moment our food-seeking genes continue to dispatch our bodies, clogged with fat, to their early graves.

Sex

'The male subject was strapped to a chair-like device with his head painlessly immobilized. In this position it was possible to insert a fine microelectrode into the hypothalamus. The female subject was then strapped into another chair that was positioned several feet away.

'The male was provided with a button that he could push to bring the chair bearing the female adjacent to his own. In this position the two were able to copulate without the male having to move his head. Recordings of neuronal activity were therefore obtained from the moment the male saw the female to completion of copulation.

'The highest neuronal activity (50 impulses per second) was recorded from a neuron in the medial preoptic area of the hypothalamus as the subject pressed the button to bring the female towards him. During copulation the discharge rate dropped and after ejaculation it ceased almost entirely. The specifically sexual nature of this activity was confirmed by a control experiment in which the female was replaced by a banana.' – *Report of experiment*[19]

Brain researchers are forced to go to extraordinary lengths to study sex, particularly in humans.

There is, for a start, the delicate problem of finding suitable subjects. If you can overcome that there is a practical difficulty: imaging equipment requires the subjects' heads to be rock-still in order not to dislodge the electrodes (in EEG experiments) or fuzz up the picture (in PET and MRI scanning). This is usually achieved by strapping the head into a brace, or getting the subject to clamp their teeth around a rubber 'bite bar'. Then there is the design of the scanning machine – definitely for one person only. Even if you can persuade someone to become sexually aroused while their teeth are clamped around a rubber bar in a clanging metal cigar tube, the confined space seriously limits the nature of the subsequent activity. The experiment above was carried out in Kyushu University and the subjects were – you may be relieved to know – macaque monkeys. In recent

THE DOPAMINE CONNECTION

Dopamine drives our behaviour towards fulfilling our urges and appetites, and when the driving doesn't stop it fuels our addictions.

The power of dopamine lies in its ability to imbue thoughts, feelings, and the things we come across in the outside world with meaning and significance. It pulls things together – the sight of an attractive person with the desire for sex; the thought of food with the urge to eat, and encourages us to see patterns and connections which help us to recognize goals and direct our behaviour. Too much, or too little of it (or greater or less sensitivity to it) therefore has a wide range of effects.

Too much of it encourages us to see links and patterns where there none – excessive dopaminergic action in the parts of the brain that govern recognition and belief therefore makes someone susceptible to hallucinations and magical thinking. In the areas concerned with motor activity too much can lead to uncontrolled movements, as in Tourette's syndrome. In the 'worry circuits' an imbalance of dopamine causes obsessions and compulsions, overexcitement, euphoria and exaggerated convictions of 'meaningfulness' (mania).

Too little dopamine is known to cause tremor and the inability to start voluntary movement (Parkinson's disease and related disorders), and is implicated in feelings of meaninglessness, lethargy and misery (depression), catatonia and social withdrawal (negative symptoms of schizophrenia), lack of attention and concentration (adult attention deficit disorder), and cravings and withdrawal.

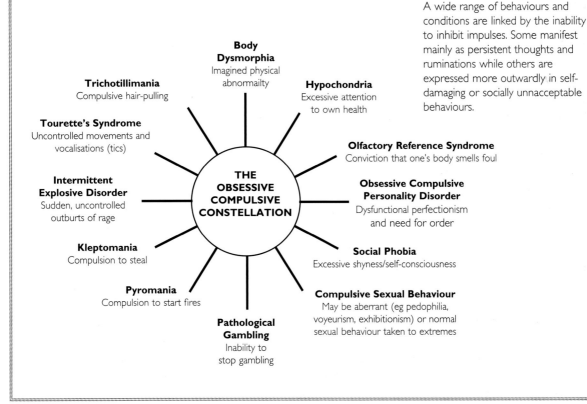

A wide range of behaviours and conditions are linked by the inability to inhibit impulses. Some manifest mainly as persistent thoughts and ruminations while others are expressed more outwardly in self-damaging or socially unnacceptable behaviours.

Body Dysmorphia
Imagined physical abnormailty

Hypochondria
Excessive attention to own health

Trichotillimania
Compulsive hair-pulling

Tourette's Syndrome
Uncontrolled movements and vocalisations (tics)

Olfactory Reference Syndrome
Conviction that one's body smells foul

THE OBSESSIVE COMPULSIVE CONSTELLATION

Intermittent Explosive Disorder
Sudden, uncontrolled outburts of rage

Obsessive Compulsive Personality Disorder
Dysfunctional perfectionism and need for order

Kleptomania
Compulsion to steal

Social Phobia
Excessive shyness/self-consciousness

Pyromania
Compulsion to start fires

Compulsive Sexual Behaviour
May be aberrant (eg pedophilia, voyeurism, exhibitionism) or normal sexual behaviour taken to extremes

Pathological Gambling
Inability to stop gambling

years, however, a few game human volunteers have also subjected their brains to scrutiny while stimulating themselves, or allowing themselves to be stimulated, one way or another, to orgasm.

Once again, the brain circuits found to be most actively involved in producing the building excitement and final ecstasy of orgasmic sex are the dopamine-driven reward circuits.[20] It is this activation, too, that generates the compulsive urge for contact and the obsessional thoughts associated with romantic love. Although romantic fantasies may take high-flown, courtly forms, the essential nature of them is sexual. Hence when the dopamine circuits are damped down sexual drive and response is also reduced. This commonly occurs when people take antidepressants of the SSRI (selective serotonin reuptake inhibitors) type. As serotonin levels rise, dopamine levels tend to fall, hence the sense of serenity and calm afforded by SSRIs (when they work) may drive out sharper emotions such as romantic yearning.[21] 'My wife constantly complains when I'm on higher doses [of a SSRI] that I show no emotions at all.' writes a commentator on a website for people who have suffered depression. 'I'm not sad or depressed, but never happy either. So if she does something special for me, I have had to learn to comment on it because otherwise she doesn't get any positive feedback.' 'It [SSRI] … has been a big help with my major depression' writes another, '…but I have a hard time feeling that 'tender, warm feeling' that used to be typical towards my husband'. A third recalls a period on an antidepressant during which 'I still wanted sex, but never felt horny, and I could go for hours without coming … I felt it numbed me to an extent mood wise, but the low, low moods virtually disappeared'. (From: http://depression.about.com/b/2009/04/17/can-ssris-make-you-fall-out-of-love.htm)

Men and women report more or less identical sensations when they describe orgasm, so it is not surprising that their brains look for the most part pretty similar while they are building up to it.

ADDICTION

The reward circuitry centres on limbic areas known as the ventral tegmental area (VTA) and the nucleus accumbens. However, many other brain areas are also involved – frontal areas are involved in seeking behaviour, for instance, the septum is responsible for some of the pleasurable feelings associated with drug use, and the amygdala produces emotional responses. Each type of drug works in a slightly different way to produce its characteristic effects.

Ecstasy, for example, stimulates serotonin-producing cells, which turn on the areas of the prefrontal cortex that give feelings of euphoria, meaning and affections.

This is similar in effect to antidepressants, but Ecstasy causes the cells to produce a greater rush of neurotransmitters than antidepressants and its mechanism puts regular users in danger of 'burning out' the cells, creating temporary withdrawal symptoms and a long-term risk of chronic depression.

Hallucinogenic drugs like LSD and magic mushrooms also stimulate serotonin production or contain chemicals that mimic its effects. As well as stimulating the brain's pleasure centres, these drugs also activate areas in the temporal lobes that give rise to hallucinations. Bad trips may be the result of stimulation of the amygdala, which produces feelings of fear.

Cocaine increases the amount of dopamine available to cells by blocking the mechanism that usually gets rid of excess dopamine. It also blocks re-uptake of noradrenaline and serotonin. The rise in these three neurotransmitters causes the feeling of euphoria (dopamine), confidence (serotonin) and energy (noradrenaline) associated with the drug. Amphetamines release dopamine and noradrenaline. This creates energy but may also produce feelings of anxiety and agitation.

Nicotine activates dopamine neurons by mimicking the effect of dopamine in binding to receptors in the cells' surface. Its initial effect is therefore similar to a dopamine rush. Nicotine quickly desensitizes the cells it works on, however, so the initial effects are no longer felt. Nicotine also affects neurons that produce a neurotransmitter called acetylcholine. This is one of the chemicals involved in alertness and is known to boost memory.

Opioids like morphine and heroin fit into receptors that normally take endorphins and enkaphelins. This triggers the reward circuit that creates the dopamine rush. The disengagement from pain produced by these drugs is thought to be caused by the deactivation of an area in the cortex called the anterior cingulate gyrus, which concentrates attention on adverse internal stimuli. The withdrawal effects of opioids are associated with a steep rise in stress hormones that activate the urge-making areas of the brain.

Alcohol and tranquillizers like benzodiazepines decrease neural activity through action on GABA (gamma amino butyric acid) neurons. Drugs that block the receptors in these cells reduce the pleasure of drinking and are effective in weaning addicts off alcohol. Alcoholism – and probably all drug addiction – is closely associated with genetic factors. Children of alcoholics, for example, are four times more likely than other people to become addicted to drink – even if they are brought up away from their natural parents.

Cocaine creates euphoria by blocking receptors in brain cells which normally mop up excess dopamine. This leaves more dopamine free to excite the areas of the brain which affect mood. The scans above show levels of dopamine absorption in a normal brain (red = high absorption, yellow = medium; green = low)
Top: *after a placebo.* Middle: *after a low dose (0.1mg per kg body weight) of cocaine.* Bottom: *after a high dose (0.6 mg per kg). As you can see, after a high dose hardly any dopamine is locked up – it is all free to work on other neurons.*

medial preoptic area

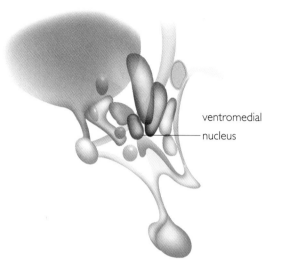

ventromedial nucleus

Typical male/female sexual responses are brought about by separate parts of the hypothalamus.
Left: The medial preoptic area orients the sex drive towards female. Signals from here are sent to the cortex, producing conscious excitement, and down to the penis, to produce an erection.
Right: Female typical sexual behaviour is prompted by the ventro-medial nucleus. This is the same cluster of cells that are involved in turning on the appetite for food. When it is stimulated in a sexual context it encourages lordosis — genital display. This gesture is also made by some animals as a sign of submission.

Several brain imaging studies show that both sexes — unsurprisingly — show fairly frenetic activity in the part of the brain that registers sensations from the genitals, as well as in the limbic areas involved in reward.

Some evidence suggests however, that there is curious diversion in brain activity between the sexes once they reach the final climax. Gert Holstege and colleagues at the University of Groningen in the Netherlands carried out a series of experiments in which couples stimulated each other to orgasm while a PET scanner recorded what was happening in their heads. In one study they recruited 13 healthy heterosexual women and their partners and then mapped the activity in the women's brains during four experiences: simply resting, faking an orgasm, having their clitoris stimulated by their partner's fingers, and clitoral self-stimulation to the point of orgasm.

Previous studies on men showed that at orgasm activity dipped in the amygdala, an area primarily concerned with emotional response and alertness, but that this and other 'emotional' parts of the brain kept ticking over. In the women, by contrast, come orgasm brain activity in large areas suddenly died away to nothing. The muted areas included neurons in the left lateral orbitofrontal cortex, which, when active, generate conscious awareness of strong emotion. An adjacent part of the frontal cortex, the dorsomedial prefrontal cortex, also dimmed to practically nothing. This area plays a key part in moral reasoning and social judgment. The researchers interpreted these findings as showing that in women, emotional awareness, judgment and reasoning are suspended during orgasm to a greater extent than in men. Given that these brain functions are primarily about self-protection — emotions to alert one to danger, judgment and reasoning to direct action in the face of it — it looks as though, for the duration of orgasm women cede responsibility for their safety to their partner, leaving themselves momentarily devoid of their normal defences.[22] This finding

SEX DIFFERENCES IN THE BRAIN

The main structural differences so far observed between men's and women's brains are:

* The hypothalamic nucleus INAH3, in the medial preoptic area, is on average 2.5 times larger in men than in women. This nucleus is responsible for male-typical sexual behaviour. It contains more cells that are sensitive to androgens (male hormones) than any other part of the brain. Some studies[23] have found a correlation in women between assertive (male-typical) and excessive heterosexual behaviour and small breasts, low voice, acne and hirsutism. The physical characteristics generally signify unusually high androgen levels, and it may be that the women's behaviour is caused by their hormones stimulating INAH3.

* The corpus callosum – the band of tissue through which the two hemispheres communicate – is relatively larger in women than in men.[24] So is the anterior commissure – a more primitive connection between the hemispheres that links the unconscious areas of the hemispheres only.[25]

This may explain why women seem to be more aware of their own and others' emotions than men – the emotionally sensitive right hemisphere is able to pass more information to the analytical, linguistically talented left side. It may also allow emotion to be incorporated more easily into speech and thought processes. Women also have more tissue in the massa intermedia, which connects the two halves of the thalamus.

* Men lose their brain tissue earlier in the ageing process than women, and overall they lose more of it. Men are particularly prone to tissue loss in the frontal and temporal lobes.[26] These areas are concerned with thinking and feeling, and loss of tissue in them is likely to cause irritability and

MALE

medial pre optic area

FEMALE

corpus callosum

anterior commissure

massa intermedia

other personality changes. Women tend to lose tissue in the hippocampus and parietal areas. These are more concerned with memory and visuo-spatial abilities, so women are more likely than men to have difficulty remembering things and finding their way about as they age.

Imaging studies show that men and women use their brains differently, too. When they do complex mental tasks there is a tendency for women to bring both sides of their brain to bear on the problem, while men often use only the side most obvi-ously suited to it. This pattern of activity suggests that in some ways women take a broader view of life, bringing more aspects of the situation into play when making decisions, for example. Men, on the other hand, are more focused.

may explain why, according to one study, women who show the socially avoidant behaviour typical of those who felt insecure as infants seem to find orgasm harder to achieve. Their emotional alarm systems may be stuck on to such an extent that even in the throes of sexual abandonment they will not damp down enough to allow orgasm to happen.[27]

Conversely, in some people orgasm comes very easily. Although it is usually brought about by genital stimulation, some people can bring themselves to sexual climax just by thinking about it, and studies of such 'all in the head' orgasms show that the associated physical responses, such as heart rate increases, blood pressure changes, pupil dilation and increased toleration of pain – are identical to those that occur during genitally induced orgasm. (Whipple, Ogden, & Komisaruk, 1992).Komisaruk, Whipple, & Alexander, 1993).

Sexual drive centres on the hypothalamus but, like other urges, it radiates out to encompass a wide range of other brain areas in both the limbic area and the cortex. Again, like other urges, it can be split into various elements, each of which is localized. The clumps of tissue that produce each aspect of sexual feeling and behaviour are affected not only by neurotransmitters but also by the sex hormones oestrogen and testosterone. These hormones help 'set' a person's sexual orientation, style and drive.

The various brain areas connected with sex differ between males and females and the underlying layout is determined – much of it prenatally – by genes. These physical differences are mirrored by observed differences in behaviour. Within any group of significant size – whether it be people, monkeys or rats – these behavioural distinctions are on average great enough for it to be accurate to talk of male-typical and female-typical sexual behaviour.

Male-typical sexual behaviour is more assertive than that of females; it is more closely linked to aggression and it involves taking the penetrative role. Female-typical is more submissive; it typically involves displaying the genitals (lordosis) and taking the receptive role in intercourse. The physical layout of male and female brains explains, in part, how these behavioural differences come about.

The medial preoptic area of the hypothalamus, which was so active in the copulating male monkey, seems to be the centre of male-specific sex behaviour. It is the area that has the largest number of androgen (male hormone)-sensitive neurons and it is bigger in men than in women. When this area is stimulated male monkeys become fanatically interested in any female that is around – providing she is in heat. However, if a female is not in heat the male is not interested. Conversely, if the medial preoptic area is removed the monkey loses interest in all females – but not in sex *per se*. Monkeys will continue to masturbate after this area of brain is removed and may show increased female-typical behaviour like lordosis.

This suggests the main function of the medial preoptic area is to respond to hormonal signals given off by receptive females. These signals come in from various areas. The olfactory system is a main source of input in monkeys, underlying the importance of smell to their sexuality, but the role of smell in humans is less certain.

The medial preoptic area also receives signals from two nuclei in the amygdala (corticomedial and basolateral), both of which are concerned in one way or another with producing aggressive or assertive behaviour. This connection may explain why sex, in the male, is sometimes coupled with aggression – the excitement of the medial pre-optic nucleus in the hypothalamus may have a knock-on effect on the areas in the amygdala that generate aggression and vice versa.

Once it is aroused by a suitable sexual stimulus, the medial preoptic hypothalamus passes the signal up to the cerebral cortex, which does (or tries to do) whatever is required to get the body it is attached to into an appropriate position for intercourse. At the same time signals are sent

Direct stimulation of the temporal lobe can produce strong erotic feelings. The swollen blood vessel seen in this brain scan produced flurries of activity which caused the patient to experience orgasms at entirely inappropriate times. The unwanted orgasms happened about once a fortnight for three years before the cause was uncovered.

[Ref: J.P. Reading and R.G. Will *Unwelcome Orgasms*, The Lancet 350 p1746, 13 December 1997)

down to the brainstem, which produces penile erection. Once intercourse begins, the motor cortex comes into play, producing appropriate thrusting movements. Finally, another hypothalamic nuclei, the dorsomedial nucleus, triggers ejaculation.

Normally, all of this takes place in an ordered sequence, but sometimes – through brain damage or dysfunction – one or another element may get out of synch, fail, or arise without the rest. If the dorsomedial nucleus is stimulated during an epileptic fit, for example, ejaculation may take place without any other sign of sexual arousal, and, in men, stimulation of the septum – an area of the limbic system that lies adjacent to the hypothalamus – has been known to produce orgasm without pleasure. This has been held to demonstrate that orgasm is, at its root, a form of 'reflex epilepsy'. Septum damage may also cause priapism – a condition in which a man has a permanent erection.

IS THERE A 'GAY BRAIN'?

In 1991 the prestigious journal *Science* published a study showing that the brains of a group of homosexual men who had died from Aids were structurally different from the brains of heterosexual men. The nucleus in the hypothalamus that triggers male-typical sexual behaviour was much smaller in the gay men and looked more like that in the brains of women. The author, Simon LeVay, from the University of California, was attacked by gay activists who feared that the recognition of homosexuality as a physical-based condition might lead to it being re-stigmatized. LeVay, who is himself gay, then went on to discover that the corpus callosum differs between gay and straight men, too – in gays it was found to be bigger. Three years later a study led by molecular biologist Dean Hamer of the National Institute of Health in Washington, DC, found evidence to suggest that a specific gene – carried on the maternal line – influenced sexual orientation in men. In 2008 Swedish scientists studied brain scans of 90 gay and straight men and women, and found that the size of the two hemispheres of gay mens' brains more closely resembled those of straight women than they did straight men. In heterosexual women, the two halves of the brain are more or less the same size. In heterosexual men, the right hemisphere is slightly larger. Scans of the brains of gay men in the study, however, showed that their hemispheres were relatively symmetrical, like those of straight women, while the brains of homosexual women were asymmetrical like those of straight men.[28] Put together, these studies provide strong evidence that homosexuality is rooted in biology – and hostility to the idea has largely disappeared.

Conversely, lack of stimulation to one or another of the sex nuclei may result in impotence: if sexual signals from the hypothalamus fail to reach the brainstem, for example, erection is impossible.

Female-typical sex behaviour is located in the ventromedial nucleus of the hypothalamus – the same one that plays a crucial part in hunger. This area is rich in oestrogen-sensitive neurons, and it is this hormone that seems to excite the ventromedial nucleus to produce lordosis – the genital display that is typical of female sexual invitation in many species. In rats lordosis is a reflex action – it occurs whenever the skin on a female animal's rump is grasped, as it would be by a mounting male. Unlike simple knee-jerk reactions, however, lordosis seems to be partially under conscious control – it is exhibited much more strongly when the stimulus comes from a male rat rather than the fingers of a laboratory researcher. In humans lordosis is generally kept firmly and completely under conscious control, though a glance through any selection of hardcore porn shows that it has by no means died out.

Although the female sex hormones seem to dictate the *type* of sexual behaviour exhibited they do not have much effect on the *strength* of the sex drive. This is controlled, in both sexes, by testosterone. These chemicals work very widely throughout the brain, and it seems likely that sex drive is brought about by the interaction of many different brain areas rather than just one.

Sex permeates the entire brain, especially the human brain. Connections from the sex-sniffing, sex-seeking and sex-reactive areas of the limbic system radiate to almost every corner of every cortical lobe, feeding the urge to our conscious minds.

The sexual traffic in the brain goes in both directions. As lascivious promptings push up from below, so the conscious brain pushes sexually stimulating information gathered in from the environment down to the limbic system. Between them the two interactive brain levels keep humans warmed up and ready for sex at any time. Other species show this degree of interest only when the female is physically ready to conceive. Humans alone have elevated sex from a periodic spree to a full-time occupation and in doing so they have turned it into something very elaborate. Sex involves practically every type of brain activity – from the high level cognition involved in imagining a rosy future with a putative romantic partner, through visual and physical recognition of sexually relevant material, down through emotion and straightforward bodily function. Because of this any fault, anywhere in the brain, may bring about some type of sexual dysfunction along with other problems. The infiltration of sex into the frontal lobes – the place where humans construct their most sophisticated, abstract ideas – has entangled it with our deepest notions of morality. Hence sexual obscenity and disinhibition are characteristic of people with the sort of frontal lobe damage that causes the destruction of a person's 'higher' cerebral functions.

Frontal lobe damage may also bring about erotomania – an obsessional delusion with a strong sexual element. Erotomaniacs believe that another person – usually someone famous – is in love with them and passing them secret messages of adoration. Sometimes they report making love to the object of their obsession, even though they have never even met them.[29] Stalkers are often erotomaniacs. They are usually harmless, but their attentions can drive their victims to exasperation. One recent case involved a man who had broken into the home of a female neighbour – whom he had followed constantly but never spoken to – and began to move in his belongings. When the police came to arrest him he informed them that the woman and he were engaged and were about to start living together. An MRI scan showed a massive (benign) growth in his left frontal lobe. When it was removed his behaviour returned to normal.[30]

Another case involved a 40-year-old schoolteacher who suddenly began secretly visiting child pornography web sites and soliciting prostitutes at massage parlours. When the man's wife found out

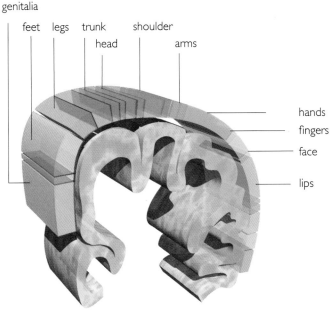

genitalia
feet legs trunk shoulder
head arms

hands
fingers
face
lips

The Brain's 'Touch Map'
The area of cortex which registers body touch is wrapped
around the cerebrum like an Alice band. The area given over to
the genitals is about as large as the rest of the chest, abdomen
and back put together.

If the area of each body part was proportionate to its sensitivity
people would look very different ...

he had made subtle sexual advances towards young children, he was legally evicted from his house, found guilty of child molestation and medicated for paedophilia. The evening before his prison sentencing he took himself to a hospital complaining of headache and saying he was afraid he would rape his landlady. An MRI scan of his brain revealed an egg-sized tumour in the right frontal area of his brain. When it was removed the sexual compulsions disappeared, but a few months later they came back. Recognising the change in himself, the man returned to hospital where the tumour was found to have re-grown.[31]

The temporal lobe is also implicated in sexual function. Damage to the cortex towards the front of that lobe, and the amygdala, which lies below it, results in a condition known as Kluver-Bucy syndrome, in which the patient tries to stuff anything in the vicinity into their mouth and/or make love to it. One unfortunate man with this condition was arrested while trying to make love to a pavement.[32]

The reason for this bizarre behaviour may be that the cortical area of the temporal lobe that is damaged in Kluver-Bucy syndrome normally sends inhibitory signals to the ventromedial nucleus in the hypothalamus. Part of the ventromedial nucleus, as we have seen, switches on the compulsion to put easily available food in the mouth, while another part triggers female-typical sexual behaviour. So cortical damage that allows the ventromedial nucleus to fire away without inhibition may create a continuous urge to eat and copulate. The strange lack of discrimination about what is eaten and copulated with may be due to disruption of the ability to recognize categories of object – another function that is localized in the temporal lobe. Put these two malfunctions together and it is quite feasible that a pavement may appear quite appetizing, as well as sexually alluring.

At the junction of the frontal and parietal lobes lie the sensory and motor cortices – the 'body map' in the brain where each individual area of the body has a corresponding area of cortex devoted to it. Here lies another demonstration of how important sex is to humans: the area of sensorimotor cortex given over to the genitals is rather more than is provided for the entire surface of the chest, abdomen and back put together. Stimulation of the area that represents the genitals produces sensations and/or action in the parts themselves, and epileptic fits that centre on this area of the brain produce strong sexual sensations. During such seizures people sometimes make thrusting movements, as in sexual intercourse.

But sex – human sex particularly – is not all about thrusting and ejaculating. In humans it gives rise to a complex package of feelings and thoughts that we label love. The intense excitement of romantic love and the more gentle affection associated with the love of a mother for her child both stem from similar brain activations – most notably those dopamine reward circuits. Maternal love, however, does not turn them on to quite the same extent. Another similarity is that both types of love turn *off* areas of the brain concerned with fear and critical judgment. The result is a 'push-me pull-me' mechanism, that creates a sense of closeness and approval both by causing us to neglect others' faults while at the same time making us feel pleasantly excited by the thought or presence of the other.[33]

A neurochemical called oxytocin is crucial to all types of love. Oxytocin is thought to be a relatively recent (in evolutionary terms) mutation of a much older hormone called vasopressin, to which it is chemically very similar. Vasopressin is an antidiuretic and its main function is to control blood volume and pressure. However, the drug is also known to help lay down new memories, and is widely used (or abused, depending on your view) as a 'smart drug' or cognitive enhancer. Oxytocin is made in the hypothalamus and released as a result of stimulation to the sex and reproductive organs. It floods the brain during orgasm and in the final stages of childbirth, and in doing so it produces a warm, floaty, loving feeling that encourages pair bonding. In the short term oxytocin seems to blunt the memory but it is possible that it has 'inherited' from vasopressin the ability to enhance the forging of new memories, so the impression left by a person who causes oxytocin to flow may be particularly strong. The mechanism may be similar to addiction: oxytocin is closely linked to endorphins – opiate-like brain chemicals – and the agitation typically felt by lovers when they are separated from the ones they adore may in part be due to their desire to push up their oxytocin level.

Countless psychological studies have shown that people in the throes of this hormonal storm are more than usually divorced from reality, particularly when it comes to making assessments about the person they love. They are – famously – blind to the other's faults and often wildly overoptimistic about the future of the relationship. Looked at coldly, romantic love is a chemically induced form of madness and a terrible basis for social organization, as the divorce rate in the Western world demonstrates.

From the brain's point of view, however, it is just about the biggest thrill there is. So long as the limbic system is still in the driver's seat sexual love will continue to disrupt, delight and occasionally ambush us when we are least expecting it. It may not keep the world going round but it certainly makes it a more interesting place to live.

Is autism an extreme form of male brain?

Dr Simon Baron-Cohen
*Department of Experimental Psychology,
University of Cambridge*

After decades of research into whether and how the sexes differ psychologically, some differences are repeatedly found that, though not true of every individual, certainly emerge when groups are compared.

Women
* score better than men on some language tasks
* show a faster rate of language development
* have a lower risk of developmental dysphasia
* score better than men on some tests of social judgement, empathy and co-operation
* are better at matching items
* are better at tests that involve generating ideas.

Men
* perform better than women on mathematical reasoning tasks (especially geometry and math -ematical word problems)
* score higher at tests that involve distinguishing between figure and background
* find it easier to rotate objects in their mind's eye
* are better at hitting targets

I am not arguing that one sex is better than another, simply that there seem to be different cognitive styles associated with being male or female – that is, not every male will have a spatial advantage but the likelihood of having this advantage is increased if you are male. Such sex differences could, of course, be the result of differential socialization, different biological

[1]

[2]

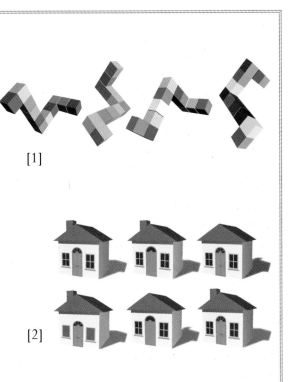

[3]

Priests, Politicians, Pundit, Physicists, Psychological, Parent, Pedagogue, Police, Philosopher, Paedology, Polymath, Palaeontologist, Palimpsest, Pagan.

[4]

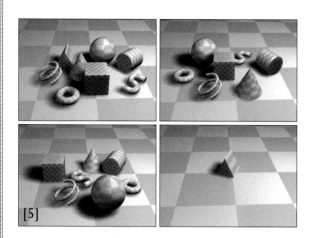

[5]

predisposition or both. I suggest that such psychological differences are in part the result of biological differences in brain development, which is itself the product of genetic and endocrinal differences. My main reason for pursuing this line of reasoning is the evidence from autism.

First, consider a model. A brain could be more developed in terms of 'folk psychology' (understanding people in terms of mental

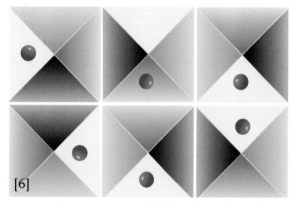

[6]

states) than in terms of 'folk physics' (understanding objects in terms of physical causality and spatial relations) or vice versa. In this box I will operationally define the male brain type as an individual whose folk physics skills are in advance of his or her folk psychology skills, and the reverse will form the operational definition

of the female brain type. Those with roughly equal folk physics and psychology skills will be called the cognitively balanced brain type.

Autism is a strongly heritable psychiatric condition characterized by abnormal social and communicative development, narrow interests, repetitive activity and limited imagination. Four times more males than females suffer from autism and nine times more from Asperger's syndrome ('pure' autism without other handicap). I will now argue that autism and Asperger's syndrome are extreme forms of male brain type.

Children with autism perform better than mental age-matched controls on the Embedded Figures Test – a test in which normal males perform better than normal females. They fare worse than controls on selective aspects of social cognition, especially on tests involving ascribing mental states to other people – an area in which normal females outstrip normal males. Indeed, even parents of children with autism show the male brain type more strongly than sex-matched controls. I suggest that this is no coincidence, rather that it might reflect the existence of sex-linked neurodevelopmental

On average....

1) Men are better than women at rotating images mentally

2) While women are quicker at spotting when two images are alike

3) and better at generating words

4) Men are more accurate in targeting tasks

5) Women can recognise missing objects

6/8) Spotting when a particular shape is embedded in a complex pattern is done more easily by men

7) but women can do fine manual tasks, like placing pegs in a board, more easily

9) mathematical calculation favours women

10) yet mathematical reasoning comes more readily to men.

[7]

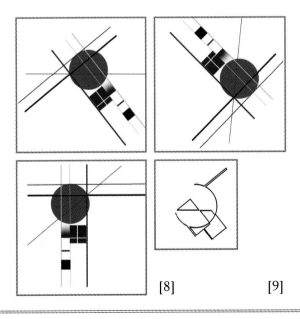

processes in the population.

What might these neurodevelopmental processes be? Here we consider the much-discussed foetal testosterone model:

In a male embryo the XY genotype controls the growth of testes, and at around eight weeks, the testes are formed and release bursts of testosterone. Testosterone has frequently been proposed to have a causal effect on foetal brain development such that by birth clear sex differences are evident. Some psychologists claim that at birth human female babies attend for longer to social stimuli such as faces and voices while male babies appear to be more interested in spatial stimuli such as mobiles. Levels of prenatal testosterone have been found to predict spatial ability at age seven.

Regarding the two brain types mentioned earlier, precisely which structures distinguish these two brain types is still controversial. Some people have found that the right hemisphere cortex is thicker in male babies than in female babies. Others show that the corpus callosum is larger in females (which could explain their superiority in verbal fluency) than in males and even smaller in individuals with autism. There is also evidence that exposure to androgens increases spatial performance in human females (and, in rats, castration decreases it), which is consistent with the notion of a male or female brain type being a function of the levels of circulating hormones during critical periods of neural development.

So one theory is that people fall into a continuum as regards male and female brain type and that autism and Asperger's syndrome are extreme forms of male brain type. Many questions have yet to be answered. What happens to cause someone at the extreme end of this postulated continuum to develop autism? Is it early hormonal events? Do these result from genetics? What does it mean in neurobiological terms for someone to be an extreme form of male brain? And if some sex differences arise for neurodevelopmental reasons, what sort of evolutionary factors have shaped such sexual dimorphism?

[8]   [9]

$$18 - 246 \div 8 =$$
$$4(18+36) + 10 - \frac{15}{5} =$$

[10]

CHAPTER FOUR
A CHANGEABLE CLIMATE

We feel as well as act ... The sunshine and shadows that play over the landscape of the mind are generated by chemicals that turn the modules of our brains on and off, creating the neural patterns that spell out our moods. The limbic structures stab out urgent messages of fear and anger, and the cortex responds by flooding our consciousness with emotion.

THERE IS A SET OF PHOTOGRAPHS THAT IS SOMETIMES USED by psychologists to provoke emotional responses. The photos show various gory accidents.

In one particular experiment the participants' bodily reactions were monitored while these images were presented to them, one by one, on a big screen and in full colour. The subjects' pulses went up, their blood pressure increased and stress hormones started to course in their blood. Asked afterwards how they felt most said they were mournful or nauseated or anxious.

One subject, however, felt none of these things. Elliott had an operation some years ago to remove a fast-growing tumour from an area near the front of his brain. A large chunk of surrounding tissue also had to be removed, and with it went his capacity to feel emotion. Antonio Damasio, the neurologist called in to assess Elliott, describes him thus:

'He was always describing scenes as a dispassionate, uninvolved spectator.'[1] A life without anger sounds dull beyond belief. But there is something, you might think, to be said for it. At the very least it would seem likely to equip a person with the ability to make rational judgements, even in the midst of a crisis.

It turns out, though, that the power of rational judgement, is not, on its own much use. The reason that Elliott was referred to Professor Damasio was because after his operation he seemed unable to function efficiently in almost any capacity. His IQ was the same as before his operation and his memory was fine. Yet he found it hard to make the simplest decision or to pursue any single plan to a fruitful conclusion. At work he might fritter away a whole day attending diligently to some unimportant detail while urgent tasks went unheeded. When he lost his job he threw himself into one wild new enterprise after another.

A battery of behavioural and neuropsychological tests finally revealed the root of Elliott's prob-

If the neural pathways from the limbic system to the cortex are blocked or severed emotions cannot register.

lem: emotions no longer registered and without them he was unable to weigh up or evaluate one thing over another. Faced with a situation that called for decisive action he could generate a full range of appropriate responses – but none of them felt any more 'right' than any other. He had no 'gut feelings' to warn him away from dodgy enterprises and no instinctive sense of who to trust. It was not that he did not know about normal emotional reactions – after seeing the pictures of people in distress he said: 'I know this is horrible – I just don't feel the horror.'

The curious dissociation between knowing and feeling was caused, in Elliott, by a severance of some of the neuronal connections that run between the frontal cortex, where emotions are consciously registered, and the limbic system, the brain's deeply buried unconscious core, where they are generated. His case and others like it demonstrate how our perceptions and behaviour are informed by brain processes of which we are not even conscious. These in turn are informed by purely visceral reactions.

Emotion also plays a crucial part in the business of making moral judgements. We tend to think of morality as one of humankind's highest achievements. Yet much of what we think of as moral

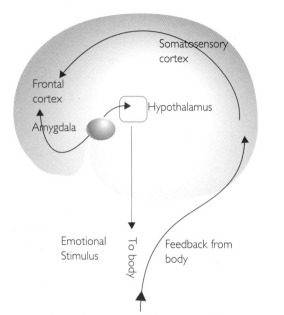

Somatosensory
cortex

Frontal
cortex

Amygdala

Hypothalamus

Emotional
Stimulus

To body

Feedback from
body

*Emotional stimuli are registered by the amygdala. Conscious
emotion is created both by direct signals from the amygdala to
the frontal cortex, and indirectly. The indirect path involves the
hypothalamus, which sends hormonal messages to the body to
create physical changes like muscle contraction, heightened
blood pressure and increased heart rate. These changes are then
fed back to the somatosensory cortex, which feeds the information
forward to the frontal cortex where it is interpreted as emotion.*

decision making turns out, on careful scrutiny, to be
simply emotional reflex.

There is a thought experiment, beloved of
moral philosophers, which can be used to tease
out the underlying biases that people are prone to
when they make value judgments about human
behaviour. It goes like this:

You happen to be standing next to a railway
line, and, looking in one direction you see in the
distance five hikers walking along the rails. For
one reason or another they are, and will remain,
oblivious to anything around them. Between you
and them there is a fork where a side-track swings
away from the main route. And down the side
track you see a single walker, also strolling along
the rails and also, for whatever reason, oblivious
to the outside world. The points at the fork are

currently set to take any oncoming train along the
main track, and when you look in the other direction you see, to your horror, that there is indeed,
an oncoming train. Furthermore, it is a train in
which, you can see, the driver happens to have
fallen asleep, so there is no chance that he will see
the obstruction ahead and put on the brake.
Hence the five walkers are inevitably going to be
killed – unless something is done. As it happens
you find you can do something: right by your side
you spot a lever which controls the points. By
throwing it you can divert the train onto the side
track, thus saving the lives of the five walkers.
Doing this, however, would mean that the single
walker on the side track would be mown down
instead. Now, the question is: should you throw
the switch?

When people are asked to decide this most
think that it would be morally correct to flip the
switch to save the five, even though it means that
one innocent person is killed. But an ingenious
twist on the story demonstrates that this rational
judgment is easily derailed by emotion.

Imagine that, instead of seeing the five reckless
pedestrians from a vantage point beside the line,
you are instead standing on a bridge over the
track, looking out over it in the company of
another, rather portly observer. Again you spot
the runaway train coming up from behind. But
this time there is no conveniently placed switch.
Rather, you realize that the only way you can stop
the train from hitting the walkers is by hoisting
your fellow observer on to the track. Being rather
overweight, his body would bring the train to a
halt before it hit the pedestrians, but the impact
would undoubtedly kill him.

The situation, of course, is fundamentally the
same as before: five people will be saved but one
will be killed. On the face of it the correct action
should therefore be to hoist the fat man over the
bridge. When people are asked to decide on the
right course of action in this case, however, far
fewer than before think this is the right thing to

do. Flipping a switch to achieve a net saving of life is supportable – presumably because it inserts a distance between the action and its consequences. Physically manipulating the victim to the same end, however, is repulsive. It seems wrong not because of the effect on other people (the fat man and the man on the side-track would suffer similarly) nor because the end result differs – it seems wrong because our 'gut' feeling says so.

People with ventromedial cortex damage, like Elliott, do not have this inhibition. The two actions seem to them to be equivalent – as, indeed, they are, in terms of consequences. Indeed it is arguable that – although their judgments may seem cold and heartless, they are actually closer to the ideally rational decisions which judges are meant to make in courts of law.

Psychopathy

Psychopaths, like people with VMPFC damage, differ from normal people in that they lack social and morally relevant emotions – empathy, guilt, remorse, shame. But, unlike Elliott's kind, they are nevertheless driven to action. The problem with them is that whereas in normal people the drive to action is fuelled by the passions, chemical and electrical eruptions in the brain that make us feel warm and inspired when we lend an altruistic hand, and disgusted when we cheat or break an established norm, psychopaths are driven only by the desire to benefit themselves.

Without the pro-social emotions to dampen their drive, they behave in a morally heinous way, lying, cheating, browbeating or threatening in order to get what they want. They *know* what they are doing is wrong, but just don't care.

As measured by standard diagnostic tests, psychopaths are (mercifully) fairly rare in the general population – about one in two hundred. In prison populations however, they are much more common.[2] They are also frequently to be found in managerial positions in hierarchical organizations, where bullying and the willingness to walk over others helps take them to the top. Indeed, although psychopathy is associated with crime, intelligent, socially advantaged psychopaths rarely need to do anything illegal because the benefits they seek – money, power, success – are easy enough to come by legally for those without conscience.

What is emotion?

What exactly is this thing that informs us so completely? We think of emotion as feeling, but the word is misleading because it describes only half of the beast – the half that we do, indeed, feel. Essentially, emotions are not feelings at all but a set of body-rooted survival mechanisms that have evolved to turn us away from danger and propel us forward to things that may be of benefit. Emotion researcher Joseph LeDoux, of New York University, calls it 'a frill – the icing on the cake'.

Emotions are generated in the limbic system, and particularly in the amygdala, a small piece of tissue buried deep in temporal lobes. Information entering the brain from the sense organs is shunted to the rest of the brain along parallel processing routes, the fastest of which takes it to the amygdala where it is assessed for significance. If it is something that needs attention – a threat, or something promising benefit, the amygdala responds by producing physiological changes which prime the body to act appropriately. The information, now 'coloured' by this assessment, is then passed on to the frontal cortex for further processing.

While this happens, the information is also being conveyed directly to the frontal cortex, so the 'thinking' part of the brain receives a double 'message': the information that arrives directly from the senses might say 'There's a large, hairy thing with big teeth approaching' while the information that arrives from the amygdala says 'Watch out! Big, hairy, BAD thing approaching'. Meanwhile the body is already starting to move away.

The amygdala generates a limited range of responses – basically it can prepare the body to

Brain scans of psychopaths suggest their behaviour may be partly due to an amygdala malfunction. When a set of scary, violent pictures are shown to a group of normal people their amygdala responds dramatically (above, left) *whereas the same images produce barely a flicker in the brains of psychopaths* (above, right).

approach, flee, fight or submit. The bodily changes themselves are not specific to a particular stimulus. Many types of stimulus will produce a shot of adrenaline, for example, and this will produce shakes and tingles, butterflies, breathlessness and muscle tension. When these come to the attention of the conscious brain it interprets them in the light of what it already knows about the current situation. The sequence is: 'I think I should be feeling angry,' followed by 'Yes! I seem to be feeling something,' followed by 'It must be anger'. Although a narrow range of bodily reactions set the background colour for the motion – essentially 'good' or 'bad' – the frontal cortex can mix them into an almost infinite range of complex mind-states.

Human emotions are rather like colours: there seems to be a handful of primary ones and a wider range of more complex concoctions created by mixing the primary ones together.

Even at this stage an emotion has not come to

full flower. To do its work as a survival mechanism it has to be expressed, and that requires yet another round of cognitive processing. Emotional expression requires some sort of bodily action. It may be a sob, a blow, a dash for safety or just the insertion of a slightly jarring tone in an otherwise neutral vocal statement.

Expressions

It is quite common for people to be able to feel emotion but to be quite unable to express it. These people, whose condition is known as alexithymia, are in a different situation to those like Elliott, who cannot express emotion because they do not feel it to start with. The inability to express felt emotion probably arises when there is some disruption in the neural connections between the cortical (conscious) emotional processing areas and the brain regions that control facial expression, speech and the other physical means by which emotions are displayed. If, for example, the break lies between the emotional brain and the speech areas in the left hemisphere, the result may be a curious flatness of voice. Such people may say, in quite a neutral tone: 'I am very angry.' Then, aware that the statement has some shortcoming, they might add: 'and I mean it.'

Alexithymia strips those who have it of an important social tool – the ability to convey, swiftly and economically, how they feel. They may know what they want to say, and find the words to say it. But the message somehow fails to hit home.

And hitting home, ultimately, is what emotions are for. At their crudest they force us to hit, flee, or scream. But at the level on which, most of the time, we experience them, their purpose is largely to bring about a corresponding emotional change in other people, which causes others to behave in a way that is beneficial to us. Just expressing emotion to another is not enough to bring that about, of course. The person who perceives the expression must also respond to it. In most people the response to seeing another expressing emotion is

The amygdala lies in the temporal lobe. It constantly 'tastes' incoming information for significance, and generates emotions in response to it.

immediate and unconscious. This is because the human brain (and that of some other primates) contains brain cells called mirror neurons which respond to the sight of an emotional expression in another person by generating the matching emotion in the observer.

In some people the effect of mirror neurons can be so strong that if they see another person expressing pain – particularly if it is someone they love – their brains show similar activity to those of people who report feeling pain themselves.[3]

Mirror neurons also cause us to match the expression we see, as well as the emotion that produces it. This automatic mimicry is so quick that it begins before we are conscious of what we have seen. In fact we don't even need to be *able* to see it. Two people who are blind in one part of the visual field due to cortical damage were found to respond in kind (at least to the point of a muscle twitching) to pictures, presented to their blind side – of people frowning and smiling. This is an example of blindsight (see pp 184–191) – a condition in which information coming in from the eyes is used by the brain to direct body movements in the absence of conscious sight. Blindsight is usually possible only for the sort of stimuli which we really *need* to know about, such as big objects flying towards one – so the fact that it also detects the tiny, subtle changes in a person's face that constitute an emotional expression suggests that the brain reads them as very important information.[4]

Human beings express their emotions in all

sorts of ways – through their actions, body language, gestures and words. But above all, they use their faces.

Imagine for one moment that you work for a fast food company that insists you dispense a bright smile with every order. You have a large family to support. And you are about to serve the two hundredth customer of the day.

Feel those muscles contract? Well done. You have composed your face into the social smile, one of the 7,000-odd facial expressions that this species has in its repertoire.[5] Between them these expressions provide us with a formidable battery of tools for easing social intercourse. Some of them – in particular the social smile – have a very specific role: they allow us to lie about our inner feelings.

The social smile is quite distinct from the genuine smile of pleasure. For a start, the one you conjured up just now has almost certainly by now disappeared without trace. A spontaneous smile lingers, and fades more evenly and slowly.[6] But the difference is more fundamental than that: the two types of smile are brought about by a different set of facial muscles, which are in turn controlled by entirely separate brain circuits. The spontaneous smile, called the Duchenne smile after the French anatomist who first identified it, emerges from the unconscious brain and is automatic,

French neurologist Guillaume Duchenne made this patient 'smile' by putting an electric current through his facial nerves as part of his investigation into the anatomy of emotional expression.

VOLUNTARY SMILE CIRCUIT

motor cortex

indirect pathway from motor cortex

direct pathway from motor cortex

SPONTANEOUS SMILE CIRCUIT

limbic system

direct pathway to smile muscles

brainstem

From left to right: The nerves which make the lips smile can be controlled consciously (left) but those that make the eyes crinkle (right) are mainly controlled by neural pathways that spring from the unconscious limbic system.

while the 'Have a Nice Day' version comes from the conscious cortex and can be summoned at will.

The conscious brain can produce a wide range of expressions to order, but they are never quite the same as those produced automatically because some facial muscles are outside cortical control. The Duchenne smile, for example, contracts a number of tiny muscles that run around the orbit of the eye socket, something the social smile rarely achieves. A smile directed at someone who is loved or sexually attractive also involves dilation of the pupils – one reason why low lighting (which also causes the pupils to dilate) is so conducive to romance.

Facial expressions of emotion are very similar the world over, suggesting that the neural circuits that create and respond to them are hard-wired into the brain rather than moulded by culture. The basic expressions are sadness, happiness, disgust, anger and fear. The thousands of other faces we make are blends of these.

Children respond appropriately to facial expressions almost from the time they are born, but they get progressively better at it as they get older.[7] The improvement matches the pattern of maturation of the frontal lobes – the cortical area concerned with emotion.

Expressions of fear[8] are picked up and identified by the amygdala. One part of the amygdala responds to facial expression and another is sensitive to tonal qualities in the voice – the give-away rasp of anger or quiver of fear. The left amygdala seems to respond more to vocal expression while the right amygdala is more sensitive to facial movement. It follows from this that people whose amygdala is oversensitive may be quick to take offence or be easily hurt, while those whose amygdala is slow to react may seem rather dull and detached.

An underactive amygdala makes any sort of social encounter difficult.[9] This is how one such man describes it:

'I have learnt to watch the mouth of the person I am talking to and to note when they show their teeth. That is how I know they are smiling. When I see their teeth I try to remember to smile back. I also look at their eyes. When people smile their eyes crinkle around the edges.

'The trouble is, by the time I have worked it out there is a time-lag. The conversation has moved on and I always return the smile that bit too late. People find this upsetting – I think it must seem to them as though I am not really connecting.

'I know I miss out on a lot when I listen in to

other people's conversations – things get transmitted without words. It makes you feel left out.

'But the worst thing is that a lot of the time people don't take me seriously. If you can't see other people's expressions, you never learn to do them yourself, so – unless I make a really big effort – I don't put out expressions with my own face. Because of this people don't think I mean what I say. Sometimes they even think I am lying.

'I used to find this very hurtful. Now I make sure to emphasise what I say with extra words. If someone gives me something to eat and I want to tell them I'm enjoying it, I make sure to say something particular about it, like 'The herbs in this are really interesting,' rather than just 'This is good.'

'Because of all this I find dealing with people is hard work. Sometimes I feel too tired to try and I shut myself away for a while. It can be lonely.'

Certain physical gestures – the Gallic shrug of contempt, the drooping shoulders of resignation – seem to be processed by the brain in a similar way to facial and tonal expressions. Clowns, mime artists and cartoonists exaggerate these gestures and when they do it well the messages they send via body posture and movement speak volumes. In everyday life, though, people tend to damp down their body language.

Some people are so sensitive to emotional expression that they are effectively equipped with a built-in lie detector. Facial expression systems based on objective measurements of muscle tone are at best 85 per cent accurate at detecting when a person is lying,[10] but a few people can spot when someone is fibbing every time. What they appear to be picking up on is what psychologist Paul Ekman has dubbed 'microexpressions' – tiny, involuntary expressions which flit across a person's face, usually when they are consciously trying to express one thing but actually feeling something else. People can be trained to see them.

Most of us, though, are surprisingly poor at detecting dishonesty from facial expression. In one experiment a group of nurses was shown a film in

which people were shown suffering horrendous injuries. Another group was shown a pleasant film. Both groups were then interviewed about what they had seen and how they felt about it. The group that had seen the pleasant film was instructed to answer all questions truthfully. The other nurses were instructed to smile brightly and pretend that they had seen the pleasant film. They were told that this was a test to see if they could keep up a nothing-to-worry-about façade in the event of a real disaster occurring.

The nurses' interrogators included psychologists, judges, detectives, customs officers, secret service agents, non-specialist adults and college students. The only group that showed a significant ability to tell those who were lying from those who were not were the secret service agents, and they mainly used techniques – cleverly constructed questions and so on – that did not depend on judging facial expression.[11]

Given the sophistication of our emotional expression system, it seems odd at first sight that we should be so bad at interpreting it. One possibility is that our ability to overlook or misread emotions is actually the most sophisticated part of it, in that it allows us to rub along together and enjoy life – laughing at jokes we have heard before; swallowing convenient white lies; and

Looking at this picture (above) of someone expressing extreme disgust triggered brain activity (right) in the viewer in the same area that lights up when disgust is experienced directly.

Information is fed to the amygdala from all over the brain, including areas concerned with reward, pain, memories and sensations. They are combined to produce a moment by moment 'commentary' of what is happening.

The amygdala is just in front of the hippocampus. If it identifies a potential threat or advantage it sends messages out to the body which prepare it to take action such as fight or flight. It also feeds information forward to the frontal cortex where it is made conscious as a 'felt emotion', such as anger, fear or joy.

Various types of input to the amygdala (pink) produce specific physiological responses which prime the body to carry out certain behaviours (red).

The degree to which a person's amygdala responds to emotionally salient stimuli has a profound effect on their behaviour. Traumatic experiences can sensitise the amygdala to danger, so that relatively small things trigger a dramatic reaction. Post Traumatic Stress Disorder is characterized by sudden, overwhelming attacks of panic which are triggered by the amygdala's over-reaction to a stimulus which 'reminds' it of the original trauma.

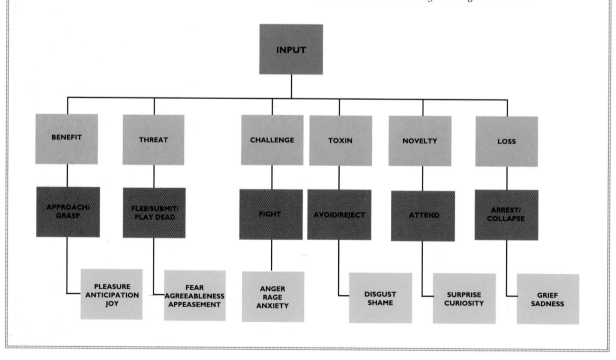

finding TV soap operas credible despite the poor acting.

Another possibility is that we use expressions to generate feelings as much as to display them, and that a little bit of deception is necessary for this to work.[12] If, for example, you contract your forehead into a frown, the nerves enervating the muscles feed back a message to the brain that effectively says: 'Something wrong here – we are worried.' Once the feeling is there, the brain then casts around for a reason for it. There is always a reason for worry if you look hard enough, and once you have found one it then fuels the feeling of concern even more, creating an ever-escalating emotional spiral. Behaviour therapy – one of the more effective forms of psychotherapy – teaches people to exploit this feedback mechanism in order to turn negative feelings, like worry, into positive ones simply by replacing the frown with a smile.

These days that can be done, very simply, by an injection. Botox, a toxin which paralyses muscles, is most commonly used as a cosmetic procedure to reduce forehead frown lines. When a group of volunteers was asked to describe their state of mind a few weeks post-Botox, they reported feeling less anxious, less depressed and generally more happy. The effect was not, apparently, due to having fewer wrinkles, but to the fact that, because they weren't frowning, their brains were duped into thinking that life was rosy.

Expressions can also transmit emotions to others – the sight of a person showing intense disgust, remember, turns on the observer's brain areas that are associated with feeling disgust.

This, presumably, is why people serving hamburgers are instructed to smile. Whether activating their major zygomatic muscles all day long keeps them in the state of perpetual cheeriness that might be expected from the foregoing studies has yet to be determined.

Anger

Emotional expression is not always as benign as a smile in a fast food joint. Rage and fear bring about a wide range of reactions – road rage, bullying, phobias – that rarely have survival value in today's world and serve only to make it a bleaker place in which to live.

Just like smiling, these reactions may either be consciously connected with some appropriate outside cue, or they may be brought about by a spasm of activity in the unconscious mind over which the person may have little or no control. It may even be possible to murder someone as a result of a such a reflex.

One in three killers claims to remember nothing about the moment when they committed the crime. Patrick – a case reported by US neurologist Richard Restak – is typical. This 42-year-old man shot his wife after 16 years of reasonably happy marriage in what appears from the outside to be a fit of jealous rage. Yet Patrick claims to remember

Mona Lisa's smile has special intrigue because it seems to change before your eyes: one moment it is gentle and sweet, the next it seems sad or sardonic. One reason for this may be that the brain is receiving mixed messages from the image. Dr Luis Martinez Otero, a neuroscientist at Institute of Neuroscience in Alicante, Spain, asked volunteers to look at the painting in varying sizes from varying distances. They found that the smile was more apparent when the image was primarily registered by retinal cells which pick up signals from the centre of the visual field rather than those which are used to scrutinize peripheral stimuli. The reason could be that the central retinal cells are the ones that are mainly used to examine emotionally salient stimuli. It may be that these signals have more effect on the amygdala than those from the periphery, causing us to be more aware of any potential meaning in them.

nothing of the episode: just a 'rushing-numb-out-of-control' feeling, followed by a blank space and then the sight of a dead body and a smoking gun.

There are several ways of viewing the selective forgetfulness of killers. The psychoanalytic approach holds that knowledge of one's appalling deeds is too much for the ego to bear and is thus repressed. The cynical view is that their amnesia is a transparent attempt to secure a soft sentence. And the latest (and most controversial) idea is that these people do indeed not remember their crimes.

Can it really be possible for an unconscious person to pull a gun, do whatever needs to be done to prime it, take aim and shoot – all while the victim presumably shouts and screams and flails? If you are to believe the perpetrators the answer is yes. Recent research into the neurobiology of what is probably our most powerful emotion – anger – suggests that some of them, at least, are telling the truth.

The amygdala, as we have seen, is the brain's alarm system – the central generator of states of mind that evolved to aid survival under threat. Stimulate one part of the amygdala and you get the typical fear reaction – a feeling of panic combined with flight. Stimulate another and you produce what people have described as a 'warm, floaty feeling' and excessively friendly behaviour – appeasement. Activity in a third region of the amygdala results in outbursts of rage.

Packing the trigger mechanisms for all three basic survival strategies – flight, fight and appeasement – into a single small nugget of tissue is advantageous in that it allows swift transition from one to another.

The drawback is that we live in a world where physical flight or fight is likely to be more catastrophic than the original threat. If you are facing an aggressive boss in a boardroom, for example, appeasement is the only non-disastrous option and even that may have its downside (there is, as we all know, a particularly derogative word for those who are excessively conciliatory towards their superiors). It is therefore essential that the emotional responses generated by the amygdala are mediated by the 'thinking' part of the brain, the cortex.

Controlling emotions is effectively the reverse of the process required to feel them. The amygdala receives emotional stimuli first via what Joseph LeDoux has termed 'the quick and dirty route': a fast track that produces an almost instantaneous automatic response – smile, jump back or lunge forward – is begun. A quarter of a second later, however, the information reaches the frontal cortex where it is placed in context and a rational plan of action is conceived to cope with it. If good sense dictates that one of the three basic survival strategies is in fact appropriate, the bodily reaction already begun will be continued. But if the rational decision is to respond verbally rather than physically, the cortex sends a 'damp things down' message to the hypothalamus, which in turn signals the body to halt or reverse the changes it has started to make. This lowering of bodily arousal is in turn sensed by the hypothalamus via a loop-back system, and the hypothalamus then sends inhibitory messages to the amygdala, calming activity there, too.

In this way, emotions are held in check by the 'higher' functions of the brain and in most people the mechanism works pretty well. So why is it that a minority is given to apparently uncontrollable outbursts of rage?

There are two fairly obvious ways in which emotional control might break down. One is if the signals sent from the cortex to the limbic system are too weak or undirected to override the activity arising from the amygdala. The other is if the amygdala is activated in the absence of any outside stimulus that would simultaneously arouse the cortex.

Of these the first is commonplace. It is the relative weakness and diffusion of cortical signals that cause children to have far more emotional outbursts than adults. Infants cannot control their emotions because the axons that carry signals from the cortex to the limbic system have yet to grow. And the cells in the prefrontal lobe, where rational processing of emotion takes place, do not mature fully until adulthood. The amygdala, by contrast, is more or less mature at birth and thus capable of full activity. The young brain is therefore essentially unbalanced – the immature cortex no match for the powerful amygdala.

Cortical maturity can be accelerated by use – children who are encouraged to exhibit self-control are likely to become more emotionally continent than those whose tantrums are allowed full rein. This is because, in general, constantly stimulating a particular group of brain cells (like those required to inhibit the amygdala) makes them more sensitive and thus more easy to activate in future. One of the saddest demonstrations of this concerns the children from Romanian orphanages who were adopted by Western families in the late 1980s. Until they were adopted the children had been given little or no individual attention from adults. Despite being doted on in their adoptive homes, many of them have grown up with profound social and emotional problems. One mother, speaking of her ten-year-old adopted daughter, says:

'Nicola has no idea what love is. She doesn't seem to connect to us any more than to anyone else – she will go and sit on a stranger's knee when she wants attention just as soon as come to one of us. She's quite intelligent, but she can't learn to show concern for other people. She never flushes the lavatory when she has used it, for example.'[13]

Harry Chugani, of the Children's Hospital in Michigan, has scanned the brains of some of these children and found that nearly all of them show distinct functional eccentricities in various areas connected with emotion. 'There is just a short window of time during development when children have to be emotionally stimulated if they are to feel those emotions in later life,' says Chugani. 'These children missed out on that, and their brains carry the evidence.'[14]

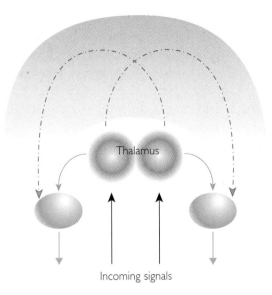

Emotional information is sent to the conscious brain and the amygdala via two routes. The path to the amygdala is shorter, so emotional reactions are faster than conscious ones.

Antisocial and emotionally incontinent behaviour is not entirely a matter of nurture, though. Studies comparing the behaviour of identical twins who have been separated at birth and brought up in different environments suggests that about 50 per cent of the variance in antisocial behaviour is due to genetic influences. One gene in particular is implicated. It is one that codes for an enzyme which breaks down monoamines in the brain, in particular dopamine – the neurotransmitter which drives people to action.

Damage to the emotional cortex may also reduce its ability to inhibit activity in the amygdala. As we have seen, amygdala activity may produce three distinct types of reaction in response to threatening or challenging stimuli: appeasement (that nervous, over-anxious friendliness that most of us recognize as insincere), fear or rage. Small irritative lesions in the area have been found to produce anger and aggressive behaviour and a number of studies of people who are given to impulsive acts of aggression have found evidence of brain damage and dysfunction. Sometimes brain damage seems to tear apart the linkage between primitive, rage-driven urges and the rational 'I' that normally controls them. On 1 August 1966 Charles Whitman, a 25-year-old student, churchgoer, charity worker and ex-Marine, climbed the Bell Tower on the University of Texas campus in Austin, US, and trained a rifle on the milling crowds below. In the course of the next 96 minutes he shot 13 people dead and wounded more than 30 others before being shot, himself, by a police officer. Whitman had already killed his wife and mother, both of whom he had previously professed to have loved dearly.

Before his hideous shooting spree Whitman had been increasingly worried by violent impulses which he was unable to control. These are well documented because he exhibited what is known as 'hypergraphia' – a compulsion to write. Many of his notes seemed to be written by one personality to another.

'CONTROL your anger' read one. 'Don't let it prove you the fool. SMILE – Its (sic) contagious. DON'T be belligerent. STOP cursing. CONTROL your passion; Don't let it LEAD you'.

Another note of Whitman's said this: 'I don't really understand myself these days … Lately I have been a victim of many unusual and irrational thoughts. These thoughts constantly recur, and it requires a tremendous mental effort to concentrate. After my death I wish that an autopsy would be performed to see if there is any visible physical disorder'.

Whitman got his wish and, as he had suspected, it revealed something very wrong with his brain. A tumour, the size of a walnut, was pressing on Whitman's amygdala, causing it to fire in a way that would normally only occur in situations of great danger, threat or challenge. Medical experts at the time disagreed about whether this accounted for Whitman's actions. (Report on the Charles J. Whitman Catastrophe at the Texas State Archives, September 8, 1966). But in 1966 neuroscience

was still really in its infancy. Psychiatry at that time was still heavily influenced by Freudian and other forms of psychoanalysis. The idea that a physical abnormality could, more or less on its own, produce a sustained and apparently intentional act of violence was not in tune with current thinking.

More dramatic still are instances in which violence occurs entirely in the absence of conscious thought. The drive to harm nevertheless manages to engage areas of the brain capable of concocting clear goals and action plans directed to achieving them.

Take the case of Kenneth Parks, a young Canadian man. Late one night Parks dozed off in his chair. An hour or so later he drove 14 miles to the home of his in-laws. There he proceeded to pummel his father-in-law to unconsciousness, before hitting his mother-in-law with an iron bar and then stabbing her to death. Parks then got back in his car and drove to a police station where he announced to the officer on duty: 'I think I have killed some people . . .'

At his trial Parks pleaded not guilty to murder because, he claimed, he was asleep when it happened. He only woke up, he said, when he found himself in the police station with blood dripping from his hands.

Sleep experts supported Parks' story with studies of his brain that showed the characteristic signs of somnambulism. The court heard that he was a man of gentle and law-abiding disposition, and that by all accounts he had been extremely fond of his in-laws. The court found him not guilty of murder on the grounds that he was not, effectively, 'there'.

Parks' case is by no means unique. Some 68 cases of apparent sleep murder have been documented, and in recent cases, brain scans which show give-away signs of a tendency to sleep-walk have helped secure a verdict of not guilty.[15]

Although the behaviour shown might look for all the world as though it is intentional (even if the intents may seem weird) the appearance is deceptive: researchers who managed to manoeuvre a sleepwalker into a brain-scanning machine found that the frontal areas of his brain were more or less entirely switched off. Although his behaviour seemed to be goal-driven there were not enough 'lights on' to suggest that it was intentional, in the sense required to hold him legally responsible for it.[16]

Frontal lobe dysfunction does not, however, explain what happened to Kenneth Parks. What mechanism could cause a person to carry out a sustained act of violence and then have no memory of it?

One possibility is that such a person's actions are the result of epileptic seizures. The amygdala is a particularly responsive part of the brain and very little electrical stimulus is required to make its cells fire. This gives it a low threshold for epilepsy – fits often begin there and radiate outwards. The stirring of activity in the amygdala prior to such a fit is probably what causes the feelings of fear and foreboding so often reported by epileptics just before they black out.

If acts of 'mindless' violence really are that – no more conscious than the kick of a leg when the knee is tapped – it seems pointless, as well as unfair, to punish the perpetrators. In the absence of any better way to deal with them it might be justified, but if brain mapping fulfils its promise of revealing exactly what is going on in rage-driven brains, it should also be able to suggest more appropriate means of dealing with them.

Fear

Phobias are among the most life-restricting of conditions. It is not so bad if your particular fear is something you can be sure to avoid: flying, for example, may limit your choice of job and holidays but you can live a perfectly full life without having to confront it. Others are more problematic.

Josephine, for example, is scared of chicken legs. On one occasion Josephine was confronted unexpectedly with a plate of *coq au vin*, which

A number of studies have found clear differences between the brains of normal people and those of criminals who have committed violent acts. The images above, for example, show PET scans derived from the brains of 41 people (39 males and 2 females) who were charged with murder and were pleading Not Guilty for Reasons of Insanity (NGRI) (above, left) compared to those of 41 normal controls (above, right). The two groups were engaged in a visual task while the scans were taken.

The results show that the murderers had less activity in the frontal part of the brain. Activity here is required to damp down emotions such as rage. This finding was particularly notable in murderers who acted impulsively rather than after premeditation. Subsequent studies have found that violent criminals have an 11 per cent reduction in the volume of prefrontal gray matter findings. The study also found that the murderers had more activity in the emotional areas on the right side of the brain, and less neural 'traffic' between the two hemispheres.

The work was done by Psychologist Adrian Raine, of the University of Southern California. He argues that the difference in limbic system activity between the murderers and controls suggests the former fail to feel fear the normal way, and lack the ability to grasp the long-term implications of a situation.

produced a reaction of such dramatic intensity that both she and her host ended up in the emergency department of the local hospital. Josephine rarely dines out nowadays.

How do phobias like this arise? And why are they so very hard to control?

The potential for certain fears seems to be hard-wired into the brain, like a faint memory trace of those things that have proved harmful to our species in the distant evolutionary past. Animal studies and careful observation of human babies show an instinctive shrinking from certain stimuli. This reaction does not necessarily occur the first time the object is encountered, but if during that first experience there is the slightest hint that the object might be something to worry about, a profound and permanent fear of it will be forged.

Baby monkeys born in captivity will not show automatic fear of a snake, for example. But if a snake is presented to them and at the same time they are shown a film of another monkey looking fearful, the snake will become an object of terror. This does not happen if the object that is presented is, say, a flower. Fear of snakes, it seems, is pre-programmed into primates' brains but may lie dormant until an appropriate signal triggers it into life. The most common phobic objects are those that once posed the greatest danger to the species. Among humans these are snakes, spiders, big swooping birds, dogs, heights and reptiles. Their roots in our evolutionary past are obvious – phobias about things that are dangerous today, like cars and guns, are far less common.

This is not to say that the newborn brain contains a rogues' gallery of potentially fearsome objects. Rather it is equipped to respond to certain fairly crude stimuli: large objects above; a certain slithering movement on the ground, base notes like those in the growl of a dog and so on.

Such 'natural' fears are not phobias, though. Once we recognize that the snake and the spider are harmless most of us can control our fear of them. Phobics cannot. Their fear is almost beyond conscious control. It bears no relation to the actual threat and may even create danger by preventing a person from acting sensibly. Someone with a phobia about heights, for example, might be literally paralysed with fear if required to climb down a ladder from the window of a burning building.

Phobias have no survival value. So what turns a fear into a phobia? Freud maintained that irrational fears arose because the feared object had come to symbolize something that really was frightening but that was for some reason too embarrassing or awful to acknowledge. One of his most famous case studies concerned little Hans, a boy who had been frightened of horses ever since he saw one fall down in the street. Freud concluded that Hans's fear came from an unconscious Oedipal complex – he secretly desired his mother but was terrified his father would castrate him for it, and this fear was displaced on to the horse.

Explanations such as this have now, at last, been shown to be ludicrously elaborate. Phobias can be produced by manipulating quite basic brain mechanisms – there is no need to involve sophisticated cognitive machinations like symbolism, guilt and covert desire.

The root of phobias lies in conditioning, the process demonstrated, famously, by the Russian physiologist Ivan Pavlov nearly a hundred years ago. Pavlov showed that dogs will salivate at the ringing of a bell once the sound of the bell has been associated in their minds with food. Countless Pavlovian-style experiments have since shown that fear can be induced by an unrelated but associated stimuli just as simply as salivation. The latest research, mainly from Joseph LeDoux, is uncovering the neural mechanisms that underlie conditioned fear. In doing so it is revealing the causes and pointing the way to new treatments for phobias, anxiety, panic and post-traumatic stress disorders.

Conditioned fear (as opposed to 'ordinary' fear, which has a rational basis) is a special type of memory. Unlike most memories, it does not need to be consciously recalled in order to have an effect. It does not even have to be registered consciously at the time it is laid down. To understand how this happens it is necessary to look at what happens to potentially fearful information once it enters the brain.

Everything coming in through the senses goes first to the thalamus where it is sorted and shunted onward to appropriate processing areas. In the case of emotional stimuli – the sight of a snake in the grass, for example – the information is split in two and sent on its way via two separate pathways. Both paths end up at the amygdala, the brain's alarm system and generator of emotional responses. The routes they take, however, are quite separate.

Pathway number one goes to the visual cortex at the back of the brain which analyses it and then sends on what it finds. At this stage it is just information – a long, thin, wriggly thing with patterns on its back, here, now. Next the recognition areas of the brain get to work on it, deciding what this long wriggly thing is. The information, now tagged as a snake, triggers the release of stored knowledge about snakes – animal/different types/dangerous? – from long-term memory. These elements are added together to create a message: 'Snake! Here, now, aargggh!' (or something to that effect). This is then sent to the amygdala where it stirs the body to action.

As you can see, pathway number one is a long and winding one with several stops along the way. Given the urgency of the situation, on its own it would be dangerously slow – a quick-response system is needed. This is provided by the second pathway to emerge from the thalamus. The thalamus is close to the amygdala and is linked by a thick band of neuronal tissue. The amygdala in turn is closely connected to the hypothalamus, which controls the body's fight or flight response. These connections form LeDoux's 'quick and dirty' route along which information can zap from eyes to body in milliseconds.

Conditioned fear seems to be formed out of information that takes this short cut. Most memories are initially encoded by the tiny but extremely important nucleus in the limbic system called the hippocampus. This is where all recent conscious memories are stored, and where those of them that are destined to become permanent brain furniture are dispatched to long-term memory. This takes a long time to do – it may be three years or so before a memory is firmly lodged in the cortical long-term store. People who have suffered serious damage to the hippocampus (a rare event) cannot recall anything in their immediate past or lay down anything new – a terrible condition to be in, as we shall see later when we meet some people to whom this has happened.

However, the hippocampus does not seem to be responsible for all memory acquisition. There is a famous case study involving a woman who had such severe hippocampal damage that she was unable to remember anything or anyone for more than a few seconds. Thus every time she saw her doctor he had to introduce himself afresh. He usually did this by shaking her hand. One day he hid a pin in his hand and when the woman grasped it she received a nasty prick. She appeared to forget all about it within a few seconds, and at the next meeting she seemed to be as unaware of the doctor's identity as ever. However, this time when he held out his hand she refused to shake it. She couldn't explain why, she was just scared of doing it. Clearly, at some level the pinprick had made a lasting impression.

Recent research suggests that unconscious memories like this are stored in the amygdala – an area of the brain never before thought of as a memory store. LeDoux for one thinks the amygdala lays down unconscious memories in much the same way that the hippocampus lays down conscious ones. Similarly, when an event is recalled the hippocampal system will come up with conscious recollections while the amygdala-based system will produce a sort of physical remi-

(4) A clear image of a snake is sent to the conscious brain for considered response

(1) Thalamus receives stimulus and shunts it to amygdala and visual cortex

(2) Amygdala registers danger

(3) Amygdala triggers fast physical reaction

niscence, reconstituting the body state – pumping heart, sweaty palms and so on – that arose with the original experience.

If a memory is burnt into the amygdala with enough force, it may be almost uncontainable, and trigger such dramatic bodily reactions that a person may re-experience the precipitating trauma, complete with full sensory replay. This condition, post-traumatic stress disorder, is quite clearly linked to a particular experience and so are most frightening memories. Sometimes, though, the amygdala-based unconscious memories flood in without the corresponding conscious recollections that could pin them to a specific event. The irrational fear felt then may be vague – a thin cloud of anxiety – or it may be sudden and intense – a panic attack. If the feeling is provoked by a conscious stimulus, it may show itself as a phobia.

Unconscious memories are particularly likely to be formed during stressful events because the hormones and neurotransmitters released at such times make the amygdala more excitable. They also affect the processing of conscious memories.

During a trauma attention is very narrowly focused and whatever happens to be the centre of attention – whether it is relevant or incidental – will be laid down as a particularly sharp 'flashbulb' memory. However, if the trauma is exceptionally severe or prolonged, the stress hormones produced may inhibit or even damage the hippocampus. The conscious memory of a traumatic event or period in someone's life is therefore likely to be fragmented or incomplete.

This has obvious implications for Recovered

Memory Syndrome. It may also explain why people often have no conscious memory of the crucial part of some terrifying experience.

LeDoux has shown that it is not necessary – in rats, at least – for a conditioned (fear-inducing) stimulus to be consciously registered at all. In one experiment he first repeatedly played a particular musical tone at the same time as giving a rat a mild shock. After a while the animal, true to Pavlovian conditioning, showed fear when the tone was played even if there was no accompanying shock. At that point LeDoux removed the animal's auditory cortex – the part of the brain that hears – while leaving the rest of its auditory mechanism, ears and so on, intact. An equivalent operation on a human would leave them without any conscious hearing whatsoever, and, to the extent that animals are conscious at all (itself a contentious issue), LeDoux's rat was left in a similar condition.

When it had recovered from its operation he played the tone to it again. The rat could not, presumably, hear anything. Yet it still exhibited fear. The noise appeared to register, unheard, in the thalamus and amygdala, creating an emotional reaction even though the animal probably did not know to what on earth it was reacting.

It is easy to see from all this how apparently irrational fears and phobias may be created. It follows, too, that they will become more troublesome in times of stress, when the amygdala is excited by circulating stress hormones. This same overexcitability may explain why people with a phobia often develop other irrational fears when they are anxious or chronically stressed. LeDoux called the short-cut route to the amygdala dirty (as well as quick) because only crude information can travel along it. His deafened rat, for example, could not easily distinguish between the fear-inducing tone and a similar sound. In the same way, memories laid down in and recalled from the amygdala are likely to be less precise than those processed by the hippocampus, and one fear may easily bleed into another when stress hormones

excite the amygdala to a frenzy.

Having seen how irrational fears may be created, how about eradicating them? Normal fears can be changed or even thought away by bringing them into consciousness and then 'overlaying' the recollection with a new vision. This is because each time a memory is reignited it becomes pliable, and the mind-state you are in when you recall it gets entangled with it. The memory is then stored again in its changed form, and becomes 'solid' again, until the next time it is brought out and experienced.

Traumatic memories are more resistant to ordinary episodic memories because it is not possible simply to yank them out of hiding and reconfigure them. It may in time be possible to extinguish such memories in a more direct way, however. Researchers have found, in rats, that traumatic events can be wiped out by stimulating the part of the pre-frontal cortex which inhibits amygdala action.[17]

It may also be possible to disrupt the normal consolidation of fear memories by altering the molecular processes by which they are encoded.

Experiments with mice show that – in them at least – a particular brain protein is required in order for fearful memories to be retained. The protein, known unmemorably, as Ras-GRF, is made by a single gene.

Ras-GRF may not work the same way in humans, and there is certainly no likelihood of human gene manipulation aimed at preventing people from developing long-term fears. However, the fact that a single chemical has been found to play such a clear and important part in memory creation suggests that one day we may have drugs that could moderate or even eradicate memories that are too painful to bear.

Meanwhile, conditioned fears are notoriously difficult to extinguish. The time-honoured way to treat them is to force the person (or animal) to confront the feared object time and again until eventually a new association is made: feared

EMOTION — ICEBERG OF THE BRAIN

JOSEPH LeDoux

Professor of Neural Science and Psycholdogy, New York University

In his book The Emotional Brain neuroscientist Joseph LeDoux describes how he has shown experimentally that emotions are survival mechanisms.

There is no such thing as an 'emotion' facility in the brain and no single system dedicated to this phantom function. If we want to understand the various phenomena we call emotion, we have to focus on specific types.

Each system evolved to solve different problems that animals face and each has a separate neural basis. The system we use to defend against danger is different from the one used in procreation; the feelings we get when these two are activated — fear and sexual pleasure — do not have a common origin.

Brain systems that generate emotional behaviours are rooted deep in our evolutionary past. All animals, including people, have to do certain things to survive as a species. At the least they have to eat, defend themselves from danger, and reproduce. This is as true of insects as it is of fish and humans — and the neural systems that achieve these ends are fairly similar in all species with brains. This suggests that if we want to know what it is to be human, we should find out how we resemble animals as well as how we differ.

No one knows if animals are conscious and so no one knows whether they 'feel'. Certainly, it is not necessary for animals to have conscious feelings for emotional systems to do their job, and it is not necessary for the functioning of basic emotion

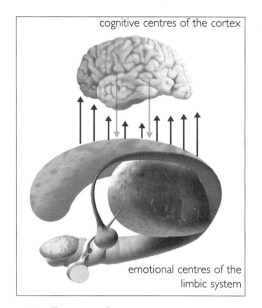

cognitive centres of the cortex

emotional centres of the limbic system

More neural traffic rises up from the limbic system than down from the cortex. This means the emotional part of our brain has more power to influence behaviour than the rational part.

systems in humans either. Emotional responses are for the most part generated unconsciously. Freud was right on the mark when he described consciousness as the tip of the mental iceberg.

Conscious emotion is in a way a red herring: the feeling and behaviour it prompts are surface responses the initial mechanism orchestrates ... Emotions are things that happen to us rather than things we make happen. We try to manipulate our emotions all the time but all we are doing is arranging the outside world so it triggers certain emotions — we cannot control our reactions directly. Anyone who has tried to fake an emotion knows how futile it is. Our conscious control over emotions is weak, and feelings often push out thinking, whereas thinking fights a mainly losing battle to banish emotions. This is because the wiring of the brain favours emotion — the connections from the emotional systems to the cognitive systems are stronger than the connections that run the other way.

object = safety, rather than feared object = danger. This, however, is a conscious association, and as such it is formed in the cortex (the middle of the prefrontal cortex, to be precise, an area directly behind the middle of the forehead). Cortically based notions can override amygdala-based tenets but they cannot eradicate them. For this reason, when stress hormones start circulating and the amygdala sparkles with activity, a person with a usually well-controlled phobia may succumb again to dreadful fear.

The darkest place

When Jennifer was at her most depressed she thought she was dead. Her doctors pointed out that her heart was still beating, her lungs were still pumping and her skin was still warm, but she was not much impressed. With the frustratingly circuitous logic of the truly deluded, Jennifer insisted that these things did not necessarily signify life because they manifested themselves in her, and she was dead.[18]

The conviction that one has died is common enough to have a name: Cotard's delusion, after a French psychiatrist who collected a dozen or so cases. Modern analysis of those studies, and of more recent cases like Jennifer, suggests that they all have some brain damage (usually in the right temporal lobe) that disrupts their perception of the world so as to give it an air of unreality. This alone does not explain their delusion, however. Many people sustain this sort of brain damage but very few think they are corpses. A second factor seems to be required to bring about this particular delusion. One thing that nearly all the dead–alive have in common is a background of severe depression.

Clinical depression is singularly life-diminishing. Its symptoms of despair, guilt, exhaustion, anxiety, pain and cognitive retardation often make sufferers wish they were dead, and one in seven of those who are severely afflicted fulfil that desire through suicide. In extremis, perhaps, depression may extinguish the life-force to such an extent that it is

Some brain areas are overactive in depression – they seem to form a vicious circle of negative feeling.
(A) Anterior cingulate cortex – locks attention on to sad feelings. (B) Lateral prefrontal lobe – holds sad memories in mind. (C) Middle thalamus – stimulates amygdala. (D) Amygdala – creates negative emotions.

easier to believe in one's own death, despite the self-evident absurdity of the notion, than it is to believe that life can consist of such misery.

Does our zest for life, and ultimately our belief in our own 'aliveness', have some physical basis in the chemistry or anatomy of our brains? The question would have seemed silly 20 years ago, but since then millions of people have been transported from death-inviting despondency to joyous rebirth via antidepressant drugs. The causal connection between brain activity and moods is no longer in serious doubt.

The feelings are different, too. Depression is more than just a mood – it also brings on physical symptoms like fatigue, pain, sleep and appetite disturbance. Memory is affected and thinking is

A

B

When asked to think of something sad women (A) *generate more activity in their emotional brains than men* (B). *This suggests that women may have stronger emotional reactions to self-generated thoughts and memories.*

slowed. Anxiety, irrational fear and agitation may be present and a depressed person typically feels guilty, worthless, unloved and unloving. Life seems pointless and the 'meaning' is missing from things. A favourite piece of music or a painting, for example, is no longer perceived of as beautiful or significant. It is just a familiar sequence of notes or a pattern of marks. At its very worst – like Jennifer – a person may feel as though they are dead.

Major depression is not a single disorder but a symptom of several different conditions, each of which probably has a slightly different brain abnormality at its root. The picture is still incomplete, and brain imaging studies have shown that trying to pinpoint the mechanisms that are involved in mood disorders is very difficult indeed.

For example, the brains of people who are depressed are generally much less active than normal – there is simply less going on than there

should be. This probably accounts for the general feeling of slowness, lethargy and lack of excitement that such people feel.

However, depression is very easily confused with, and very often goes hand in hand with, anxiety, which shows up (at least in certain brain areas) as *increased* neural activity.

Then there is the puzzling behaviour of the part of the brain known as the anterior cingulate cortex (ACC) which lies right at the front of the brain, along the bottom inside edge of the central chasm that runs from the back to the front of the brain. This area is older, in evolutionary terms, than the outer surface of the brain, and is welded to the limbic structures beneath by thick neural connections. It is thus on the receiving end of myriad pathways that run up from the unconscious brain as well as down from the cortical areas that process thoughts. A huge amount of traffic passes along these routes: urges, desires and wordless memories from beneath, and news of plans, ideas and fantasies from above.

The ACC generates self-willed actions and plays a central part in creating the feeling of 'agency' that goes along with self-willed behaviour. It also seems to create the essential feeling of 'aliveness' that we usually take for granted and it seems likely that it is this spot that is turned off in people who develop Cotard's delusion. Early studies showed that the very front part of the ACC, where it tucks under the frontal cortex, was underactive in depression.[20] These were followed by other studies that showed that this same spot (or a spot so close to it as to be practically indistinguishable) is *over* active in depressed people.[21] Indeed, stimulating this spot, by placing little electrodes next to it and applying a small current, has subsequently been found to relieve depressive symptoms.[22]

The most likely explanation for the apparent contradiction is that the relevant spot may show greater activity in response to positive events in optimistic subjects – therefore suggesting that it is mainly concerned with generating good feelings. But in people who are depressed, it may respond more to bad events – hence suggesting that it is about negative feelings.

Other 'dead' areas in depressed people include parts of the parietal and upper temporal lobes that are associated with attention, and particularly with attending to what is going on in the outside world. This suggests that the depressed brain is turned inward, tuned in to its own thoughts rather than to what is going on around it. This may explain why depressed people are less reactive to outside stimuli and more 'bound up in their own problems'.[23]

High activity in this area is associated with mania – a condition of overexcitement, euphoria and buoyant confidence – the very opposite of depression. One of the hallmarks of mania is an increased sense of meaningfulness. People in an advanced manic state see significance in every little thing and often think they have insight into some Grand Scheme in which each incident and thing is bound together in a mystical wholeness. The feeling of interconnectedness and enhanced significance is also experienced in paranoia, into which mania sometimes tips. Paranoia is one of the symptoms of certain types of schizophrenia, which in turn is associated with fluctuations in dopamine, the neurotransmitter that activates the prefrontal cortex. The finding of prefrontal abnormality in depression therefore fits well with other findings.[24]

It is conceivable that depression once had some survival value. Something that looks very much like depression occurs in animals trapped in nasty situations over which they have no control. And in the wild normally dominant animals may become subservient – and again appear to be depressed – if they are successfully challenged by a stronger adversary. In these cases depression may help the animals survive, either by conserving energy, in the first example, or, in the second, by forcing withdrawal from situations in which the animal is

People who are depressed show abnormal patterns of activity in the areas of the frontal cortex coloured above. The side section of the frontal cortex – which is concerned with generating actions – is underactive while the middle part – which registers conscious emotion – is overactive. As a result the depressed person is without drive or desire to do anything, yet abnormally fixated on their intense emotional state.

over-faced and therefore at risk. This might explain why today depression is so commonly triggered by events that undermine a person's self-belief – the human equivalent of losing control over one's circumstances or being beaten on one's own ground by a stronger adversary.

In today's world, though, depression is very rarely helpful when a person is stuck in a bad situation or confronted by an overwhelming challenge; it usually makes things worse. If it was ever a survival mechanism, it is now one that should be sloughed off along with full body hair and prehensile toes. Natural selection is a slow worker, but human ingenuity in inventing effective psychological and pharmaceutical therapies for depression is mercifully starting to overtake it.

IS THERE A MORAL ORGAN?

PROFESSOR MARC D. HAUSER
Director, Cognitive Evolution Laboratory
Harvard University

An alternative to the view of morality as emotionally driven comes from thinking about the problem in the same way that the linguist Noam Chomsky has thought about language — an alternative that I have adopted in my own research. This idea supposes that all humans are equipped with a moral faculty, a cold computational system that evaluates the moral permissibility of an action based on what an individual believes and intends, together with an evaluation of how his actions cause particular consequences, some good, some bad. Thus, in the same way that a Chomskyan perspective proposes a universal grammar to account for the similarities in structure and patterns of acquisition of all languages, as well as to the nature of neural breakdown, so too may we propose a universal grammar to explain similar aspects of our moral systems. Only recently has this view been explored on empirical grounds.

If the analogy to language is at least partly right, then the moral faculty operates independent of the emotions, is a cold computational system that provides a set of abstract principles for building moral systems, and should be subject to systematic breakdown when injury arises. Several recent studies are consistent with this perspective, but there are important challenges ahead.

Studies of psychopaths that my collaborators and I have carried out suggest normal patterns of judgments when presented with moral dilemmas. Thus, when asked whether it is morally permissible to push a man in front of a trolley to save five others, psychopaths are more likely to say no than when five people can be saved from the trolley by flipping a switch to turn the trolley onto a track where it will kill one person. This result, together with imaging experiments and studies of patients with frontal lobe damage, suggest that for a wide variety of moral problems, the computation is cold, running without input from the emotional systems of the brain.

Behavioural studies, many conducted by my students and collaborators, suggest that there are at least six principles that may represent part of the universal moral grammar, operating outside of our awareness, automatically, like a reflex:

- Actions causing harm are worse than omissions causing the same harm

- Harming someone as a means to a greater good is worse than harming someone as a side-effect

- Harming someone by physical contact is worse than harming by non-physical contact

- Harmful outcomes that arise by a linear causal route from the agent's intentions are worse than non-linear routes

- Harms that arise from use of personal force are worse than harms involving a mediating, impersonal cause

- Harming someone as a means to a greater good, and making them worse off, is worse than harming someone as a means and not making them worse off.

To illustrate, consider the runaway train problem (see pp 82–3). Principle 1 arises in contrasting pushing the man in front as opposed to failing to warn the man from walking in front of the trolley. Principle 2 arises in the comparison of pushing the man (which is necessary to save the five) versus flipping the switch (the man on the side-track is unfortunate side effect, and if he was off the track, it would be obligatory to flip the switch). Principles 3, 4 and 5 arise, again, contrasting pushing (contact, personal force) with flipping the switch (no contact, mediating impersonal cause). With respect to linearity, the push is direct from an intent to move the man onto the track, ending his life, but saving the five. In contrast, if the man was on a looped track that diverged from the main track and then returned before the five, flipping the switch first redirects the threat of the trolley, then it kills the man, and then it slows down before the five (indirect, non-linear). Lastly, Principle 6 is illustrated by the push case (making the man worse off) versus pushing the body of a dead man on to the tracks (not making the man worse off).

Whether these principles are universal, and whether they operate automatically, immune to reflection or cultural changes, are fascinating and presently unanswered questions. But they are answerable, and that is what makes the science of moral decision making an exciting frontier. It is an opportunity to link basic understanding of how the brain works with applied issues that are relevant to mental health, education, and the law.

ANATOMY OF JOY

Happiness is not a single, or a simple, state of mind. People have very different ideas of what it means, for a start, and it is very difficult to pin down the neural mechanisms which give rise to it. Its main components are:

* physical pleasure
* absence of negative emotion
* meaning

Pleasure is the result of a rush of dopamine in the reward system. It can be brought on by a simple sensory or sexual thrill, or by a more complex route – the sight of someone you love, perhaps. It lasts, however, only as long as the neurotransmitters continue to flow.

Absence of negative emotion is essential for happiness because as soon as strong fear, anger or sadness enters, pleasure is reduced. The amygdala is responsible for generating negative emotions, so to prevent them flooding the brain this part of the limbic system must be quiet. Working hard on non-emotional mental tasks inhibits the amygdala, which is why keeping busy is often said to be the source of happiness.

The amygdala also plays a role in generating good feelings, though, as with bad ones, it takes the involvement of the frontal cortex to make them conscious.[19] An activity is required in the ventromedial area of the prefrontal cortex – one of the areas that is deadened in depression. The ventromedial cortex creates a feeling of cohesiveness – without it the world seems pointless and fragmentary. Overactivity in this area is associated with mania.

KAY REDFIELD JAMISON

Professor of Psychiatry, Johns Hopkins University School of Medicine

Author of Touched by Fire (Free Press, 1996)

People with manic-depressive illness and those who are creative share certain features: the ability to function well on a few hours' sleep, the focus to work intensively and an ability to experience depth and variety of emotions. Where depression questions, ruminates and hesitates, mania answers with vigour and certainty.

Robert Schumann's musical works, charted by year and opus number, show a striking relation between his moods and his productivity. He composed most when hypomanic and least when depressed. Both his parents were clinically depressed, and two other relatives committed suicide. Schumann himself attempted suicide twice and died in an insane asylum. One of his sons spent more than 30 years in a mental institution.

In the late 1980s, while on sabbatical in England, I began a study of 47 writers and artists: painters and sculptors were Associates of the Royal Academy; playwrights had won the New York Drama Critics Award, or the *Evening Standard* (London) Drama Award. Half the poets were in *The Oxford Book of 20th-Century Verse*. As against the 5 per cent of the general population who met the diagnostic criteria for a mood disorder, I found that 30 per cent of these artists and writers needed treatment. And 50 per cent of the poets – the largest fraction from any one group – had needed much extensive care.

The Creative Life of Robert Schumann

THE PAIN OF REJECTION

HELEN E. FISHER

Research Professor and member of the Center for Human Evolution Studies, Rutgers University

Helen E. Fisher, a biological anthropologist, has written five books on the evolution and the future of human sexuality, monogamy, adultery and divorce, gender differences in the brain, the chemistry of romantic love, and most recently, human personality types and why we fall in love with one person rather than another.

He loves me; he loves me not. Breaking up is hard to do. But when a beloved finally departs, the pain can be hard to bear. Hopelessness, fear, rage, loneliness and craving can swamp the mind. What is happening in a person's brain as they ride the rollercoaster of lost love and rejection? Perhaps worst of all, the rejected man or woman often becomes obsessed, relentlessly pining for 'him' or 'her'. Known as 'frustration attraction', feelings of romantic love intensify when barriers obstruct a passionate personal connection. Many rejected lovers also protest. In fact, psychiatrists now divide romantic rejection into two general phases:

'Protest' and 'Resignation/despair'. And it is likely that these broad general (regularly intermixed) responses are both associated with the dopamine system in the brain.

During the Protest phase, the deserted lover tries to win the beloved back. Many find it difficult to sleep; many lose weight too. But overcome by longing and nostalgia, they devote almost all their time, energy and attention on their departing mate. They call, write, even show up uninvited – to try to reason, plead, bargain, or seduce their abandoner. When they fail, they often get angry too, what psychologists call 'abandonment rage'. And it is likely that the brain's dopamine system fuels this passion, as elevated activity of this neurotransmitter produces energy, alertness, focus and motivation – in this case the motivation to win back life's greatest prize, a mating partner. This tumult of emotions seems impractical, unadaptive. Yet this Protest response may actually succeed, winning back the lover. Moreover, if this tactic fails, the rejected person's rage may drive the would-be partner away even faster, thus freeing him or her to start afresh.

Nevertheless, at some point resignation sets in. The rejected lover gives up entirely, engulfed in feelings of melancholia and sadness. A study of 114 individuals who had been rejected in the past eight weeks showed that 40 per cent were clinically depressed, and 12 per cent were 'moderately to severely depressed'. This response may also be caused, at least in part, by the activities of dopamine. As this neurotransmitter plummets, it contributes to feelings of lethargy, sorrow and despair. Yet, as painful as depression is, this response may also make evolutionary sense: depression is an honest signal that the rejected lover needs the support of family and friends. Depression also

The foremost part of the anterior cingulate cortex is overactive in depression (above, left). When electrodes are placed in the brain in a position that inhibits this activity the person reports a lift in mood.

enables a person to make a more honest assessment of their situation, pushing the rejected lover to make the tough decisions he or she must make to heal.

So the behaviours of rejected men or women suggest that dopamine is involved; perhaps first it soars, then it plummets. But to see what is actually happening in the rejected brain, my colleagues, Lucy Brown of the Albert Einstein College of Medicine, Arthur Aron of State University of New York Stony Brook and I have now put 17 rejected men and women into a brain scanner (fMRI). Sure enough, we found activity in the ventral tegmental area, in a region that produces dopamine and distributes this neurotransmitter to many brain regions – particularly to the 'Reward System', the brain's network for focus, energy and motivation. However, we also found activity in the nucleus accumbens and other brain regions associated with craving and addiction. Indeed, romantic love has many characteristics of an addiction – a wonderful addiction when all is well, a dangerous and excruciatingly painful addiction when a person is rejected.

CHAPTER FIVE
A World of One's Own

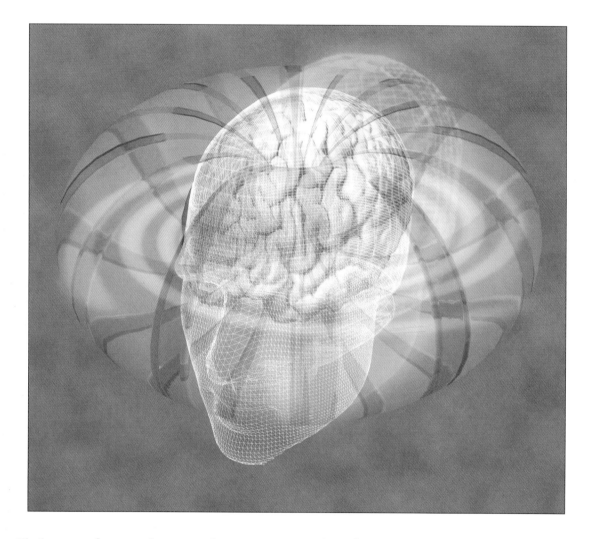

The brain is a factory with many products. Its raw material is information: the length of light waves hitting the retina; the duration of sound waves pulsing in the ear; the effect of a molecule in the olfactory canal. From this the sensory areas of the brain create an idea of what lies outside. But that basic perception is not the brain's finished product. The final construct is a perception that is invested with meaning. The meanings we attach to our perceptions are usually useful: they transform mere patterns of light into objects we can use, people we can love; places we can go. But sometimes they are misleading: the pool of water in the desert turns out to be a mirage; the axeman in the dark corner a mere shadow...

Your name, Richard, tastes like a chocolate bar – warm and melting on my tongue.' It is the sort of thing one might say to a lover as an extravagant declaration of affection, but in fact the woman who said it was speaking literally. At the time, she was the subject of a research study, and the chocolate sensation produced by the name of Richard owed nothing to her feelings for neurologist Richard Cytowic, to whom the remark was addressed.

The woman has a condition called synaesthesia. It causes sensory perceptions – sound, sight, touch, taste and smell – to blend. Some synaesthetes see sounds; others smell sights. Practically every combination has been reported. One boy found words had distinct 'postures' that he was able to demonstrate by contorting his body into various poses. There are even people who are assaulted by intense emotion when faced with a particular sensation: depression at the touch of denim, embarrassment at the feel of wax.

Most people know what it is like to get a fleeting suggestion of colour or pattern when they hear a piece of music, and everyone can imagine how synaesthesia feels; our sensory similes – the 'sharp' taste of lemon – all depend on drawing parallels between various senses. But only about one in 25,000 people consistently experiences two or more senses together.[1]

Synaesthesia is of more than idle interest because it undermines some of our most basic assumptions, both about sensory perception and about the nature of the external world.

What makes smell smell? Molecular structure? Think again. If one person tastes chocolate in response to the sound waves made by a spoken name, who is to say that light waves create vision rather than taste or that molecules, rather than sound waves, create smells? All we seem to have by way of authority on the subject is a majority vote.

Nonetheless, in a standard issue, one-sense-at-a-time brain, a particular type of stimulus consistently registers as sound while another is experienced as vision. How come?

The obvious place to look for clues is at our sense organs – eyes, ears, nose, tongue and somatosensory receptors in the skin. Each one is intricately adapted to deal with its own type of stimulus: molecules, waves or vibrations. But the answer does not lie here, because despite their wonderful variety, each organ does essentially the same job: it translates its particular type of stimulus into electrical pulses. A pulse is a pulse is a pulse. It is not the colour red, or the first notes of Beethoven's Fifth – it is a bit of electrical energy. Indeed, rather than discriminating one type of sensory input from another, the sense organs actually make them more alike.

All sensory stimuli, then, enter the brain in more or less undifferentiated form as a stream of electrical pulses created by neurons firing, domino-fashion, along a certain route. This is all that happens. There is no reverse transformer that at some stage turns this electrical activity back into light waves or molecules. What makes one stream into vision and another into smell depends, rather, on *which* neurons are stimulated.

In normal brains incoming sensory stimuli follow well-worn neural paths from the sensory organ to specific brain destinations. As the stimulus passes through the brain it is split into several different streams which are processed in parallel by different brain modules. Some of these modules are in the cerebral cortex. Others are in the limbic system where the stimuli generate the bodily reactions that give them an emotional quality – the thing that turns noise into music and a pattern of lines and contrasts into a thing of beauty.

The cortical area for each sense is made up of a patchwork of smaller regions, each of which deals with a specific facet of sensory perception. The visual cortex, for example, has separate areas for colour, movement, shape and so on. Once the incoming information has been assembled in these areas it is shunted forward to the large cortical regions known as association areas. Here the sensory perceptions are married with appropriate cognitive associations – the perception of a knife, for example, is joined with the concepts of stabbing and eating. It is only at this stage that the incoming information becomes a fully fledged, meaningful perception. What we now have in mind was triggered by stimuli from the outside world, but it is not a faithful reflection of that world – rather it is a unique construction.

Every brain constructs the world in a slightly different way from any other because every brain is different. The sight of an external object will vary from person to person because no two people have precisely the same number of motion cells, magenta-sensitive cells, or straight line cells. For example, one person – someone with a particularly well-developed colour area (V4), say – may look at a bowl of fruit and be struck by the gleaming colours and the way they relate to each other. Another – with a more active depth discriminatory area (V2) – may be caught instead by the three-dimensional form of the display. In each case the raw data would be identical but the image brought to consciousness would be different.

Everyone sees the world in a slightly different way according to the make-up of their visuo-perceptual system.

Sometimes a person with a particularly striking way of looking at things manages to convey it to others by representing their view in a work of art. That person's view may be seen as more beautiful than our own and by absorbing it – and perhaps stimulating our own visual pathways in such a way that they start to function more like the artist's – we may start to see things that way for ourselves. One reason that new works of art are often so shocking is that they present the world in a way that clashes with our own view.

An individual's view is formed both by their genes and by how their brain has been moulded by experience. Musicians, for instance, have brains which are physically different from others and which work differently when they play or hear music.[2] One study, for instance found that the part of the brain that responds to sounds was on average 130 per cent larger in those who played music and that the increased volume related directly to their musical experience.[3] The differing 'view' this gives them of the world doesn't seem to stop at a heightened response to music, though. They also seem to be more sensitive to emotions. They pick up more quickly on the desperation in a baby's cry, for instance, which must make their world a more emotionally drenched place.[4]

Animals that are deprived in infancy of the sight of one particular visual element – horizontal

Rows of Signs by Wassily Kandinsky, 1931 (Photo: Giraudon).

Artists have often tried to represent synaesthesia: Rimbaud assigned colours to the five vowels, translating impressions into visual ones and Whistler and Mondrian were among those who tried to paint sound. Wassily Kandinsky here places images on musical staves.

lines, say — are bad at or even incapable of discerning them in adulthood because the cells that would normally detect that visual component fail to develop if they are not stimulated at a particular time in infancy.[7]

Extraordinarily individual ways of seeing things may also arise from strange 'quirks' of brain development. Albert Einstein, for instance, had a very oddly constructed brain which might account for his astonishing insights into the nature of space and time. When he died, in 1955, Einstein's brain was preserved, and distributed among various scientists — the idea being that the fleshy chunks might give some clues to his genius. This notion, it turns out, was quite right, but at the time most of the researchers hadn't a clue what to look for. Half a century later, however, researchers at McMaster University in Ontario, Canada, examined the reconstructed brain using modern techniques. They found that the brain was different from most in several ways, the most notable being that two sulci (infolds) in the parietal cortex had merged during development, creating a single enlarged patch of tissue where usually there would be a division. In normal people, one of these areas is primarily involved in spatial

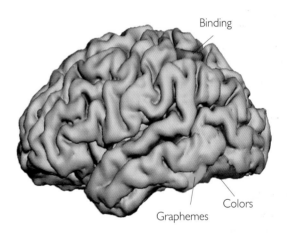

Grapheme-colour synaesthesia occurs when people see each letter in a different, distinct colour. Brain imaging shows that in such people, seeing a letter activates the area of the brain which distinguishes letter forms (green) and also the colour area of the brain (red) whereas in most people these two areas are activated independently. The blue area is thought to be a region concerned with binding the sensations produced by the green and red brain areas into a single experience.

A FINE CASE OF COLOURED HEARING

The writer Vladimir Nabokov describes himself as a 'fine case of coloured hearing' in his autobiography *Speak, Memory*:[5]

'The long "aaa" of the English alphabet has for me the tint of weathered wood, but a French "a" evokes polished ebony. This black group [of sound] includes hard "g" (vulcanized rubber); and "r" (a sooty rag being ripped). Oatmeal "n", noodle-limp "l", and the ivory-backed handmirror of "o" take care of the whites. I am puzzled by my French "on" which I see as the brimming tension-surface of alcohol in a small glass. Passing on to the blue group there is steely "x", thundercloud "z", and buckle-berry "k". Since a subtle interaction exists between sound and shape, I see "q" as browner than "k", while "s" is not the light blue of "c", but a curious mixture of azure and mother-of-pearl.'

Nabokov 'saw' the sound of each letter as a different colour or texture...

awareness, while the other does (among other things) mathematical calculation. The merging of these two areas in Einstein's brain may well account for his unique ability to translate his 'vision' of space-time into the most famous mathematical equation of all time: $e = mc^2$.[6]

Most differences between brains are too subtle to be clearly seen by imaging machines but the extraordinarily different sensory-processing styles of people with synaesthesia show up quite clearly in brain imaging studies.

A growing body of evidence suggests that adult synaesthesia is not so much an oddity as a reflection of a prototype sensory perception that is done at subcortical level but that the normal adult brain learns to over-ride. As babies we experience everything this way, but as our cortex develops it effectively hijacks the incoming information and subjects it to a ruthless categorizing, shunting each stimulus into one or another sensory modality only. In doing so, connections between the parts of the brain that are preferentially sensitive to specific types of stimulus (sound or light waves, say) die away for lack of use, and the cortical neurons in each sensory area become more and more habituated to presenting their information in a single modality. Hence as adults we mostly end up with brains that rigidly carve up the world into the familiar handful of senses.[8]

If this is correct, our strict categorization of information into its different sensory modalities probably developed in order to speed up our identification of incoming stimuli. If a wasp is experienced as a taste and a smell as well as a buzzing yellow thing, it must take that little bit longer to work out that you should swat it. Like many of our cortex-derived sophistications, however, it also impoverishes us slightly. Apart from living in a more densely sensational world, synaesthesia also seems to aid certain aspects of creativity[9] and some types of synaesthesia may even make people more empathetic towards others[10]. No doubt, if we could all switch off our cortical categorization

Diffusion Tensor Imaging of people with grapheme-colour synaeshesia shows that they have more connections than others between the two brain areas that create each element of the experience (colour and word form).

process from time to time we might discover a richer sensual world by far. At the moment, unfortunately, the only reliable way to do it is by taking drugs, most of which are illegal. Perhaps when the mechanisms of synaesthesia are better understood, someone will invent a safer way of opening this particular door of perception.

Recognition

However well constructed a sensory perception may be it is meaningless until the brain recognizes it.

There are two distinct types of recognition: one is the cerebral snap of the fingers that happens when you hear a familiar piece of music. Getting a joke is a form of this type of recognition – a good punchline delivers a sudden jolt of recognition. So is coming up with a solution to some problem that you just 'know' is right. The penny drops. Eureka!

This type of recognition is quite different from the other – the conscious acknowledgement of a correct answer that you arrive at if, say, you add a string of figures together. You 'know' the sum of the figures because your conscious brain created the knowledge by a process of deduction. The deduction involves a sequence of rule-bound cognitive moves in which other knowledge – the

decimal system, the rules of arithmetic, the way to use a pocket calculator – is brought to bear. It is a process, and those who are unpractised at it may fancy they can almost hear cogs and wheels in their brains creaking to turn out the answer. But (with the possible exception of *idiot savants*) everyone has to arrive at this sort of knowing by a conscious effort. Automatic recognition, by contrast, is instant, effortless and unavoidable.

The automatic type of recognition happens when one of the many parallel streams of incoming information passes through the limbic system. Modules here register the emotional content of the information, including familiarity. It happens so fast that the unconscious brain recognizes something is known to it before the conscious brain has even decided what the thing is.

This form of recognition does not extend to consciousness. It may make itself felt, at its strongest, as a vague feeling. But in order to *know* that you recognize something, and to say what it is, the conscious brain has to be brought into the process.

Conscious recognition takes place along the pathway that runs from the appropriate cortical sensory area to the association area that abuts it. Here the stimulus starts to take on identity. If you are looking at an object, say, the association areas in the lower temporal lobes begin the process of classification, starting with rough divisions like living/non-living, and perhaps human/non-human. The left temporal lobe then assigns a name to it. Meanwhile, higher up in the brain, in the parietal lobes, the object is fixed in space. If you are listening to something, a similar process – language/animal cry?; near/ far? – takes place in the auditory association area. For recognition to be complete information is then brought in from memory stores throughout the brain to flesh out the stimulus with the associations that give it meaning. 'My house' becomes 'my home'. Finally, feedback from the limbic area is included so the perception is clothed with emotion. 'My home' is

SENSING THE WORLD

VISION   Light from a visual stimulus is inverted as it passes through the lens. It then hits the retina at the back of the eye, where light-sensitive cells turn it into a message of electrical pulses. These are carried along the optic nerve from each eye and cross over at the optic chiasma – a major anatomical landmark.

The optic track then carries the information to the lateral geniculate body, part of the thalamus. This shunts it on to V1 at the back of the brain. The visual cortex is split into many areas, each processing an aspect of sight, such as colour, shape, size and so on.

V1 mirrors the world outside in which each point in the external visual field matches a corresponding point on the V1 cortex. When a person stares at a simple pattern like a grating the image is reflected by a matching pattern of neuronal activity on the surface of the brain.

The 'map' is distorted, as the neurons responding to the central area of the visual field take up a much greater cortical area – so the 'picture' painted on V1 is a little like that seen through a fish-eye camera lens.

The centre of the retina, the fovea, is much more densely packed with neurons and sees far more detail. The eyes therefore dart around, in a series of leaps called saccades, in order to scan the visual field in detail. Saccades are triggered by the attention system of the brain and are not generally under conscious control. It is the visual cortex that sees, not our eyes. Indeed, although it is helpful to have a pair of eyes connected to the right part of the brain, it is not an absolute necessity for sight. People who are blind, yet have an intact visual cortex, can experience a representation of the world around them using devices which send information to the visual cortex via another route – the ears,

Below, top: *Awareness of sighted objects is conveyed to the limbic system but is not consciously visual.*

Below, bottom: *Each visual element is processed by a separate brain area.*

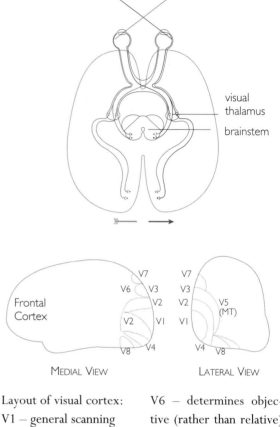

Layout of visual cortex:
V1 – general scanning
V2 – stereo vision
V3 – depth and distance
V4 – colour
V5 – motion

V6 – determines objective (rather than relative) position of object
'Where?' path: V1-V2-V3-V5-V6
'What?' path: V1-V2-V4

say, or the nerves which usually convey tactile experience.

For example, one group of blind people were fitted with a device that turned low level video pictures into vibrating pulses that could be 'read' tactilely, rather like Braille. A camera mounted next to the subjects' eyes, spread the pulses – which felt like a grid of tingles – over their backs, so they had continuous sensory

Heschi's gyrus

medial genicu-late body

inferior collicus

cochlear nucleus

The neural pathways that convey sound information to different parts of the brain.

input from the visual world. The patients soon started to behave as though they were 'really' seeing. They ceased to be aware of the tingles and their 'point of view' shifted to the camera. One of the devices had a zoom lens, and when an experimenter – without warning – operated the zoom, causing the image on the subject's back to expand suddenly as though the world was looming in, the subject ducked and raised his arms to protect his head.

Other novel ways of producing sight in blind people include turning light information into sound 'patterns' which the person learns to understand by matching the patterns to touch. A vertical wall, for example, might be turned into a single low pitch, which the person then learns to associate with the feeling of a surface. Once people are very familiar with their sound patterns they report experiencing the world in a way that is indistinguishable from normal sight,

and brain scanning studies show that this is achieved not by the part of the cortex that hears the sound but by the visual brain. Indeed, when the visual cortex is 'turned off' in such people while they are receiving the sound patterns their 'view' of the world ceases, even though the sounds are still getting through.[11] A similar experiment using a device that turns video signals into tingles on the tongue found that both blind and sighted people could be trained to 'read' letters that were transmitted to them in this way. The reading seemed to be done in rather different ways, though, according to whether the people could see or not. In the blind subjects the tingles activated the visual part of the brain, whereas in the sighted subjects the tingles impacted only on the bit of brain that deals with information from the tongue.[12]

However, there seemed to be a limit to the impact of visual information presented in this way. After the (male) subjects became practiced 'viewers', an erotic picture was projected – the subjects were able to describe it accurately but were unmoved by it.

HEARING   The neural pathways carrying sound information from each ear divide into unequal parts once they leave the ear.

On each side the broader path goes off to the brain hemisphere opposite the ear from which it came, so sound from each ear reaches both hemispheres – but most of the left ear's signals go to the right hemisphere and vice versa.

Both hemispheres have a distinct role in sound processing, and this means that sounds are dealt with (and therefore experienced) slightly differently according to which ear they enter. For example a person deaf in the left ear will receive most sound signals in the left auditory cortex (the side of the brain opposite the 'good' ear). This is the side that deals mainly with the identification and naming of sounds rather than their musical quality, so rhythm and melody perception may be blunted.

Conversely, a person deaf in the right ear may find that words are more difficult to distinguish than music, irrespective of loudness.

SMELL   Flavour perception seems to be processed separately from either smell or taste. In one study students who learnt new words while sniffing an unusual smell and then sniffed the smell again when they had to recall the words showed a 20 per cent boost in memory power. Scanning studies suggest that pleasant odours mainly light up the frontal lobes' smell area, particularly on the right-hand side. Unpleasant odours activate the amygdala and the cortex in the temporal lobe (insula). Unlike other senses smell passes directly to the limbic

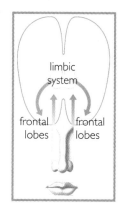

Smell is different from other senses because it goes straight to the limbic system – a fast route to the brain's emotional centre. Unlike other senses it does not cross from nostril to opposite hemisphere.

limbic system

frontal lobes   frontal lobes

system. This fast route to the brain's emotional centre gives smell its power to elicit strong emotional memories.

TASTE   Damage to the frontal lobe of the right hemisphere may turn ordinarily hungry people into fanatic seekers of fine food. Gourmand syndrome has been identified by Swiss researchers who first suspected it when two of their patients developed foodie obses-

sions after sustaining brain injuries. The researchers subsequently scanned 36 gourmands: 34 of them had lesions in the right frontal lobes. The mechanism causing the new interest in food has yet to be revealed – serotonin levels in the frontal lobe may play a part.

SENSATION   Sensation travels along several different types of nerves to the brain. Pain is carried by two types of nerve – fast, which carries sharp pain; and slow, which carries deep, burning pain. Stimulation of one type blocks messages from the other by closing a 'gate' in the spine. That is why 'rubbing it better' is effective.

The anterior cingulate cortex – an area primarily associated with emotion and attention – is essential for conscious pain. Opioid-type analgesics (including morphine and codeine) are the most effective type of painkillers. They block the receptors in brain neurons normally be filled by enkephalins – the brain's own painkilling chemicals, which are released by acute pain stimuli. Opioids also damp down activity in the anterior cingulate cortex.

The importance of the anterior cingulate cortex in pain perception is demonstrated by brain scans showing that people with cardiovascular disease appear to get angina – the chest pains associated with lack of oxygen to the heart – only when the anterior cingulate cortex is active. In some people, it seems, the anterior cingulate cortex lights up as soon as the heart is short of oxygen. This creates conscious pain. In others the heart can be severely short of oxygen before the anterior cingulate cortex is activated. These people can develop potentially dangerous heart disease without angina, making them vulnerable to surprise heart attacks.

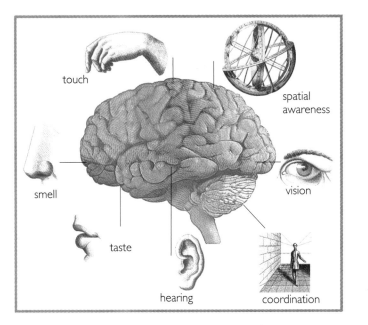

touch

spatial awareness

smell

vision

taste

hearing

coordination

Left: *The vast majority of the cortex is given over to sensory processing — only the frontal lobes are dedicated to non-sensual tasks.*

Below: *All incoming sensory information (except smell) goes first to the thalamus. This limbic nucleus acts like a relay station, shunting the data onto appropriate cortical areas for processing.*

THE SIXTH SENSE   Proprioception is the sense of body awareness telling us the position of our limbs, our posture and equilibrium. It involves the integration of several sensory inputs: pressure sensations from skin and muscles; visual and motor information from the brain; and data about our balance from the inner ear. Proprioception uses so many different brain areas that it is very rare for it to be lost altogether. Occasionally, though, people suffer brain injuries that so disturb proprioception that they lose all sense of having a body. Certain meditative states involve dissociating the conscious brain from proprioceptive input, inducing a feeling of disembodiment Out-of-body experiences, in which people report becoming detached from their bodies and floating around in mid-air can be induced by disrupting the part of the brain that usually blends our body awareness into a stable 'here-and-now' experience.

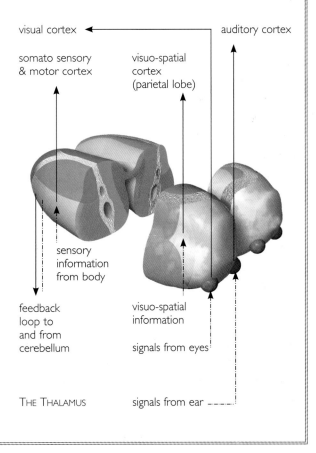

visual cortex

auditory cortex

somato sensory & motor cortex

visuo-spatial cortex (parietal lobe)

sensory information from body

feedback loop to and from cerebellum

visuo-spatial information

signals from eyes

THE THALAMUS

signals from ear

now a place of warmth, love, shelter or loathing as well as the place you hang your hat. The process of recognition is complete.

That is how recognition should take place, but occasionally, in nearly everyone, it falters. A disruption in the recognition process accounts for those embarrassing 'know the face – can't quite recall the name' moments. But these are momentary glitches – a source of mild embarrassment at worst. For people with serious recognition problems the world is a frightening and alien place.

Altered views

'Sorry – no idea.' The patient shook her head in frustration. In front of her was a large, clear picture of a cat. 'It's a cat,' said the doctor. 'Does that mean anything to you?' 'Not a thing,' was the reply. 'Is a cat, say, an animal?' urged someone else. 'Is a cat an animal?' repeated the patient. 'I only wish I could remember what an animal was.' – *Patient study*[11]

A babbling infant knows what a cat is. But the 69-year-old woman quoted above had no idea. Her world had become furnished with ever-increasing numbers of strange objects – things with odd textured surfaces that ran and jumped and slithered and made odd noises. Psychological investigation revealed she had a condition called agnosia (literally, 'without knowledge') and one of its manifestations in her was the inability to recognize all living things other than people.

Agnosia is a fundamental lack of recognition – a dreadful condition that sometimes affects stroke patients or marks the early stages of dementia.

As we have seen, recognition is what rolls off the end of a long and complex assembly line. Agnosia is brought about by a fault somewhere along the line, and the point and place at which the fault occurs dictates the type of agnosia that results. Any sense may be affected by agnosia. Visual agnosia – the inability to recognize things that are seen – is the best documented, but there

are also people who cannot recognize sounds, smells or bodily sensations.

Cognitive processes can be affected, too. Abstract concepts like 'morality', 'co-operation' and 'revolution' may lose their meaning.

Agnosia is generally divided into two main types:

Apperceptive agnosia results from damage fairly early on in the recognition assembly line, before the perception is properly constructed. If the raw material is not put together correctly, the resulting perception will be so weak or wonky that the brain will not be able to match it with anything it already knows.

Associative agnosia is caused by a fault in the later stages of recognition. Here the perception may be perfect but the memories that are associated with it (and that are essential if it is to have meaning) cannot be retrieved.

People with apperceptive agnosia are often affected in one modality only. For example, they may be unable to make anything of objects when they see them but are quite able to recognize them when they are given their names or asked to feel them.

Loss of recognition may be wide-ranging or extraordinarily specific. One well-studied agnosic, a businessman who had suffered widespread brain damage after a stroke, was flummoxed by most things. Shown a carrot he said: 'I have not the glimmerings of an idea [of what it is]. The bottom point seems solid and the other bits are feathery. It doesn't seem logical unless it is some sort of brush.' An onion, he thought, might be 'a necklace of sorts' and a nose he (rather confidently) identified as a soup ladle.[12]

Other people lose the ability to recognize certain categories of things. For example, anything with a proper name may be lost, so a patient may be quite familiar with the notion of a queen but draw a complete blank if asked about Queen Elizabeth I.[13] Faces (prosopagnosia) are a specific category and body parts are another. 'Is it a

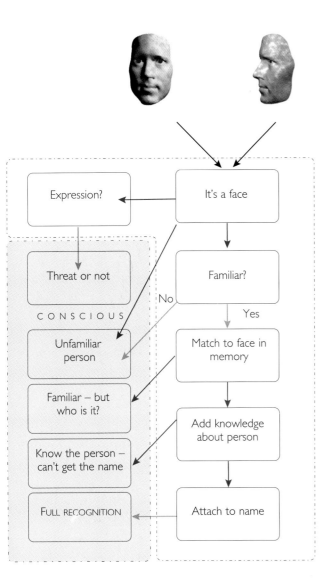

Recognizing someone is a process, most of which is done unconsciously. If the procedure is disrupted the conscious mind cannot achieve full recognition, however well they should 'know' the person.

wrist?' asked a patient looking at a picture of an elbow. Then, correcting himself: 'No, of course it's not. It's someone's backside.'

The discovery that a single brain lesion can erase all knowledge of, say, man-made artefacts while another may take away all knowledge of animals suggests that these categories are somehow hard-wired into the human brain – that we all have a set of memory pigeonholes pre-labelled 'proper nouns', 'edible items', 'abstract concepts' and so on.

This seems so unlikely that researchers have expended a lot of time and trouble trying to find an alternative explanation for category-specific recognition deficits. The most hotly debated category is the living/non-living division. Quite a few agnosic patients have come to light who can recognize non-living things but not living. They also tend to fail to recognize food, even when the foodstuff – a block of ice-cream, say – is visually closer to a (non-living) brick than a leopard. Oddly, such agnosics are often particularly bad at recognizing musical instruments, too.[14] Other man-made objects, by contrast, are easily named and so are human body parts.

These patients suggest that the brain, for some reason, puts food, animals and musical instruments into one compartment and man-made objects and human body parts into another. At first sight it seems bizarre. What does the brain make of these disparate objects so that it lumps them together?

The currently favoured explanation for category-specific recognition failure arises from the idea that the brain sorts and stores things according to the relationship we have with them rather than how they look or what they do.

Our relationships with things – even quite simple objects – are multifaceted. Food, for example, is something to be seen, smelt, handled and purchased, as well as eaten. An animal may be seen, touched, loved, feared, pursued – or eaten. A musical instrument may be heard, manipulated, seen and played.

Each facet of these memories of things may be stored in a separate, appropriate area of the brain. Let's call each fragment a 'recognition unit' (RU). A flute, probably has a shape RU in the visual cortex, a word RU in the temporal cortex, a sound RU in the auditory cortex, and a tactile RU – the feeling of something smooth and cylindrical requiring fine hand manipulation – in the somato-sensory and premotor cortices.

Each area of the brain is packed with RUs of disparate objects brought together not because the objects they relate to are similar to one another in any overall way, but because they are similar in the particular aspect that concerns that part of the brain. Thus the tactile RU of a flute may nestle up against the tactile RU of a cigarette, and the flute's auditory RU may be next to the RU of a whistling kettle. When we think of a flute all the flute RUs are pulled together to create an aggregate concept, but the facet of the flute with which we are most familiar is likely to be accessed most readily. Which one this is will differ from person to person. A flautist would have a strong flute memory in the premotor cortex (handling) and somatosensory (mouth feel) areas. A concert-goer would have a strong auditory memory. And the flute RUs of someone who never listens to music would be mainly visual and verbal.

It may be, then, that the curious categories that seem to emerge during studies of agnosics are essentially the result of an accident of cortical geography. Animals, food and musical instruments may be recognizable to one patient while body parts and tools are not, because – in that particular patient – the first three happen to have their strongest RUs in an undamaged part or parts of the brain, whereas the others do not. The groupings that arise as a result of a system like this would be similar for most people but not universal. For example, animals may be linked to food in one person's mind because, for that person, a picture of a cow triggers the taste (as in a steak) RU of a cow. Vegetarians would presumably make different connections and Hindus who believe cows to be sacred might make yet others. The imaging experiment required to test this thesis has yet to be done.

Face blindness
'When I was about six I told my brother I thought robbers were really dumb to cover their faces with masks when they held up a bank. Why bother, I said, when

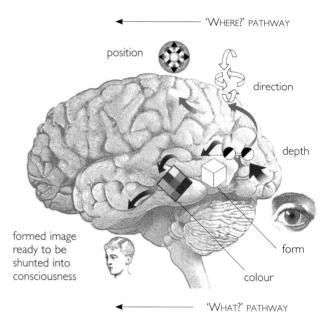

Raw visual material is constructed into recognizable things by unconscious assembly lines. A separate pathway works out where the thing is.

the rest of their bodies still showed? It took me a long time to realize that faces were special to most people' – *Bill, 50-year-old prosopagnosic.*[15]

Faces are very special to most people. So much so that it seems we have a special brain system dedicated to identifying them. People like Bill, quoted above, have a fault in the system that causes a condition known as prosopagnosia or face blindness. They can see perfectly clearly but a person's face makes no more impression on them than, say, their kneecap. As he recalls:

'Once, around midday, I met my mother on the sidewalk and I didn't recognize her. We walked towards each other and passed within two feet, on a not-too-busy sidewalk in a neighbourhood shopping district. The only way I know about this is because she told me about it that night. She was not amused.'

Face blindness may be caused by a dysfunction along any point on the cortical recognition pathway. The severity and guise of the condition depend on precisely where the fault lies. If it is early in the process and affects both left and right hemispheres the effect may be catastrophic: one such patient gave neurologist Oliver Sacks the title for his celebrated case study, *The Man Who Mistook His Wife for a Hat.*

Milder damage to early processing areas may cause faces to be identifiable as faces but to look peculiar – one patient was only able to tell a person's sex by looking at the hairstyle and said all faces looked like 'strange white, flat ovals with dark discs where the eyes are'. If the problem lies towards the end of the pathway, on the other hand, it may just appear that a person is 'bad with faces'.

The ability to recognize people is so important for normal social functioning that even a mild deficit can make life difficult. Those with severe face blindness, on the other hand, can find themselves right out on society's outer edges, perpetually puzzled and lonely. Bill again:

'An ordinary social evening with a group of people sitting round a table is pretty boring for me. It is like it would be for a normal person to sit around all night with only their companions' feet on show. I didn't even know how many people worked in the last office I was at because they all looked the same so I never knew if I was seeing the same guy as had been in the room earlier, or another one.'

The brain area that recognizes faces is specific for our own kind: one man, a farmer, became entirely incapable of recognizing people after a brain injury but was able to name every one of his flock of 36 sheep without hesitation. The acquired face blindness even seemed to enhance his recognition of the animals – other equally dedicated but non-prosopagnosic sheep farmers were unable to identify more than a few of their sheep without error.[16] Some face-blind people find they can identify faces only when the images are upside down – the opposite of normal.

Prosopagnosia does not usually involve the emotional recognition pathways. This has been demonstrated in studies in which face-blind people have been shown familiar faces while linked up to a machine that measures emotional responses like skin conductivity and heart rate. The subjects typically claim not to recognize the faces, yet when an emotionally significant face is shown their body reacts to it normally.[17] This is called covert recognition – a type of unconscious emotion.

Face-blind people confront endless obstacles: how to negotiate a social occasion without giving offence or embarrassment; how to follow the plot of a play or film when one character is indistinguishable from the next. But essentially these are practical problems – once they have established a person's identity they are capable of forming normal emotional attachment to them. Awkward though their lives are, they are better off than people who have faults in the *emotional* recognition system – that is, along the pathway that carries facial images into the limbic system where they are clothed in appropriate emotion before being sent back up to the conscious mind.

Profound dysfunction of the emotional recognition system can cause weird sensory experiences. When it occurs in a person who also has a deranged belief system, the result may be pathological.

Fregoli's delusion, for example, is a condition in which sufferers constantly mistake strangers for people who are familiar to them even though they can see the strangers look nothing like the people they believe them to be. The sense of recognition Fregoli patients feel for these strangers is profound – so profound that they find it easier to believe that the strangers are the people they know in disguise than that their own sense of recognition is false.

A typical case was Miss C., a 66-year-old woman who became convinced that her ex-lover and his girlfriend were spying on her. She claimed the couple disguised themselves. Sometimes one of them would pretend to be the gas man, she

THE SEARCHING BRAIN

RICHARD L. GREGORY
Professor of Neuropsychology,
University of Bristol

The following is an extract from Eye and Brain
(4th ed.) by Richard L. Gregory.

The regions of the cerebral cortex concerned with thought are comparatively juvenile, and they are self-opinionated by comparison with the ancient regions of the brain giving survival by seeing.

The perceptual system does not always agree with the rational thinking cortex. For the cortex educated by physics, the moon's distance is 390,000 km; to the visual brain it is a few hundred metres. The visual brain has its own logic and preferences, not yet understood by us cortically. Some objects look beautiful, others ugly; but we have no idea for all the theories which have been put forward why this should be so. The answer lies a long way back in the history of the visual part of the brain, and is lost to the new mechanisms which give our intellectual view of the world.

We think of perception as an active process of using information to suggest and test hypotheses. Clearly this involves learning, and ... it [seems] clear that knowledge of non-visual characteristics affects how objects are seen. This is true even of people's faces: a friend or lover looks quite different from other people; a smile is not just a baring of teeth, but an invitation to share a joke ... Hunters can recognize birds in flight at incredible distance by the way each species flies: they have learned to use such subtle differences to distinguish objects which look the same to other people. There is no doubt that perceptual learning of this sort does take place; but ... we still do not know for certain how far learning is required for the basis of perception.

It is not difficult to guess why the visual system has developed the ability to use non-visual information and to go beyond the immediate evidence of the senses. By building and testing hypotheses, action is directed not only to what is sensed but to what is likely to happen, and it is this that matters.

MAKING UP THE WORLD

CHRIS FRITH
Emeritus Professor of Neuropsychology,
University College London

The way we experience the world is misleading. It feels like a one-way process: light reflected from objects outside in the world strikes our eyes, signals are transmitted to our brain and we then see the objects. But how is it possible to have hallucinations, to see something when no signals are striking the eyes? The answer is that perception is a two-way process. The crude light signals striking our eyes are never sufficient to tell us what is out there. We have to interpret the signals on the basis of our long-term experience and our current expectations. Then our brain can predict what signals should strike our senses. Our predictions will not be quite right. But errors are vitally important since they enable us to improve our guesses.

This mechanism is extraordinarily flexible, but hallucinations are the price we pay for this flexibility. Hallucinations can occur if the mechanism is working perfectly well. If we lie in a dark, sound-proof room our senses rapidly adapt to the lack of stimulation and we become aware of random variations in low level light, sound and touch. After a little time our brain succeeds in imposing structure on this random noise and we start to experience hallucinations. At the other extreme our expectation of what we are going to see becomes so strong that this determines our perception rather than the evidence of our senses.

There are also many ways in which the perception mechanism can go wrong. Cataracts or damage to the retina in the eye cause the sensory input to become unreliable. Some sufferers from these problems experience visual hallucinations in which they see colour and shapes (Charles Bonnet syndrome). Damage to hearing can cause auditory hallucinations. Drugs such as mescaline and LSD can cause visual hallucinations, probably by disrupting the interplay between the sensory signals and the prior expectations that create our perceptions.

However, hallucinations are mostly frequently associated with schizophrenia. Typically the patient hears the voices of people speaking to them or about them. Schizophrenia is also frequently associated with delusions. Indeed hallucinations and delusions often occur together. While hallucinations are false perceptions, delusions are false beliefs. Patients may believe that they are being spied on by the CIA (delusion of persecution), or that the news-readers on television are speaking directly to them (delusion of reference).

prefrontal cortex

B   A

C

Facial recognition (A)

B   A

C

prefrontal cortex

D

Facial recognition (B)

D

Above, top: The face recognition pathway runs from the visual cortex (A) to the prefrontal cortex (B). En route it passes through an area which is specifically dedicated to faces (C). Above, bottom: Information about faces is also shunted to the amygdala (D), where it is endowed with emotional meaning. This is then fed back to the prefrontal cortex to give full recognition.

I SEE YOUR FACE ...

Familiar faces are stored in the brain in neural circuits — memories — known as Face Recognition Units (FRU). When a new image of a person enters consciousness these FRUs are scanned for a match. If one is found the appropriate FRU is activated, retrieved and attached to the new image. This merging of memory and stimulus is a crucial part of the process of recognition. New images may come from outside or they may be generated inside the mind — the brain activity is the same in both cases. So imagining a picture of someone you know will activate that person's FRU.

FRUs are kept alive by constant use. Each time one is activated it becomes more deeply etched into the brain through the process of long-term potentiation. If an FRU is activated frequently, it will also stay 'warm'. Normally, an FRU needs quite a strong stimulus to be activated – typically the sight of the person it represents, or the sight of something closely connected to them. But an FRU that is already warm needs only a weak stimulus to spark it off. In extreme cases – when an FRU has been kept almost permanently turned on for days – almost anything can serve as a visual reminder of the person.

Everyone has experienced this from time to time: when you are in love, or grieving, you see the person who is on your mind everywhere. Then you look again and see it was actually a stranger with only the slightest similarity to the one for whom you mistook them. This is what it means to have someone 'on your mind' – their recognition unit is 'warm' and hair-trigger ready for action.

THE BAYSIEN BRAIN

Human brains are constructed along fairly standard lines and so we all tend to see the world in a pretty standard way. Individuals may disagree over whether an object is beautiful but when two or more of us look at the same object it is very unlikely that one will proclaim it to be a banana while another says 'Hey! a parrot!'

Human brains have certain pre-existing hypotheses about the world 'built-in'. They don't have to learn, for example, that an object flying towards them at great speed is best avoided. Others are the result of things we learn – a four year old who has been told that a fat man in a red suit will be delivering presents to them on Christmas Eve may project that hypothesis so strongly that a rustle and shadow at the end of the bed at roughly the right time is seen quite clearly as a magical visitation from Father Christmas. In time though she will change her hypothesis. So how does she get from that first hypothesis to the second?

One strong theory is that human brains employ a form of statistical reasoning first described by an eighteenth-century cleric, Thomas Bayes, and known now as Baysien induction.

The Baysien approach goes like this: imagine you are in a strange land and you spot a cat with red eyes. You wonder if this is a one-off, or whether all the cats in this place are like that. For the moment you decide to keep an open mind – in statistical terms you assign equal prior probabilities to both possible outcomes. Now let's say you represent this by placing one white and one black marble into a bag. The following day you see another red-eyed cat. To represent this sighting, you place another white marble in the bag. The probability, now, that a marble plucked randomly from the bag will be white (i.e., your belief that the cats in this place have red eyes) has thus gone from a half to two-thirds. Next day, upon encountering a third red-eyed feline, you add another white marble, and so the probability (and thus your degree of belief) goes from two-thirds to three-quarters. Gradually, your initial belief that cats around here are as likely not to have red eyes as to have them is modified to become a near-certainty that red eyes is the norm.

Given that each marble deposit is represented in the brain by a change in the neural structure (albeit a change on a minuscule level) you can imagine that over time a brain is physically changed by experience – its beliefs literally etched into the flesh.

explained, so they could get into her house on pretence of reading the meter. At night she saw them passing by her window and by day they lurked at street corners. Miss C. reported their activities to the police, and sometimes she would approach strangers and demand that they remove their disguises. On the day of her first appointment with a psychiatrist she was hours late because, she explained, she had to do a complicated detour around town to throw the couple off her trail.

Miss C.'s pursuers disappeared when she was treated with a dopamine-blocking drug. Dopamine excites many subcortical areas, and the strong sense of recognition that was constantly triggered in Miss C.'s brain was probably due to over-stimulation of the right-hemisphere limbic system pathways that pick up on familiarity.[18]

In Capgras delusion the emotional recognition system is under- rather than over-active. Capgras patients can see that people look like themselves, but they do not feel right emotionally. The 'ah-ha!' of recognition is missing and without it Capgras patients cannot believe that their nearest and dearest are really whom they claim to be.

In order to explain the mismatch between appearance and feeling, these patients often come to believe that members of their family have been 'taken over' by aliens. One man was so convinced that his father had been abducted and replaced with a humanoid robot that he ended up slitting the man's throat to look for the wires that animated him.[19]

As with those who develop Fregoli's delusion, Capgras patients have cognitive dysfunction in addition to their recognition fault, and it is this – their shaky thinking – that causes them to create weird explanations for their distorted perceptions. The cognitive deficit in such cases can usually be traced to fairly obvious cortical damage: a CAT scan of Miss C.'s brain, for example, showed she had lost quite a large area of cerebral cortex as a result of a stroke.

This raises a question: what would it be like to have an emotional recognition dysfunction in the

The cortical 'who?' recognition pathway ends in the frontal area with the conscious acknowledgement that a person is familiar.

visual cortex

The emotional recognition pathway passes through limbic structures which give a feeling of familiarity.

These two types of knowing usually come together in consciousness, but if the emotional message does not get through to the conscious brain the person may look familiar but not 'feel' right – a condition known as Capgras' delusion.

absence of a cognitive deficit? Say you had an overactive emotional recognition system, so the circuit usually reserved for activation by those who are emotionally important to you is triggered by a much wider range of people. The result of this might be that you would keep spotting people you know, only to discover on closer scrutiny that they look nothing like whom you thought them to be. However, unlike poor Miss C., your intact grasp of reality would prevent you interpreting this as evidence that you are being stalked by people in disguise, so in time you would learn to recognize only those people who trigger an exceptionally strong sense of familiarity.

You would still feel a twinge of recognition towards others, though, and it seems likely that this would give you a sense of connection, emotional attachment and interest in others that would be greater than that felt by most people. Talking to people would generate a continuous emotional charge; just seeing a friend would give a jolt of pleasure; pictures of familiar people – celebrities, say – would create interest.

If, on the other hand, your emotional recognition system was underactive, you would be slow to recognize those you know and might therefore appear to be aloof. Talking face to face to a person would be only as engaging for you as the content of the conversation – you might find communicating by e-mail just as good. You would probably shun social gatherings, both out of boredom and for fear of accidentally snubbing someone you know. And you may well feel a lack of emotional attachment even to those who are closest to you, as well as detachment from people in general.

These two behavioural profiles match up, of course, with our idea of what it is like to be an extravert or an introvert. So could the degree of activity in the emotional recognition system be a measure of extra/introversion? Could it even dictate which type of person we are?

A recent brain scanning study showed that extraverts, when shown happy faces, have greater activation in the right amygdala than introverts, and those who show up in personality tests as 'neurotic'. It is this activity rather than any difference in cortical areas, that seems to determine a person's personality type.[20] Emotional recognition, as we have seen, is a function of the limbic system, so the greater the activation in that area the more active our emotional recognition system is likely to be.

Whatever its role in shaping personality may turn out to be, the emotional recognition system is clearly an important means of forging the emotional connections that are so vital for survival in a highly social species like ours. Without them we cannot truly say we know who's who.

The phantom factory

A Dutch eye specialist sent a follow-up survey to patients who had undergone a particular surgical procedure. The questions were compiled, in Dutch, by an English assistant. One of them was intended to ask if the patients saw distortions, and if so, what they were like. However, a slight mistranslation of 'distortion' made it seem that the enquiry was about visual hallucinations.

The doctor was subsequently astonished to receive dozens of accounts of detailed, dramatic phantom sightings – the sort of things that, in certain circles, would be held up as incontrovertible evidence of some Other World. Most of the sightings were clear images of people going about their normal daily business. Sometimes they were complete strangers, sometimes they were familiar. One man kept coming across his wife as he moved from room to room. He found that if he walked straight through the phantom it would disappear. Unfortunately, this led to some painful encounters with the real thing who was alive and well and also living in the house. Eventually, the couple worked out an elaborate identification ritual to avoid collisions.

Some people reported coming across huge buildings in what they knew was empty moorland; others saw whole crowds of people. The images often persisted for hours.

Many of the patients said they kept their experiences to themselves for fear of ridicule, and expressed relief at being asked about hallucinations because they assumed this indicated that 'seeing things' was a recognized side-effect of the particular eye operation they had undergone. In fact, it is not. Although phantom sightings are much more common among people with damaged sight, the visual system in these patients was generally intact. The error in the questionnaire revealed that hallucinations – at least among middle-aged Dutch people – are far more common than you might expect.

So how do they come about?

The brain does not 'see', 'hear' or 'feel' the outside world. It constructs it in response to stimuli. The stimuli usually come from outside –

light waves, for example, bounce off objects and then hit the light-sensitive neurons in the eye. These stimulate the brain to create an image that accords with the information it is receiving.

Sometimes, however, the brain either misreads the incoming information (creating an illusion) or generates its own stimuli, which it then interprets as coming from outside. When this happens there may be no way – other than by deduction – for someone to work out whether what they are sensing is really in the outside world or only in their own mind.

Look at this inverted picture of Barack Obama. Looks normal enough, does it not? Now turn it right side up.

The distortions leap out and hit you only when you turn the picture around because the face recognition system of the brain is designed to work right side up and inverted faces are not processed as 'faces' – just objects. Object processing happens in a different area of the brain which is not equipped to give images as fine as fine scrutiny as the face processing area. Small differences like a droopy mouth are therefore easily overlooked. Incidentally – that little jolt you got when you saw the distorted face registered came from the emotional face recognition area of your brain. If your brain had been scanned at the moment you felt it the area around your amygdala would have been seen to light up.

'Phantom limb' sensation affects 69 per cent of people who undergo amputation.[21] Sometimes it fades after a few months but often it lasts a lifetime. People may simply feel the lost limb in the way that they felt it when it was there. It is quite common for patients with recently amputated legs to cause themselves further injuries by momentarily forgetting their loss and trying to walk on the lost leg. Sometimes a lost limb feels as though it is stuck in an awkward position. A young man who lost his arm in a horrific motorcycle accident cannot sleep on his back because it feels as though his arm is still bent behind him in the position it was forced into when he was spreadeagled across the road.[22]

Hallucinations, imagination, and 'real' seeing are essentially the same thing as far as the brain is concerned. If you look at a scan of a person's brain while they create an internal picture of, say, their bedroom, you will see activity in the same vision and recognition areas that would be activated if they were actually looking at the room. Usually, however, more sensory neurons are activated in response to outside stimuli than in self-generated sensory experience.

You can measure the difference by looking up from this book, memorizing the scene in front of you for a minute or two, then closing your eyes and trying to recreate it in your mind's eye. The first impression probably seems very strong but if you home in on details – the titles on the spines of books in the bookcase, for example you will probably find they go fuzzy. This is because enough neurons are firing in your visual cortex to give an impression of the scene but not enough to provide the details.

This is not the case with everyone. Some people have eidetic – photographic – memory, which allows them to create visualizations that are just as intense as those brought about by the original stimuli. Eidetic memory may be something we all start off with. Studies suggest that up to 50 per cent of five-year-olds[23] have the ability to 'read off' an imagined image as though it was really there. If they look at a picture of a zebra, for example, and then close their eyes, they can count the stripes along its back – the equivalent of reading the spines on the books.

A few adults retain the ability to imagine things with this intensity. Psychiatrist Morton Schatzman reported the case of a woman called Ruth who was 'haunted' by her abusive father. She would wake in bed and find him leering over her, or walk into her living room and find him ensconced in her favourite chair. Sometimes she would lean over to pick up her baby and find her father's face superimposed on the child's. The man was still alive when this happened, but the experience was otherwise very similar to the classic tales told by people who see ghosts, right down to the accompanying feeling of a presence.[24]

Ruth was subsequently found to be able to create such intense images that they completely blocked out the real world. In one experiment she was linked to a machine that measured the electrical activity created in her brain by certain stimuli. When she was placed in front of a light her brain at first reacted in the expected way. But when she imagined a person sitting between her and the light her brain no longer responded to the light waves coming from the bulb. The figure she had conjured up actually blocked her vision of the real world. This image differed from the 'hauntings' in one way only: she knew she had produced it herself. Once she recognized that her father's unwelcome visitations were similarly self-generated, they ceased to affect her and eventually disappeared.

Hallucinations can therefore best be understood as exceptionally intense self-generated sensory experiences. People with eidetic memory are likely to experience them more frequently than others. Children who play with seemingly invisible playmates, for example, may actually be seeing these friends as clearly as they see real people.

All types of sensory experience can be generated internally. Tinnitus, for example, may be caused by stimulation of the auditory cortex in the absence of outside stimuli. Some people report hearing a full orchestra playing, just as loudly and clearly as if they were in a concert hall. The Soviet composer Dmitri Shostakovich is said to have been able to hear music by tipping his head to one side, and claims to have come by several melodies by listening in to it. The music appeared after a shell exploded near him during the Second World War, embedding a splinter of metal in his brain. By tipping his head to one side, the splinter presumably came into contact with the auditory cortex and triggered activity in it.[26]

Voices are perhaps the most common type of auditory hallucination. Work with schizophrenics – 75 per cent of whom report hearing voices in their heads – has demonstrated that the voices heard by them are in fact their own. What happens is that they generate speech in one part of their brain and experience it as auditory input in another.[27] This does not usually happen with normal people because the brain generally monitors its own speech production area and signals to the speech recognition area when it is active. This prevents one's own words being mistaken for those of someone else.

Sometimes, however, this automatic distinction between outside voices and one's own breaks down even in normal people. It is quite common for people in mourning to report hearing the voice of the person who has died.

Phantom tastes and smells are also well documented. Imaginary smells, for example, are a common feature in early Parkinson's disease, and people who are depressed often report that they can smell themselves or that they have a 'bad taste' in their mouth.

Bodily sensations may also be generated internally. We take mild bodily hallucinations for granted: when we itch, for example, we do not necessarily expect to see something scratching us. False messages from the brain centres that keep

People with phantom hands have been helped by 'mirror-hand' therapy, devised by neuroscientist V.S. Ramachandran of the University of California in San Diego. The patient puts their real hand in one side of a box, which is divided by a mirror. They are then instructed to 'place' their phantom hand in the other side, and to move their real hand while watching the movements in a mirror. Then they are asked to match the observed movements by doing the same with the phantom. The effect is that the person feels the two hands to be moving together, and the image in the mirror confirms the illusion. This breaks the uncomfortable mismatch between what they feel in their phantom, and what they see, and the result, in many cases, is that the phantom ceases to be painful.[25]

track of one's own body can also produce profoundly upsetting hallucinations: doppelgangers, for example – apparitions that look precisely like onself – are probably produced by disruption to areas where the body map infringes on the visual association area.

Doppelgangers (properly known as autoscopic delusions) are traditionally seen as harbingers of death and so are regarded as terrible. Yet people who actually experience them usually report being curiously unmoved by the experience. Ms B., a retired schoolteacher whose case is reported by a doctor in Bristol, first saw her 'other self' when she returned home after her husband's funeral. She opened the door to her bedroom and was confronted by the shadowy shape of a woman facing her. Ms B. reached out with her right hand to switch on the light, and the figure did the same with her left hand, so their hands touched on the light switch. 'My hand immediately felt icy cold, and where it touched me I felt as though all the blood drained out of me,' she told the doctor. Despite this, Ms B. said she did not feel scared, just 'mildly surprised'. Without bothering about the intruder, she went about removing her hat and coat, and noticed that the other woman did precisely the same thing in mirror image. It was only then that she realized she was looking at her double. At that moment she suddenly felt exhausted and frozen, and lay down on the bed. As soon as she closed her eyes she lost sight of the figure – at which point her warmth and strength returned.

'It was as if the life of this astral body flowed back into me,' she explained. Ms B. was subsequently visited almost daily by her double. She found that she did not just see the figure – she felt it as well. Just as normal people are aware of two legs, two arms and so on, she was aware of four. 'It is me,' she explained, 'split and divided.'[28]

Some hallucinations may be brought about by a change in attention – a de-focusing on the outside world that allows internally generated stimuli to flood the brain. People with damage to the tegmentum – an area just above the reticular formation, which is part of the attention control mechanism – sometimes report having very elaborate, richly coloured hallucinations of everyday scenes. Sometimes these are familiar while at other times they seem to be new creations. Some are much bigger than life-size, others are tiny. One patient reported watching an entire circus performance, with clowns, jugglers and high-wire artists, all taking place in the palm of her hand.

Although such hallucinations are usually sharp-edged and quite solid-looking, they often seem to lack emotional impact – people typically say they observe them with detached amusement.

A similar matter-of-fact attitude is usually shown by children towards their imaginary friends. It is also characteristic of people who claim to be visionaries. This suggests that certain hallucinations are created by stimulation of the cortical areas of the brain and do not activate the limbic areas. They may look exactly like real entities but at an unconscious level the brain 'knows' that they do not pose a material threat. Hence – whether or not the person consciously recognizes them to be self-generated – they carry relatively little emotional punch.

Flashbacks, like those experienced in post-traumatic stress disorder, are just the opposite. These, too, take the form of intensely clear and lifelike scenes but their defining quality is terror. Flashbacks (as the name suggests) are not fresh creations but memories. Sometimes the memories are fragmented, sometimes they are precise replays of some traumatic event. They differ from other hallucinations in that they are triggered by memories laid down in the amygdala, and bring with them their full cargo of both sensory and emotional associations. In contrast to other hallucinations these may be consciously recognized as being false, but they feel more real than reality itself.

Migraine, epilepsy and a huge range of chemicals can create the changes in brain activity associated with hallucinations. Some of them increase or mimic the effect of excitatory neurotransmitters like dopamine, amplifying imagined sensations until they are indistinguishable from those generated by outside stimuli. Others inhibit areas of the brain involved in reality testing. Illicit drugs are often taken specifically for their ability to produce hallucinations, while therapeutic drugs often produce them as a (generally) unwanted side-effect.

Phantom sights and sounds are particularly likely to occur when people are deprived of normal outside sensory stimuli. People who lose all or part of their sight or hearing often find that they experience hallucinations for this reason. It also explains why ghosts are more commonly seen at night. In the absence of competing visual stimuli the brain picks up the shadow in the corner and moulds it into a sinister figure clothed with whatever visual associations – monk's habit, funereal gown – leap up from the memory storage areas.

Why does this happen? The brain evolved to keep constant watch on the outside world, sensing, sorting and shaping every stimulus in order to ensure that no danger creeps up unannounced, or opportunity pass by unnoticed. It needs to keep active so if the usual stream of clamouring external stimuli is turned off, it searches desperately for something to take its place. The slightest sound, sight or sensation is seized upon, amplified and shaped to make something meaningful, and if

PATTERNS IN THE MIND

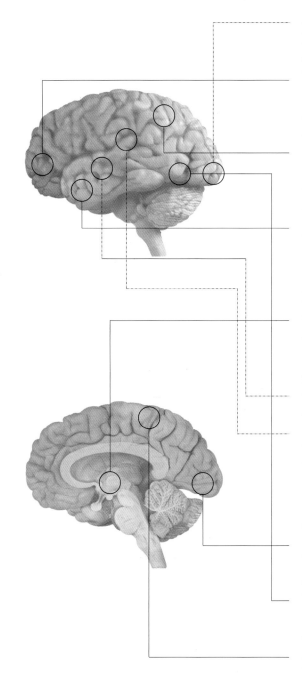

<u>Eyes and V1</u>: 15 per cent of people who lose part of their sight report having hallucinations.

<u>Left frontal lobe</u>: reality testing area – damage to this area may reduce the brain's ability to distinguish between externally and internally generated stimuli.

<u>Occipito-parietal area</u>: damage may make objects seem to appear or disappear due to simultagnosia – an inability to hold two objects in vision at the same time.

<u>Temporal lobe</u>: stimulation in this lobe – by epilepsy or drugs – may produce intense flash-backs and feelings of a 'presence'. Objects may appear strange or change from one form to another.

<u>Temporal/limbic system</u>: stimulation here may produce intense feelings of joy, and a feeling of being in the presence of God. Religious visions may occur.

<u>Auditory cortex/speech areas</u>: stimulation here produces hallucinatory voices.

<u>Superior auditory cortex</u>: sounds and noises, such as hissing, clicks and crashes, may occur if this area is stimulated. The brain may interpret them as meaningful noises. Tinnitus may be caused by activity here in the absence of outside sounds.

<u>Visual shape area</u> (right hemisphere): 'Ghostly outlines' may be triggered by overstimulation of the visual area that detects shape.

<u>Visual face recognition area</u>: images of faces may linger after they have 'really' gone due to overactivity here.

<u>Parietal/sensory cortex margin</u>: doppel-gangers – a spectral version of oneself – may be the result of disturbance to this area.

absolutely nothing comes in from outside, the brain will generate its own excitement. Hallucinations, like dreams, are part of a continuous cabaret that keeps us primed and ready for action. If the stage falls empty, the ghosts will come in to fill it.

Illusions

In July 1985 a group of Irish teenage girls claimed to have seen a statue of the Virgin Mary move. The figure, in Ballinspittle, Co. Cork, was wringing her hands as though in grief, said the girls. Other people saw it, too. The story – coming as it did in the midst of the annual 'silly season', when hard news is thin on the ground was picked up and made much of in the newspapers. Within 24 hours at least 40 other statues of the Virgin were reported to be on the move as well – busily waving, blessing and, in some cases, having a good look around. That summer more than a million people claimed to have seen these miracles. For a short while the Second Coming was confidently predicted to be nigh.[29]

Moving Madonnas are now two-a-penny. Since that major outbreak in 1985, they have popped up with monotonous regularity. This is not surprising because, if you look hard enough at a statue under the right circumstances, you will indeed see it move.

Try this experiment. Block out all the light in the room then place a lighted cigarette in an ashtray at one end of it. Then take a seat at the other end and concentrate hard on the glowing tip. After a while you will see it start to wander. Sometimes it will swoop in one direction, sometimes in the other. It may circle gently, or describe graceful arcs and curves as though spelling letters in a neon thread. The harder you look, the more it moves.

A similar effect is achieved if you stare at any distant object illuminated against a dark background. The phenomenon is known as the autokinetic effect and it occurs when the eye muscles become tired from straining to fixate on a single

Whether you see a goblet or two faces depends on which part of this figure your brain selects as background and which as figure. If you expect to see either a face or a goblet, you will probably see that image first and more persistently.

point. The fatigue would normally cause the eyes to wander away from the fixation point, so, to continue to hold them on the target, the brain sends a stream of 'correction' commands to the eye muscles. These are the same signals it would send, if the muscles were not tired, to instruct them to move. The signals are therefore interpreted by the brain as eye movements. Hence the point of light registers as a moving object, activating neurons in the areas of the brain – mainly V5 – that are responsible for registering motion. Divine intervention is not required.

Illusions like this differ from hallucinations in that they are errors of perception and/or construction, rather than false constructions. A great deal of the perceived world is in fact illusory – the moving pictures of a film or video image are actually a series of stills or pulsating dots, for example – but we generally notice such falsities only when they jump out at us or produce an effect that fails to fit our expectations.

Some illusions are caused by fairly mechanical processes: the halo of brightness that persists after a strong light has been switched off, for example, is due to residual firing of the light-sensitive neurons in the retina. Others, though, give an insight into the way our brains work at the highest level: what may at first appear to be an error of the senses is actually created by an error of cognition. Sometimes the two are combined: the Virgin Mary, for example, may move owing to the physiological effect of staring too hard at a fixed point. But it is a cognitive error that translates the illusory movements into hand-wringing and blessings.

Cognitive illusions come about because the brain is full of prejudices: habits of thought, knee-jerk emotional reactions and automatic orderings of perception. These are so deeply ingrained that we are usually unaware that they exist, and when we do become aware of them we think of them as common sense assumptions or intuition. These prejudices are, to some extent, hard-wired into our brains. As we have seen, even infants have strong expectations about how objects should behave. This is why babies are so gripped by games in which things are made to 'disappear'. The concept that material things take up space and do not just dematerialize is clearly very much part of our neural blueprint.

Such pre-programmed theories about the world are useful because they allow us to make quick, practical decisions about how to react to what we perceive. Most of the time they work fine (which is, of course, why they evolved). Sometimes, though, we are caught out by them.

Take, for example, our simple prejudice about object size. If you see two cars ahead, one big and the other tiny, you assume the bigger one is closer. Your experiences of perspective have woven a neural pathway in your brain that transforms the sight of 'little object/big object' into 'far object/ near object'. There is no pre-operative checkpoint at the start of this pathway to question whether the tiny car may in fact be some child's toy cunningly placed to look like a real distant vehicle. Such a test, if it was run each time you encountered two cars of differing size, would take up so much time you would never get around to crossing the road. No, when the stimulus 'big car/little car' gets through the primary vision areas and into the visual association areas the automatic perspective processor trips into action without pause. We are so used to it delivering the right answer that when we find it is wrong – the little car really *is* a child's toy – we receive a jolt.

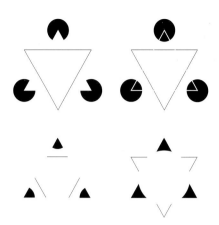

The phantom triangle is constructed in a different way, and in a different area of the brain, from the 'real' one.

Similarly, when we see a curved oval object lit from above the brain automatically responds to it as though it is a face. As faces stick out rather than in, we therefore construct a perception of a concave object – even when it is in fact convex. If the lighting is changed so the object is lit from below, the brain no longer sees it as a face (presumably because faces are usually downlit by sunlight) and the object suddenly pops out.

The prejudices that give rise to sensory illusions are generally benign. The illusion of a mirage in a desert may be a cruel trick but it is not one that takes many lives nowadays and magicians may use our various blind spots to deceive but it is usually done by happy collusion with the deceived. As a scientific tool they are very useful, but as individuals there is not much to be gained, in practical terms, by becoming aware of the mechanisms by which we falsify the evidence of our senses.

Prejudices of thought are a different matter. The illusions created by our own cognitive misconstructions make bigger fools of us than any stage magician may contrive. 'Purely' cognitive illusions – those in which the affected perceptions are ideas rather than sensory phenomena – may have arisen for the same reason as sensory illusions: they help us deal quickly and practically with complex challenges. But ideas

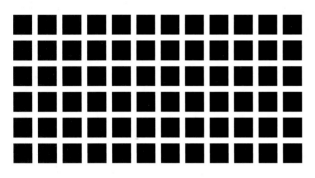

Hermann's Grid

If you look at the grid you see little grey blobs at the intersections of the white lines. This is due to a physiological mechanism affecting the retinal neurons. It is called lateral inhibition. When you look at the intersection of the white lines – the place where the blobs appear – you will see that the blobby area is surrounded on four sides by white but if you shift your gaze to the vertical bands of white between the intersections you will see that there are only two neighbouring white areas. Lateral inhibition causes light-receiving cells in the retina to shut down when the light-receiving cells around them are activated. When you look at the intersection, the cells focused on that area are surrounded on four sides by others which are also firing. When you look at the bands, by contrast, the cells adjacent to those focused on the bands are activated only on two sides.

The cells are therefore more inhibited when they focus on the intersections than they are when they focus on the white bands. The result – dark patches. Magicians take advantage of lateral inhibition to obscure their apparatus. For example, if they want to hide the struts of a floating body they might surround it with brightly shining metallic objects, white cloth, and so on. The parts they want to hide would be black, placed against a black background. The dazzle from the bright objects would cause the cells which would normally spot the darker objects to be inhibited – so the struts would not be seen.

are more slippery than material objects. If we process them according to rigid prejudices they are very likely to trip us up – and the cost may be high.

Take, for example, the 'common sense' approach to the following scenario. You are a member of a jury that is trying a man for murder. The prosecution has no evidence against him bar this single item: his DNA matches traces of genetic material left by the murderer on the victim's body. The chances of the DNA found at the scene matching any single person plucked at random are, you are informed, ten million to one. Do you find him guilty?

You probably do. Such evidence has, in the past, sent many suspects to jail, while the juries that convicted them went home to sleep peacefully in their beds, convinced that 'statistically' a guilty verdict was in order.

The apparent unlikeliness of the person in the dock being innocent is, however, illusory. Even if his DNA pattern is seen only once in every ten million in a country with a population of, say, 100 million people, that means it is shared by ten other men. If all ten were in dock, would you have any reason to single out the one that is now before you? The prosecution, remember, has *no other evidence against him.* Logically, then, the chances of his being guilty are one in ten, not (as you might have thought) one in ten million.

This, like many sensory illusions, is one that persists even when we have spotted the error. Our prejudice – in this case the assumption of guilt until proved innocent – is so deeply entrenched that we find ourselves struggling to fit the facts to match it rather than vice versa. 'Ah,' we say, 'but the suspect wouldn't be in the dock if he hadn't given the police cause to suspect him, would he?'

In the past this particular prejudice probably had high survival value. The fact is, in the messy, 'real' world in which we evolved, it was generally safer to assume guilt in anyone who came under suspicion and not to bother with fancy ideas about admissable and inadmissable evidence. Our concern for the rights of the individual, not to mention our ability to analyse statistics, came a whole lot later. They do not therefore come naturally to us. In the example above, furthermore, it is easy to rationalize the assumption of guilt. We know that the legal system puts strong constraints on what evidence may be presented so it is quite possible that there is other evidence against the suspect, even though it is not admissible in court. We also know that the police are unlikely to have picked on an entirely random member of the public to put in the dock. So we make our decision in our time-honoured, prejudicial way, and justify it with a veneer of rationality.

There are real, practical considerations here. For one, things change in the world of ideas and prejudices that were fair enough yesterday may be terribly misguided today. In our example, a computerized database of every person's DNA — not such a distant possibility — would remove one of the major justifications of the assumption of guilt. This is because such a database would make it relatively easy for the police to run a check against almost anyone, not just people they had reason to suspect. So the chances of them effectively placing a 'random member of the public' in the dock are greatly increased.

Cognitive illusions about statistics leave us open to costly errors. Whole financial markets have been known to collapse under the weight of instinctual irrational buying and selling, and many decisions about how to use public money have been found, on analysis, to be based on misreading of statistics. Cognitive illusions cause us to take extreme precautionary measures against obscure risks and to be

A concave mask appears to be convex once enough of it is visible for us to realize it is a face. As it rotates (anticlockwise) the concave side springs out and appears to be convex. This is because the face recognition area 'knows' that faces are convex — and constructs the image accordingly.

reckless about the day-to-day dangers that are actually likely to cause us harm.

Take the way that people select their numbers for the British lottery. They can choose 6 numbers ranging from 1 to 50. Everyone knows that every number is as likely to come up as any other. Yet most people 'intuitively' — and insistently — choose a nice even spread — typically one number in every ten. A few, determined not to be taken in by that particular illusion, choose 1, 2, 3, 4, 5, 6; or 35, 36, 37, 38, 39, 40. These choices certainly stand the same chance of winning as any other but they both stand *less* chance of attracting the Big Win — the multimillion-pound prize that everyone lusts for. The reason? If two or more people select the winning numbers, the prize money is divided between them. So the really big prizes only go to single winners. With so many people looking for 'a nice even spread' the chances of two or more of them coming up with the same particular spread is quite high. Similarly, the idea of putting 1, 2, 3, 4, 5, 6 has occurred to many people. So the best string of numbers to select is slightly bunched, skew-whiff and *unusual* – the string you can least imagine coming up.

What has all this to do with the construction of the brain? Probably almost everything. Such evidence as there is suggests that the brain constructs its ideas – even its most sophisticated notions – in much the same way as it constructs sensory perceptions. Our essential prejudices of thought (not what we think, but how we think it) are created by the layout and connectivity of our neurons, much of it probably laid down before we are born.

Hence we arrive in the world with a set of hypotheses which we update only if the incoming evidence conflicts with them. We also have a built-in 'confirmation bias' that encourages us to be more alert to the evidence that supports our prejudice than to that which contradicts it. So, for example, if we come across unpalatable truths about someone we want to admire, we override the impact of it by sheer emotional force. Psychologists at Emory University demonstrated this in a sample of committed Democrats and Republicans during the three months prior to the U.S. Presidential election of 2004. The Democrats and Republicans were each given information about their chosen candidate which – had they been operating in a purely reasonable way – would have given them second thoughts about their preference. While they took in the information the researchers scanned their brains with fMRI to see what was happening in them. What they found was that the frontal lobe areas which are known to be involved in reasoning were strangely quiet. Instead increased activation was seen in a network of emotion circuits, including those activated by sadness, disgust, and – most tellingly, perhaps – conflict. The subjects' brains looked for all the world as though they were fighting the incoming information, struggling to block it out or minimize its impact. The subjects were then invited to comment on what they had learned and more or less all of them reported that their essential preference was unchanged, and that the information they had received was less important than it seemed or – by various acts of mental athletics – actually supportive of their views. Having arrived at their convoluted conclusions, the activity in the subjects' brains altered. Now the areas that lit up were those in the reward circuit. Not only, it seems, do we find ways to support our prejudices but, having done so, we reward ourselves for it![30]

There is an important difference between these higher illusion-creating mechanisms and those that make us see sticky-out noses on concave faces. It is that they are much more malleable. Try as you might, you will not get rid of the illusory grey square in Hermann's grid (on page 132). But you can work at the illusion of the guilty man, or the illusion of the 'nice, even, winning-type' string of lottery numbers. You can chip away at your political prejudices; force yourself to assess rationally evidence you would normally fight to dismiss.

Thinking alters thinking. We can actually change the structure and activity in our brains, just by deciding to. It is the greatest accomplishment of our species.

THE CONVERGENCE OF AUNT MAGGIE

 ANTONIO DAMASIO
Professor of Neurology, University of Iowa College of Medicine

The following is an adapted extract from Descartes' Error *by Antonio Damasio.*

Images are not stored as facsimile pictures of things, events, words or sentences. If the brain were like a conventional library, we would run out of shelves just as conventional libraries do. Furthermore, facsimile storage poses difficult problems of retrieval efficiency. Whenever we recall a given object, face or scene, we do not get an exact reproduction but rather an interpretation, a newly reconstructed version of the original, which evolves with our changing age and experience.

And yet we all feel that we can conjure up, in our mind's eye or ear, approximations of images previously experienced. Maybe these mental images are momentary constructions held in consciousness only fleetingly. Although they may appear to be good replicas, they are often inaccurate or incomplete. I suspect that explicit recalled mental images arise from the transient synchronous activation of neural firing patterns largely in the same early sensory cortices where the firing patterns corresponding to perceptual representations once occurred.

But how do we form the topographically organized representation needed to experience recalled images? I believe those representations are constructed momentarily under the command of neural patterns elsewhere in the brain that quite literally order other neural patterns about.

These representations exist as potential patterns of neuron activity in small ensembles of neurons that I call 'convergence zones', which consist of a set of neuron firing dispositions within the ensemble. The dispositions related to recallable images were acquired through learning and can thus be said to constitute a memory. The convergence zones whose dispositional representations can result in images when they fire back to early sensory cortices are located throughout the higher-order association cortices (in occipital, temporal, parietal and frontal regions) and in basal ganglia and limbic structures.

What dispositional representations hold in store in their little commune of synapses is not a picture per se, but a means to reconstitute 'a picture'. If you have a dispositional representation for the face of Aunt Maggie, that representation contains not her face as such, but rather the firing patterns that trigger the momentary reconstruction of an approximate representation of Aunt Maggie's face in the early visual cortices.

The disparate dispositional representations that would need to fire back more or less simultaneously for Aunt Maggie's face to show up in your mind's eye are located in several visual and higher-order association cortices. And the same arrangement would apply in the auditory realm.

There is not just one hidden formula for this reconstruction. Aunt Maggie does not exist in one single site of your brain – she is distributed all over it in the form of many dispositional representations. When you conjure up remembrances of things Maggie she is present only in separate views during the time window in which you construct the meaning of her person.

CHAPTER SIX

CROSSING THE CHASM

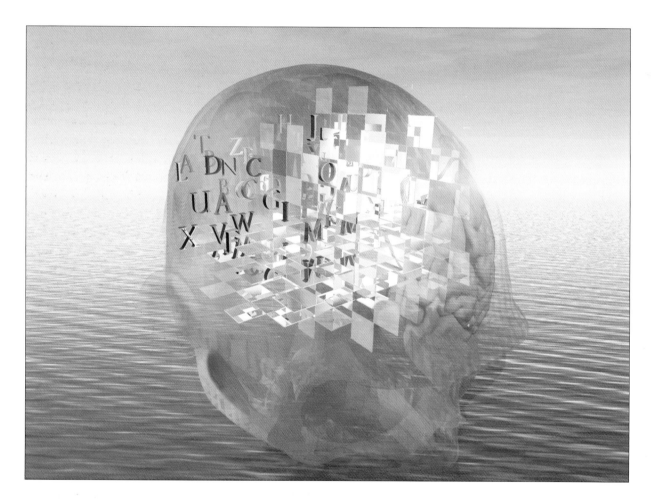

Just as each separate brain cell reaches out to make contact with others, so each brain is designed to communicate with its like. Our ability to enter the minds of others, by intuition and by speech, gives human beings a singular advantage over other species. It allows us to create and live in the highly organized hives we call civilization, and as a species we can join in endeavours so grandiose that they alter our environment on a global scale. Language allows us to juggle ideas in a uniquely creative way, and our intuitive knowledge of others' mental machinations makes our relationships complex, subtle and deep.

Language development changed the landscape of the brain radically because it annexed huge cerebral areas once used for movement and sensation. In doing so it created the asymmetry that distinguishes the human brain from that of any other animal.

OMMUNICATION IS NOT a bolt-on extra; for most species it is a matter of survival. Most of the constant information exchange that goes on between living things is unconscious: hormones waft from one creature's gland to another's nose carrying messages about territorial rights and sexual receptivity; reflex pricked ears and swivelled eyes give mute warning of approaching danger within herds; a bee's complex dance, dictated by some mysterious genetic imperative, directs the hive to a cache of pollen.

Once, no doubt, all living things communicated only to the extent that they reacted to changes in others' behaviour or appearance in much the same way as they reacted to other environmental signs. Those who were good at reading these changes must have had a major advantage. If you react to your neighbour's reaction to a rustle in the bushes rather than wait to hear the rustle yourself, you speed up the process of fleeing from a potential predator. Similarly, those who gave big, noticeable reactions must have given a survival benefit to those who hung around and mated with them, so their genes were passed on preferentially. In this way Darwinian selection must constantly have improved communication between individuals until some species became adept at reading the slightest facial expression, body movement or visible physiological change in others of their kind.

Some species, at some point in their development, took communication one step further – they started to do it deliberately. This brought with it all manner of survival benefits. Say you are a dog with a lively litter and you want one of your offspring to stop jumping on your back. You could stop the game by biting the culprit. This would be effective but it might hurt the precious vessel of your genes and thus prejudice its (and your) genes' survival. So instead you snap, giving a deliberate warning that

has the same effect but without the risk. Similarly, a horse or a dog or a fish may fake a fighting stance to scare off a would-be aggressor. If it does it convincingly enough it will succeed without involving either of them in potentially dangerous combat.

Hominids, blessed with their free-moving, flexible hands, developed a particularly useful form of deliberate signing: gesture. Gesture is still going strong in humans and can often be more effective than words: try describing a spiral without using your hands, or conveying a Gallic shrug in words. As well as acting as an adjunct to verbal expression it seems to function as a fall-back language when no other is made available. Deaf children who are not taught to sign develop a wide range of gestures spontaneously and they also string the gestures together to form what seem at first to be sentences. However, such children do not develop structured language and without it they do not seem able to make the leap into the world of abstract thought. For that they have to be taught a formal signing language – one that has similar rules and structure to spoken language.

Gesture gave way to 'proper' language about one and a half to two million years ago. The development of language gave humans the tool needed to lift themselves up to a higher level of consciousness. Deliberate communication of the posturing, mimicry sort provided the first step up from the concrete world of the here and now because it created the possibility of an alternative world: a world in which the puppy gets hurt and the audacious horse is attacked. But the range of options that could be conjured up in this way were pretty limited. Language, by contrast, opened up a universe of endless possibilities.

Think – what sort of memory would you have without words? What if you needed to remember that bananas, say, were good food? You can't store

nerve fibres connect Wernicke's
area (comprehension) with
Broca's area (speech production)

angular gyrus

the visula, tucked inside the
fold, makes language areas
work in concert

The language areas of the brain are mainly in the left hemisphere,
around and above the ear. The main ones are Wernicke's area,
which makes spoken language comprehensible, Broca's area, which
generates speech (and may contain a 'grammar module') and the
angular gyrus which is concerned with meaning.

an actual fruit in your head for later reference so what would be lodged is a sensory impression: the shape and colour, the smooth feel of its skin and the sweet smell of the flesh. Next time you come across a long, smooth, yellow object with a banana-like smell you would match these sensory memories to your bounty and know that it is good.

So far so good, this is (very roughly) how memories are laid down, with or without language, and it works fine in so far as it goes. But what if you wanted to titillate yourself with the idea of a banana? How would you bring those sensory memories to consciousness? Without some symbol, like a name, for an object you have nothing with which to hook the memories of it from storage. They may be brought to mind by sensory reminders – a flash of yellow, perhaps – but voluntary access to them, on demand, would be much harder. Once you can label things, however, you can make your mind into a filing cabinet and pack it with representations

of the outside world. You can then pluck out these representations seemingly at will and juggle and juxtapose them, creating new ideas in the process. This creates a template within which ideas can be ordered and structured, giving shape and stability to notions that would otherwise remain nebulous. Thus it provides the means to consider abstractions: honesty, fairness, authority and so on.

What it once did for the species, it does for individuals, too. Neurologist Oliver Sacks, in *Seeing Voices*, his book about the deaf community and their language, describes a deaf boy who was reared without access to sign language:

'Joseph saw, categorized, distinguished, used... but he could not, it seemed, go much beyond this, hold abstract ideas in mind, reflect, play, plan. He seemed completely literal – unable to juggle images or hypotheses or possibilities, unable to enter an imaginative or figurative realm.'[1]

Once you can make that jump into the realm of imagination there need be no limit to the mental concepts you create: morality, justice, God... Then, by communicating these ideas to others, you can create social constructs: codes of behaviour, legal systems, religions – and so give your lofty notions practical expression. Such things could never be achieved by grunts and gestures.

The reason for the emergence of language is mysterious, but the brain itself provides some clues. The main language areas are situated in the left hemisphere of the brain, in the temporal (side) and frontal lobes. If you look down on a slice of brain cut horizontally at a certain level, you will see these areas are marked by a distinct, one-sided bulge (see illustration on p. 154). The equivalent areas in the right hemisphere are concerned mainly with processing environmental noises and with spatial skills: the rhythm and melody of music impacts here; the 'where' of things in the outside world is registered and fine hand movements – including gestures (but not formal sign language) – are processed. Apart from what seems like a tiny budding in some primates, animals do not have language areas.

Instead their brains are more or less symmetrical, and their noises are produced and processed along with environmental noises on both sides.

The region where language developed is also rich in connections to deeper brain structures that process sensory stimuli, and it is one of the places where stored impressions from different senses, particularly touch and hearing, are brought together and reassembled into coherent memories. Assuming that man's immediate ancestors were wired in a similar way to today's primates, it seems that language sprung up in a region where several different and important functions converged. Perhaps the brain of *h. habilis* – the hominid in which language first seems to have blossomed – had already started to expand and was compressed within the skull in such a way that these abutting areas, with their different skills, started to merge. Sound would then become linked to hand gestures and gestures would become associated with the synthesizing of sensual memories into wholes.

The evolution of language may have been aided by a particular type of genetic mutation. The gene known as FOXP2 is found in many primates, but the human version differs at two links in the chain of amino acids that make up the protein. These two tiny molecular differences alter the activity of at least 116 genes in brain cells grown in laboratory dishes, many of which are involved in neural development and the production of collagen, cartilage and soft tissues. This in turn suggests that the protein helps shape both the brain and the vocal apparatus that makes speech possible.[2]

Once language had taken hold in our early ancestors it rapidly annexed large parts of the left hemisphere, growing so fast that it pushed the visual functions back and appropriated most of the locality previously given over to spatial skills. The visuo-spatial functions were still enormously important, of course, and in the right hemisphere they held their own. This was the beginning of the hemisphere differentiation that led to each side of the human brain developing clear specialisations – far more markedly than in other species.

The language vehicle

As far as the brain is concerned the essential thing about language is not that it is a means of communication but that it is a means of communication that follows certain rules. Hence body language is not dealt with in the language areas, gestures are not dealt with in the language areas and nor are screams, sighs or gasps. Formal sign language is processed in the language department, however, and so are formal gestures such as placing a finger to the lips for silence, because although these things do not have what we think of as the components of language – words – they have a formal structure and that is what matters to the brain.[3]

The skill that builds and understands structured language is something quite apart from general intelligence. It does not develop in line with the emergence of important and complex ideas. Rather it seems to be there, potentially at least, in advance of any ideas. It is wired in at such a fundamental level that in normal children a minimal amount of exposure to language at the right time will cause it to flower in all its complexity. Even the most monosyllabic teenage grunt-head is capable of composing grammatically accurate sentences when pushed.

In some people the linguistic vehicle is grander than the ideas it has to convey, and the flimsiest of notions are inflated in order to fill it. Most of us know people who seem to be effortlessly articulate and can talk fluently and expressively without ever actually *saying* anything. At first sight such people may seem socially adept and even gifted, but close acquaintance reveals them to be vacuous.

There is a very extreme form of this condition known as Williams syndrome. Alex is a fairly typical example. He did not babble like a normal baby, nor did he say 'ma-ma' or 'da-da' at the appointed time. At three he was showing signs of mental retardation and he had still not uttered a word.

However, when, at five, Alex finally came out with his first words, they were astonishing. It happened on a hot day in his doctor's waiting room. Alex was restless and toddled over to investigate a portable electric fan that had been brought in to keep the area cool. His mother removed him to a safe distance, but the boy kept returning and sticking his fingers perilously close to the blades. The receptionist, spotting the danger, turned the machine off. Clearly irritated, Alex turned it back on. The receptionist turned it off at the mains. A few minutes later Alex crawled up to the socket and flipped the switch back down. The receptionist responded by pulling out the plug and placing it out of the boy's reach.

Alex was now stymied. Looking severely displeased, he fiddled with the switch, flipped the mains and shook the base of the fan. The other people braced themselves for a wail of anger or some similar infant protest. Instead Alex chose that moment to come out with his maiden speech: 'Jesus Christ!' he said. 'This fan doesn't work!'[4]

From that moment on full-fledged, adult-sounding speech flooded out of Alex's mouth as though it had been stored there, complete and ready-learned, just waiting for the right moment to erupt. By the time he was nine his vocabulary and his grasp of grammar, syntax, modulation and emphasis were as good as any adult's. He has since been supremely confident and outward going, circulating rooms like a seasoned diplomat at a cocktail party. In terms of content, though, his conversation has never become much more consequential than his observation about the fan. Nor, most probably, will it ever.

Williams syndrome is caused by a genetic mutation that produces marked mental retardation (as well as other physical peculiarities) along with extraordinary linguistic skill. Although they often show remarkable intuition and empathy, the average IQ of Williams people is between 50 and 70, around the Down's syndrome mark. Ask a 10-year-old with Williams syndrome to fetch a couple of things from a cupboard and they will get confused and bring the wrong items. They may not be able to tie their shoelaces or add 15 and 20, and if you get them to draw a picture of someone riding a bike they will typically produce an incoherent melange of spokes and wheels, chains and legs. If you ask them to list all the animals they can think of, however, you will get an entrancingly imaginative and fulsome catalogue: one little girl's list included brontosaurus, tyranadon, zebra, ibex, yak, koala, dragon, whale and hippopotamus.[5]

Williams children are unstoppable chatterboxes, endlessly engaging strangers in conversation and taking off on long, expressive narratives interspersed with eccentric exclamations and verbatim inserts:

'…then she said to me: "Oh no! I've left the cake in the oven" and I said: "Heavens to Betsy! That will make for an unfortunate teatime!" and she said: "Well, I think I'll just pop back home and see if I can rescue it before it burns to a crisp," and I said: "Right-ho!"…'

Captivating though the style may be, such stories are nearly always banal, and sometimes they are entirely fabricated. Williams children have no desire to deceive and their confabulations are not designed to bring them any material advantage. It is just that language, for them, is not so much a vehicle for conveying information as a way of forging links between themselves and others and maintaining closeness.

Mirror Neurons

Closeness to and understanding of others is a central need for all normal people, and, indeed, for members of every species which depend on some sort of co-operation for survival. So important is it that it evolved way in advance of the intellectual skills required to seek co-operation consciously. Indeed, it seems to be built in to the very fabric of the mammalian brain.

One mechanism that drives social integration — perhaps the most important one — is the mirror neuron system. Mirror neurons are brain cells which are activated both when a person (or animal) does a particular act, and when they observe that action being done by another. A similar effect occurs with neurons that code for emotions and thoughts – some of the brain cells that would normally be activated when a person feels a particular emotion, or thinks a particular thought, also become active when the emotion or thought is discerned in others. The effect of mirror neurons and the broader 'mirroring' of emotions and thoughts is to provide the observer with immediate, automatic knowledge of what is going on in the other's mind. So for example, when you see someone lifting a heaving object, mirror neurons which would normally produce the action of lifting (and the sensation of effort and weight) spring into action and so give you the feeling – albeit perhaps so faintly that you are not aware of it – that you too are lifting a heavy weight. Hence you don't have to *think* about how the other person is feeling – you have the answer right there in your own, immediate experience.

The ability to know, intuitively, what another person is feeling or thinking is thought to be the basis of mimicry and empathy. It is how we learn to do things just by watching someone else do them, and how we do not just know, but *feel* the pain when we see someone else suffering it. It may also play an important part in the development of morality.

Mirror neurons were discovered, in 1995, by accident. A group of researchers led by Giacomo Rizzolatti at the University of Parma were trying to find out exactly which neurons in the motor cortex of monkeys were activated when they did certain movements. On one particular day they had electrodes implanted in the pre-motor cortex of a monkey to measure the nerve cell activity when the animal picked up a piece of food. During a lull in the experiments, one of the experimenters, feeling a bit peckish, picked up the monkey's titbit and put in his own mouth, just as the monkey had been doing.

The monkey was doing nothing but watching.

Mirror neurons were first discovered in the premotor area of monkeys (A). In humans they seem to extend into frontal lobe areas which are concerned also with intentions and emotions (B).

But suddenly the equipment registered activity in some of the same cortical cells that had been active when the monkey was picking up the morsel himself. Rather than writing off the event as some problem with the equipment – as might easily have happened – the researchers tried making other actions in front of the monkey. Each time they found that neurons which would normally fire if the animal was doing the act itself, became active when the animal was merely observing the act.

Mirroring touch

Mirror neurons allow us to know what another person feels when they are making an action, and also to know what they are feeling when they are touched. In one study subjects' brains were scanned, first while their leg was brushed, and then while they watched a video of someone else's leg being touched.

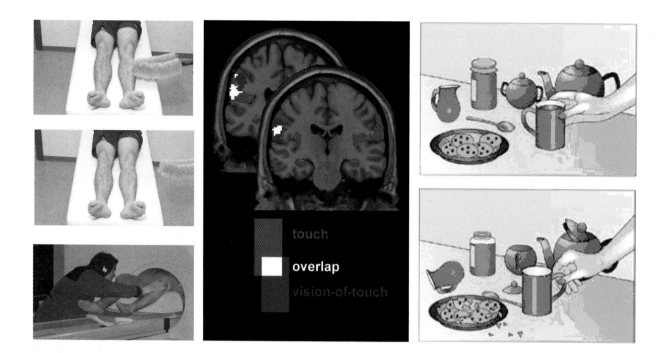

The brain scan in the centre (above) shows the overlap between areas activated by touch and areas activated by seeing someone else being touched. Areas activated only by the touch of the right or left leg are shown in red, areas activated only by the vision-of-touch are shown in blue and areas activated by both the touch and the vision-of-touch – the mirror areas – are shown in white. In this experiment the mirror neurons seemed to be limited to the left hemisphere though in others experiments they have been detected in both.[6]

Another study showed that human mirror neurons can even give us automatic understanding of another's person's intentions, as a clever experiment demonstrated. In it, researchers showed volunteers pictures of a hand grasping a cup in two different contexts. One was that of a newly-laid 'treat' of cookies, while the other showed the remnants of the meal. As the volunteers looked at the pictures (similar to those above, right) a measure was taken of the activity in their frontal cortex – the area of the brain which works out the meaning of actions (rather than just mimics them). Different neurons were activated in each case, suggesting that, although the physical action of grasping the cup was more or less identical, the brain understood the two actions entirely differently. In the first case the action was (presumably) taken to signify that the cup was being lifted to drink from, whereas in the second picture the cup was being taken away to wash up.[7]

Eye talk

'People talk to each other with their eyes, don't they? What are they saying?' – *Asperger's syndrome subject to a researcher*[8]

Autism is in many ways the mirror image of Williams syndrome. While the chatterboxes seek endlessly to bind non-related and imagined events into cohesive narrative and draw people together in warm community, those with autism see the world as fragmented and alien. They are unable to communicate, either effectively or, in some cases, at all.

There is a spectrum of conditions that can be considered autistic. At one end there are individuals whose only visible function is to make weird, repetitive body movements. At the other there are people who have high IQs, successful professional careers and outwardly normal domestic lives. A few combine extraordinary gifts for drawing, calculating or playing music with a very low IQ. One hallmark of them all, however, is a lack of empathy: autistics do not intuitively understand that other people have minds that may contain an entirely different view of the world to theirs and they cannot 'get into' another person's head.

Some brain imaging research suggests – controversially – that autistic 'mind-blindness' may, at least in part, be due to a defect in the mirror neurons system. One study looked at mirror neuron activity in high-functioning children with autism and matched controls. Both underwent fMRI while imitating and observing emotional expressions. Although both groups performed the tasks equally well, children with autism showed little or no mirror neuron activity in the frontal area critical for processing emotions. The children with the most severe problems showed the least activity.[9] Another study showed that in adults with autistic spectrum disorder the cortex in the areas associated with mirror neuron activity was significantly thinner than in controls.[10] This makes sense: more

than anything, autism is a defect of communication – an inability to share feelings, beliefs and knowledge with other people.

The instinctive ability to know what is in another person's mind is known as 'theory of mind'. It is simply illustrated – or rather its lack is illustrated – by a poignant story recounted by the father of an autistic boy. Autistic children do not automatically understand that their desires are subject to constraints; to them their wanting is all-consuming, so they tend to grab what they want when they want it. This particular child had been taught, by painstaking repetition, that he must not just help himself to biscuits. Instead his father trained him to point at what he wanted and then wait for an adult to give it to him. Generally, this worked quite well, and on the whole the child seemed happy living within this and other rules. From time to time, however, the child would throw a massive tantrum for no apparent reason.

Brain scans show that when normal people read a story which involves inferring someone else's state of mind the left medial prefrontal cortex lights up (hatched area, top). But when the same story is read to Asperger's subjects a different area just below it is activated.

A) *shows normal brain activity, including mirroring in frontal lobes,* B) *shows reduced activity in children with autistic spectrum disorder.*

One day the father caught sight of his son through a window. The boy was standing alone in a room, pointing at the cupboard where the biscuits were kept. The child could not have known that he was overlooked, and the father decided to stay at the window and watch. After about 5 minutes of hopeless pointing, the boy started to get upset and after 10 he was distraught. Within 15 minutes he was gripped by a full-scale tantrum. Evidently, the child had been waiting for a biscuit to be given to him. He failed to recognize that this would not happen in the absence of an obliging adult because he had not grasped that the purpose of pointing was to put an idea into someone else's mind. And the reason he failed to grasp that was that he did not have the concept of another person's mind to begin with.

Although we take it for granted, the conceptualizing required to have a theory of mind is really quite complex. It involves first, that you recognize yourself as something *apart* from the thoughts and feelings and perceptions that you are experiencing. You have to be able to project your point of view outside your own mind, and then look back on yourself as an object in the world. Once you have made that, huge, conceptual leap, you have to recognize that some objects in the world – the ones that seem to be sentient – have entire worlds of experience in their heads, just as you do in yours.

In normal people, all of this difficult conceptual work is carried out by unconscious processes. The only people who have to engage their neocortex to do it are those with autistic spectrum disorders, as the following study by psychologists Uta Frith and Francesca Happé, together with researchers at the Wellcome Department of Cognitive Neurology, seems to show.

A group of normal people read a series of two types of story as they lay in a PET scanner. The following is an example of the first type:

A burglar who has just robbed a shop is making his getaway. As he is running home a policeman on the beat sees him drop his glove. He doesn't know the man is a burglar, he just wants to tell him he dropped his glove. But when the policeman shouts out to the burglar: 'Hey! You! Stop!' the burglar turns round, sees the policeman and gives himself up. He puts his hands up and admits he did the break-in at the local shop.

The following is an example of the second type of story:

A burglar is about to break into a jeweller's shop. He skilfully picks the lock, then crawls under the electronic detector beam. If he breaks this beam, he knows it will set off an alarm. Quietly, he opens the door to the storehouse and sees the gems glittering. As he reaches out, however, he steps on something soft. He hears a screech and something small and furry runs out past him towards the shop door. Immediately the alarm sounds.

After listening to each story the participants were asked a question, and their brains were scanned as they thought about the answer. The question relating to the first story was: 'Why did the burglar give himself up?' The question relating to the second was: 'Why did the alarm go off?' The first question required the participants to have insight into the burglar's mind, while the second required only general knowledge.

The brain scans showed that the normal participants used quite separate regions of their brains to work out each answer. The question that called for a calculation about another person's mental state (in this case the burglar's false belief) lit up a spot in the middle of the prefrontal cortex – one of the most 'evolved' parts of the brain. This did not happen when the subjects worked out the answer to the second question.

The prefrontal area that lit up during the story has wide-ranging connections to many other areas of the brain, in particular those needed to pull in stored information and personal memories in order to 'read between the lines' of a story or 'see behind' the face value of what is presented. These skills are closely related to theory of mind, and are also starkly absent in autism.

A second brain scanning study shows that the reason for this lack may be that the crucial region of brain required for these skills to be activated is not turned on in autistics. In this experiment a group of people with Asperger's syndrome were recruited to listen to the two types of story. Asperger's syndrome is a condition that is characterized by autistic qualities combined with a normal or high IQ. Predictably, these subjects took longer than normal subjects to answer the questions which called on them to see into the burglar's mind, but they got there in the end. The brain activity they used was, however, strikingly different from that of the normal subjects. The prefrontal area identified in the previous scans did not light up at all. Instead a part of the brain below it came into play. This area is known from previous studies to be concerned with general cognitive abilities.[11]

This suggests that the Asperger's subjects worked out what was in the burglar's head by using a brain module that most of us use to work out straightforward causes and effects like those in the second story. They arrived at the answer by working it out like a crossword clue.

Along with their inability to read other people's minds intuitively, people with Asperger's syndrome are extremely poor at reading body language and facial expression. Simon Baron-Cohen and colleagues at the Department of Experimental Psychology at Cambridge recently found an actress with the rare talent of accurately expressing a wide range of mental states. They took photos of her face while she expressed ten basic emotions (such as sadness, happiness and anger) and ten complicated ones (such as scheming, admiration and interest). They then showed both the whole face and separate parts of it – the eyes or the mouth – to groups made up both of normal people and those with Asperger's syndrome. The participants were asked to identify the expressions.[12]

Animal noises, including birdsong, differ from language in that they are largely 'hard-wired' and generated by the unconscious brain.

The results revealed what seems to be two tiers of expression reading, each of which uses a different mechanism. For basic emotions the technique seemed to be to read the whole face – seeing the eyes or the mouth alone was less helpful. However, when expressions became complicated, normal people found it just as easy to read the expression by looking at the eyes alone as by looking at the whole face. This suggests that at a certain level of complexity a new communication method comes into play – what Baron-Cohen has called the 'language of the eyes'. People with Asperger's syndrome do not seem to know this language. On basic expressions they could read faces as well as normal people, but when expressions became complicated they could not make them out. They were particularly perplexed when they tried to read the eyes alone.

Once you know what is happening in their brains it is easy to see why people with autistic tendencies are slow on the uptake and

THE LONELY BRAIN

VILAYANUR S. RAMACHANDRAN
Director, Center for Brain and Cognition
University of California, San Diego

Is language mediated by a sophisticated and highly specialized 'language organ' that is unique to humans and emerged completely out of the blue as suggested by Chomsky? Or was there a more primitive gestural communication system already in place that provided a scaffolding for the emergence of vocal language?

Rizzolatti's discovery of mirror neurons gives us the basis for understanding 'mind reading', empathy, and even the evolution of language. Anytime you watch someone else doing something, the corresponding mirror neuron might fire in your brain, thereby allowing you to 'read' and understand another's intentions.

Mirror neurons can also enable you to imitate the movements of others thereby setting the stage for the complex cultural inheritance that characterizes our species and liberates us from the constraints of a purely gene-based evolution. Moreover, as Rizzolati has noted, these neurons may also enable you to mime – and possibly understand – the lip and tongue movements of others which, in turn, could provide the opportunity for language to evolve. Once you have these two abilities in place then you have set in motion the evolution of language. You need no longer speak of a unique language organ.

These arguments do not negate the idea that there are specialized brain areas for language in humans. We are dealing, here, with the question of how such areas may have evolved, not whether they exist or not.

Mirror neurons were discovered in monkeys but how do we know they exist in the human brain? To find out we studied patients with a strange disorder called anosognosia. Most patients with a right hemisphere stroke have complete paralysis of the left side of their body. But about five per cent of them will vehemently deny their paralysis. To our amazement, we found that some of these patients not only denied their own paralysis, but also denied the paralysis of another patient whose inability to move his arm was clearly visible. This bizarre observation is best understood in terms of damage to mirror neurons. It is as if anytime you want to make a judgment about someone else's movements you have to run a VR (virtual reality) simulation of the corresponding movements in your own brain and without mirror neurons you cannot do this. The second piece of evidence comes from studying brain waves (EEG) in humans. When people move their hands a brain wave called the MU wave disappears completely. We found that such a suppression also occurs when a person watches someone else moving his hand but not if he watches a similar movement by an inanimate object.

Mirror neurons obviously cannot be the only answer to all these riddles of evolution. After all rhesus monkeys and apes have them, yet they lack the cultural sophistication of humans. I would argue, though, that mirror neurons are necessary but not sufficient: their emergence and further development in hominids was a decisive step. The reason is that once you have a certain minimum amount of 'imitation learning' in place, this culture can, in turn, exert the selection pressure for developing those additional mental traits that make us human. And once this starts happening you have set in motion the auto-catalytic process that culminated in modern human consciousness.

language   music

Above: *Words and music are processed in different parts of the brain: the scan on the left shows the left auditory cortex lighting up when a subject listens to words while the scan on the right shows the right auditory cortex springing into life at the sound of music. The language centre of the brain in the left hemisphere is divided into different regions, each of which does a specific task.*

exasperating to live with. Asperger's syndrome is thought to affect as many as one in 300 men (nearly all are male) but most of them are unlikely to be formally diagnosed because their general intelligence usually gets them by, despite their lack of intuition. Nevertheless, their behaviour tends to be very odd: they are usually obsessionally wedded to routine, and may indulge in all-consuming hobbies that typically involve collecting or categorizing (train-spotting is, of course, the classic example). Socially, they are a disaster: they do not get jokes based on human foibles and fail to be captivated by gossip. They may drone on for hours about things that are of no interest to others, outstay their welcome or doze off when others are talking. Mercifully for them, they are not given to embarrassment because they are not generally conscious of what other people might be thinking about them.

Some people with autistic tendencies are very high achievers and their oddness may show up only in their preference for being alone, lack of empathy and single-minded pursuit of their own interests.[13] Many very successful academics are thought to fall into this category.

Although most people with subtle forms of autism find it easier to be alone, they often have a strong desire to abide by social convention and some of them get married. Much of the closeness in any partnership stems from the ability of each partner to see into the other's mind, and those who marry people with Asperger's syndrome often feel there is something fundamentally wrong with their relationship, even though they may not realize quite what it is. Psychiatrist John Ratey, in his book *Shadow Syndromes*,[14] quotes Susan, whose husband, Dan, displays typical autistic characteristics:

'It's the inappropriate responses when there is emotional news or bad stuff going on [that is difficult]. Yesterday I found out that I didn't get the job I applied for and I was really upset and crying. Dan said in a little-boy voice: "Oh, better luck next time" and then moved right on to the next topic. Once when I had a devastating blow Dan just said: "Oh. Want to go swimming?" I realize he can't help it – but it gets very lonely here [in this marriage] sometimes.'

Music

Music is generally regarded as one of the more elevated endowments of the human world. It seems to be one of the few things we do simply for pleasure – a pure piece of hedonistic icing on a cake of necessities. Yet evidence is accumulating to suggest that our brains are moulded by our genes to create and understand music rather as they are made to form language. Children as young as five months are aware of tiny shifts in musical pitch and by eight months they can remember a melody well enough to show surprise if a single note in a familiar tune is altered.[15]

There is no known mechanism by which purposeless functions come to evolve. Music is therefore likely once to have had some survival benefit, and the most probable one is that it is a prototype communication system. Support for this idea comes from the hearing   seeing   left   right

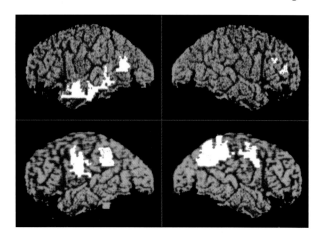

speaking   thinking

Above, left: *The brain responds differently to a word according to whether it is* (top, left) *hearing it spoken;* (top, right) *seeing it written down;* (bottom, left) *speaking it or* (bottom, right) *considering which other words it relates to.* Right: *When you look at a word you may see it as a word — that is, a component of language — or it may act as a trigger for the concepts which it represents. In each case a different part of the brain comes into play. The scans, above, show*

(top) *how the language areas are activated when a person is shown a word and asked how many syllables it contains and* (bottom) *how the same word sparks activity in completely different areas (including those concerned with memory retrieval) when the person is asked to consider what the word means.*

fact that music appreciation seems to be wired into some of the dumbest creatures on earth.

A short while ago Jaak Panksepp, a psychologist played various pieces of music to a flock of chickens and noted their reactions. Of all the musical delights, Pink Floyd's 'The Final Cut' brought the most notable response. The birds ruffled their feathers and shook their heads slowly from side to side.[16]

Panksepp concluded that the feather-ruffling was the avian equivalent of the musical 'chill' or 'tingle' experienced by people when they hear certain musical effects. Nearly everyone knows how it feels: an ecstatic sub-orgasmic ripple of tension and release.

The particular musical moments that are most frequently reported as tingle triggers are sudden shifts of harmony, or sequences that set up an expectation of a particular resolution, then delay

or subvert it. The emotional pattern in all such moments is relaxation–arousal–tension–relief–relaxation.

As well as sending momentary shivers up the spine, music can prompt us to dance or put us to sleep. The right sort can even dictate what type of wine we buy in a supermarket.[17]

The brain has to do a great deal of construction work to make music from the mere beat of sound waves against a membrane in the ear. Each component of the incoming information — pitch, melody, rhythm, location and loudness — is processed separately, then the parts are reassembled, along with whatever emotional response they elicit. Glitches in this production line produce the musical equivalent of agnosia — a person may hear a tune clearly, yet be unable to tell if it is 'Jingle Bells' or the '1812 Overture'. Nor can they tell two tunes apart or spot a wrong note. And yet such people can nearly always say whether a piece of music is happy or sad. This is because the sound is processed in parallel by the limbic system, which notes only its emotional tone. The tingle factor probably arises from this primarily unconscious emotional processing. The fact that it is not a function of the conscious brain explains why it seems to work for chickens as well as people.

One reason for the emotion-tugging effect of certain types of music may lie in their similarity to vocal (but not verbal) signals that carry emotional messages between animals. The tension- building sequence with delayed resolution that typically brings about the chilly spine feeling, for example, has features in common with the sounds made by infants – both human and animal – when they are parted from their mothers. In animals these cries have been found to trigger a drop in oxytocin – the brain chemical most closely associated with parental bonding – and they also bring about a drop in the mother's body temperature. When the mother is reunited with her baby, the child responds by 'resolving' the cry – a vocal performance not dissimilar to closing a phrase of music with a satisfyingly final note. At the same time the mother's oxytocin level goes up, and her body becomes warmer. Women have been found to feel the tingle more keenly than men, which fits in neatly with this theory.

Perhaps, then, the tingle is a faint echo of the shiver that helps to motivate a mother to seek out her lost infant. Other emotional frissons we experience when notes take a particular turn may relate to similar signals.

Music can have a powerful bonding effect on people. Those who are most sensitive to it – by nature or training – have been found to be quicker to pick up on emotional tone in language, and to be generally more empathetic.[18] Once again, mirror neurons may be at work here. Researchers have found that *hearing* the sounds of everyday actions, as well seeing people do them, sparks activity in the same brain cells that would light

Auditory mirror neurons are far more active in normal people (above) than in people with autistic spectrum disorders (below).

up if the listener herself were doing the action. Hearing someone crunching an apple, say, provokes similar activity in the listeners brain to that seen when they are themselves eating an apple.[19] As with mirroring by observation, mirroring by sound is strongest if the action involved is one that is familiar. In another study pianists and non-musicians listened to piano music while their brains were scanned. Both groups showed the expected activity in the 'hearing' part of the brain, but the pianists' brains also showed activity in the motor areas of the brain corresponding to finger movements. The pianists, it seems, were 'playing along' with the music, while the non-playing group were just listening.[20]

Words

Although children do not generally speak until they are two or three, the stamp of language is present in the very first noises they make. Babies cries may sound similar the world over to the untrained ear, but careful study has shown that they actually take on the melody of their native

A B

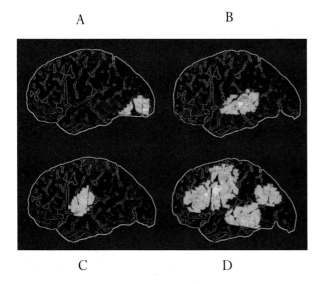

C D

A: reading activates part of the visual cortex
B: listening to speech makes the auditory cortex light up
C: thinking about words makes Broca's area – the articulation
   centre – light up
D: thinking about words and speaking generates widespread
   activity

language. During the last few months of gestation, it seems that babies hear the sounds of speech from the world outside the womb, and learn to mimic it. Hence when they are born, German babies cry in a falling tone typical of the tonal speech patterns of that country, while French babies bawl on an upward curving note.

Making sense of a stream of spoken words is a formidably complicated business. First, the brain has to recognize that what is coming in is in fact language. This preliminary discrimination may be done in part by the thalamus[21] and completed by the primary auditory cortex. Speech is then shunted to the language areas to be processed, while environmental noises, music and non-verbal messages – grunts, screams, laughs, sighs and exclamations like 'ugh!' – go elsewhere.

Most of what we know about the brain locations concerned with language comes from studying people who have language problems caused by strokes or other types of brain injury. Some of these people have oddly specific symptoms: they

may be able to speak fluently, for example, but have no idea what they are saying, or be able to read but not write.

The language cortex – situated on the left side in 95 per cent of people – surrounds the auditory cortex in all directions. It is spread over most of the temporal lobes and edges into the parietal and frontal lobes. Two main areas – Wernicke's and Broca's – have been recognized for more than a century, but brain imaging studies have recently suggested that other areas are also involved. These include part of the insula – a hidden expanse of cortex that lies within the great infold, known as the Sylvian fissure, that divides the temporal and frontal lobes.[22] Each main area of language cortex is probably split, like the sensory cortices, into many different processing regions and sub-regions, but it is only in the last few years that brain imaging studies have started to reveal what they are.

Once speech has been identified, the words are assigned some sort of meaning, and, at the same time the gappy, slurry, tangled ribbon of sound is broken down into its elements – separate words or phrases. The two things are necessarily done together (another example of the brain's parallel processing ability) because without meaning it is almost impossible to make out language construction. Try listening to someone speaking at normal conversational speed in a foreign language and you will be hard pushed to tell when the sentences begin and end, let alone the clauses. Similarly, without awareness of construction it is difficult to make out meaning. there is no punctuation for example in this and already I expect you are finding it hard going yet punctuation is only one aspect of construction if I the words jumbled this like not clue a have would you what of going on about I was so important construction to meaning is. You as see can.

One essential skill required at an early stage is that of discriminating very fast-changing sounds. The difference between two spoken consonants – the 'p' in 'pa' and the 'b' in 'baa', for instance – is

> ## FINISHED FILES ARE THE RE SULT OF YEARS OF SCIENTIF- IC STUDY COMBINED WITH THE EXPERIENCE OF YEARS

Count the 'F's in this sentence...overpage for answer

only distinguishable for a tiny fraction of a second. If you miss it, there's no knowing whether you are hearing about your father or a sheep. An inability to make these quick distinctions between sounds is thought to be the root cause of specific language impairment (SLI) – a condition in which other- wise bright, attentive children fail to pick up lan- guage in the normal way.[23] Neurologists have found a tiny area of tissue – about one centimetre square – near to Wernicke's area that lights up only when consonants are heard. When this area is deactivated by electromagnetic inhibition, patients have difficulty understanding words that depend on consonants for identification, whereas they can still make out words in which the crucial distinguishing sounds are vowels. Lack of normal activity in this area may account for SLI.

The cortical area that imposes structure on incoming speech – assuming there is one – has yet to be identified. The eminent linguist Noam Chomsky and his colleague Steven Pinker have argued persuasively for some form of 'language organ' in the brain, but what form it might take and where it might be located are not known. People who lose the ability to structure sentences through brain injury tend to have lesions towards the front of the language cortex[24] and one possibil- ity is that syntax is produced somewhere around Broca's area – the more frontal of the two main language regions. Or it may be something that is dealt with in a subcortical area between the two language areas. Steven Pinker has suggested that the language organ may not be a neat module at all – more a smear of neuronal activity resembling road-kill. Alternatively, it may be that there is no

physical 'module' for syntax at all – rather that it is produced by some neural interactions or pat- tern that involve activity in many different areas.

Analysis of word meaning is carried out either in or very close to Wernicke's area – a patch of cortex that is splayed over the top and back of the temporal lobe, edging up to the parietal lobe. Damage to the connections between the primary auditory cortex and Wernicke's area can result in a peculiar language disorder known as word deaf- ness. People with this condition cannot under- stand spoken words, yet they may still be able to read, write and speak quite normally. 'Voices come, but not words,' says one patient. 'Speech sounds like an undifferentiated continuous hum- ming noise without any rhythm,' says another.[25]

Damage to Wernicke's area itself causes anoth- er type of disorder. Wernicke's aphasia patients retain perfectly fluent speech and their grammati- cal construction is fine; if you listen to them talk- ing from a distance, you'll think there is nothing wrong. Attend to the actual words, though, and you realize that much of what they say is nonsense. Wrong words or non-words are substi- tuted for right ones and much of the content may be made up of meaningless jargon. People with Wernicke's aphasia do not understand their own spoken words either, so they cannot monitor their own speech. For this reason they often seem to be blithely unaware that they are talking nonsense.

angular gyrus

Broca's area

insula

Wernicke's area   arcuate fasciculus

Some types of dyslexia may be due to what is known as a dissociation disorder – a missing or inactive connection between two brain modules. A study in which PET scans were made of dyslexics' and non-dyslexics' brains while they attempted a complex reading task, suggests that the two main language areas, Wernicke's and Broca's, do not work in concert in dyslexics. This appears to be because an important neural link in the vicinity of the insula cortex is not activated during such tasks as it is in others. The result of the 'dead' connection is that the words cannot be understood (a function of Wernicke's area) and articulated (a function of Broca's) at the same time.

The communication breakdown makes it difficult to assess Wernicke's patients' general intelligence, but as far as can be gathered their ability to reason is generally unaffected.

The rather surreal drawing on the previous page is one of the tools used by psychologists to test for various intellectual impairments. This is an example of the description of the drawing given by a patient with Wernicke's aphasia:

'Well this is…mother is away here working her work out of here to get her better, but when she's looking, the two boys looking in the other part. One their small tile into her time here. She's working another time because she's getting to. So two boys work together and one is sneaking around here making his work and his further fun-

nas [sic] his time he had.'[26]

The jargon generated by Wernicke's aphasics can sound impressive. One patient, trying to explain what he used to do for a living, told a researcher: '[I was] an executive of this, and the complaint was to discuss the tonations as to what type they were…and kept from the different tricula to get me from the attribute convenshements.[27]

This type of speech flows effortlessly from the mouths of Wernicke's patients – odd though its content might be, they have no difficulty producing it. This is because speech production is governed by a different part of the brain altogether.

Broca's area is further forward, in the side of the frontal lobe. It abuts the motor cortex, just by the part that controls the jaw, larynx, tongue and lips. This area of cortex seems to hold the programmes that instruct the neighbouring motor cortex to articulate speech. People with damage to this part of the brain can understand what is said to them perfectly well, and they know what they want to say. They just cannot say it. Those words they can get out tend to be concrete nouns or verbs, delivered in staccato 'telegramese'. A Broca's aphasic described the cookie-theft picture: 'cookie jar… fall over… chair… water… empty.' Some people with Broca's aphasia are unable to say anything. Often, though, their economic use of the odd apt word can convey volumes. Professor Christine

FINISHED FILES ARE THE RESULT OF YEARS OF SCIENTIFIC STUDY COMBINED WITH THE EXPERIENCE OF YEARS

Did you spot six 'Fs'? Probably not. Most people see only four – they skip the 'fs' in 'of' because the brain processes short familiar words as a single, whole, symbol rather than breaking them down into smaller units as they do with longer or less familiar words. The two types of words are thus probably processed in different brain areas.

Temple, in her book *The Brain*, reports visiting a Broca's patient who had a bad head cold. 'Nose,' said the patient, by way of greeting.[28] The meaning, apparently, was crystal clear.

Damage to cortical areas adjacent to these two main ones can cause a wide range of very specific language problems. If the connections between Wernicke's area and Broca's area are damaged, for example, a person may be unable to repeat what is said to them. This is because the incoming words (which are registered in Wernicke's area) cannot be passed on to Broca's area for articulation. Then there are people who seem to be unable to stop repeating what is said to them – the affliction known as echolalia. This may be caused by overactivity of the connections between the two language areas so that what goes into one is automatically shunted on to the other before other areas of the cortex can step in to inhibit it.

Occasionally, a severe stroke or similar cerebral injury can damage the areas surrounding the language cortex and leave it cut off from the other parts of the brain. Such patients are typically mute and appear not to understand anything that is said to them. Yet they can repeat words and finish well-known phrases. 'Roses are red', for example, will bring the response 'violets are blue'. This shows again how elements of language can exist in isolation from other intellectual functions.

Reading and writing come to children after speech is established, as children have to be taught to read – it does not come so naturally to them. This may be because it is a latecomer in evolutionary terms and, unlike spoken language, we have probably not evolved a specific system with which to read and write. Rather we produce and understand written language by pressing into use the language system as evolved for speech, together with parts of the object identification and gesturing systems.[29]

As with speech, processing the written word takes place in several different areas. Reading and writing pull on the brain's capacity to see (or

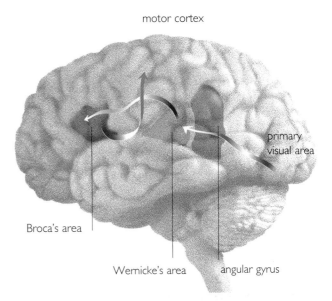

Reading and writing involves more than just the language areas – the visual cortex feeds information in from the page and the motor cortex is required to activate the muscles used for writing. It is therefore important that information flows freely between these areas – if it is blocked or disrupted a form of dyslexia may result.

touch, in the case of Braille) and to use fine hand movements to manipulate a writing instrument, as well as on the language areas. It is not surprising, then, that the areas dedicated to it are situated around the junctions between the areas given over to these different skills.

Just behind and slightly up from Wernicke's area lies a region of brain where vision, spatial skills and language jostle together on the margins of the occipital, parietal and temporal lobes. It is marked by a bulge called the angular gyrus, which seems to act as a bridge between the visual word recognition system and the rest of the language process. Damage to the angular gyrus itself is likely to disrupt both reading and writing. If the area around it is damaged, by contrast, a person may be left in the peculiar position of being able to write but unable to read silently. One woman, left   right

In the human brain the area which processes language, in the left hemisphere, is visibly larger than the equivalent area in the right hemisphere. There is no such asymmetry, generally, in animals' brains – though some studies have detected what looks like the beginning of extra left hemisphere development in some primates.

identified by researchers as J.O., is able to understand spoken words and write quite normally, but when she tries to read back silently what she has written she can't make head or tail of it. If she is asked to read the words aloud, however, she can – and can then understand their meaning by listening to her own voice.[30] 'I see the words but nothing comes in,' she says. This odd condition seems to come about when the neural path between the visual cortex and the angular gyrus is blocked or broken so visual information about words cannot be matched to their meanings. They can be read, though, because the visual information can still be matched to their sounds – presumably by another route.

The importance of language skills in a literate society can hardly be exaggerated. People are judged on how they speak and nearly all academic teaching is done by means of language. So anyone who is not 100 per cent up to scratch in this area is likely to be seen as deficient across a whole range of skills. This used to happen as a matter of course to people with dyslexia, and it still happens to some extent today.

Dyslexia takes many different forms and probably has many different causes. One form, however, seems to be caused by a particular brain module failing to fire. PET scans of dyslexic people doing word tasks have shown that, unlike in normal people, the language processing areas in dyslexics' brains fail to work in concert so the incoming words get jumbled up and disjointed. The scans, which were done on dyslexic and non-dyslexic volunteers of above-average intelligence, showed that the word tasks caused the language areas in the non-dyslexics to fire in unison, together with a spot in the insula, the deep infold that lies in between them. This spot appeared to act like a bridge between the language areas, orchestrating their activity. In dyslexics, however, the insula did not fire and each language area was activated singly.[31]

The discovery of a distinctive physiological sign for dyslexia should make the condition easier to recognize. Brain scans are not yet practical for general diagnosis, but the discovery of the precise neurological mechanism involved in at least one form of the condition should make it possible to devise functional tests that show up the fault more clearly than the broad-based reading and writing tests used now.

It also raises the possibility that dyslexia may one day be susceptible to a physical cure. As the main problem appears to lie in the link between two brain areas, perhaps it would be possible to insert a tiny artificial bridge – a pacemaker for the brain.

supplementary motor area lights up to turn intended words to speech

mouth cortex lights up to prepare speech action

auditory cortex left lights up to monitor own speech

cerebellum activity

NORMAL
left hemisphere

intense activity SMA

little activity auditory cortex

intense activity in cerebellum

STUTTERER
left hemisphere

little activity in right auditory cortex

cerebellum activity

NORMAL
right hemisphere

intense activity SMA

mouth cortex on right lights up

intense activity in cerebellum

STUTTERER
right hemisphere

Speech development

Babies are tuned in to speech from birth — or even, perhaps, in utero. If kicks and squirms are taken as reliable markers of approval, they seem to prefer familiar stories to those they have not heard before.[32] Most of them seem to love the sound of the human voice, particularly their mother's, and play an active part in promoting 'conversations' — 'motherspeak' on one side, burbles and grunts on the other — from a few weeks of age.

'Proper' language starts in the second year with the activation of the two major speech areas that occupy separate but neighbouring areas on the side of the brain. One – Wernicke's area – is specialized for language comprehension, while the other –

When reading aloud, people who stutter show different patterns of brain activity from non-stutterers. In particular, the right hemisphere is more active in stutterers. This suggests that stuttering may be due to competition for dominance between left and right hemispheres. Neither side can decide which is in control, so the two both try to produce words, with disastrous results. Stutterers' brains also show lack of auditory feedback – the loop that usually plays their own voice back to them is underactive. When stutterers read in chorus with other non-stutterers their speech impediment disappears, probably because the auditory feedback is supplied by the other readers.

Broca's area – deals with speech articulation. Language initially develops in both hemispheres, but in 95 per cent of cases it shifts by the age of five to lodge in the left hemisphere only and the abandoned speech areas in the right hemisphere are given over to other things, including gesture.

One of the clearest precursors to language is babbling – the speech-like torrent of sounds that babies typically start generating at about 18 months. This is followed within a couple of months by a rapidly expanding vocabulary of proper words. This sudden explosion of language coincides with a flourishing of activity in the frontal lobes. Around this same time children seem to develop self-consciousness.

The simultaneous emergence of speech and self-consciousness may simply reflect the parallel maturation of the two relevant brain areas: language and frontal lobes. Or it may be that the two things are inevitably connected. Language gives the child the tool it needs to form a concept of itself that it can then place outside its own experience and regard in relationship to others. Once it can do that it can start to make plans, and to make plans it needs functioning frontal lobes. So perhaps the language areas, as they stir into life, send wake-up messages forward to the frontal cortex.

Language comes naturally to children – provided they are exposed to it during infancy. But if they are deprived of the sound of speech, their brains may be physically disordered.

In 1970 in Los Angeles a child was discovered who had been locked away, practically from birth, in a featureless room with minimal human contact and nothing to watch, do or play with.[33] When she was found, aged 13, she could not hop, skip or extend her limbs, she was unable to focus her eyes beyond the width of her prison, and the only words she knew to utter were 'stopit' and 'nomore'. She was encouraged to learn language and her vocabulary increased dramatically. But grammar – which comes so instinctively to a young child – escaped her.

Brain imaging revealed why: the child had a highly unusual arrangement of cerebral functions. Most notably, when she spoke it was with the right side of her brain, not the more usual left. This is not in itself pathological – about 5 per cent of people (most of whom are left-handed) do this and all it usually signifies is that their language areas have developed in the opposite side of the brain to normal. But in this girl's case something else had happened. Deprived as it was of human speech, her language area had effectively atrophied. When she finally encountered spoken words her brain processed them in the area normally reserved for environmental noises. This area, presumably, had been kept active by the sad little symphony of noises that had reached her during her incarceration: distant birdsong, noises from the bathroom next door, the odd creak of floorboards.

Foreign tongues

We all start off with the potential to speak any language, but if we are only exposed to a single tongue our options soon narrow because the neurological wiring needed to distinguish sounds atrophies if it is not stimulated early in life. Therefore people who learn foreign languages as adults rarely speak them without an accent – Japanese adults cannot reproduce the English 'l' and 'r', for example, because these are sounds not heard in Japanese. Conversely, English speakers cannot manage certain Japanese phonemes.[34]

Second languages are processed in a different section of the language area to the mother tongue.[35] This is why people who suffer very localized stroke damage sometimes lose their ability to speak their native language, while retaining their ability to speak those they learnt as adults.

THE IMPORTANCE OF GOSSIP

 PROFESSOR JOHN MAYNARD SMITH
Emeritus Professor of Biology,
University of Sussex

Something very puzzling happened about 50,000 to 100,000 years ago. The fossil evidence is patchy, but it seems that hominids suddenly developed brains that, in terms of size, were much like ours. Yet this apparent growth spurt was not reflected immediately by any great cultural changes. That came 50,000 years later, when a whole variety of artefacts – tools and musical instruments and cave drawings – suddenly came on the scene.

Something must have happened between the physical changes in the brain and the cultural expression of such changes. Most linguists now argue that the something was the development of language. I am sure that our ancestors had been communicating for a long time (half a million years or so) before they became linguistically competent, so perhaps there is something about language itself that led to this acceleration of cultural complexity.

Or could it be the other way around? Could cultural changes have brought about the development of language?

Brain size in primates is closely associated with the size of the social group in which the animal lives. The initial expansion of what was to become the human brain may have been prompted by a growth in numbers that required

The skull of hominids was pushed into its present shape by the evolving brain

greater social skills: remembering who various members were, whether they were friends or enemies and so on. One social skill that would have been increasingly required as the social group grew was gossip – the need to swap information about each other. This may have brought about the initial expansion of the frontal cortex and, in its wake, the development of language.

At the moment this is still speculative but I believe that the answer will be found through genetics. If, as some suggest, there is a specific gene or genes for grammatical language, we may be able to identify them and then find out their origin by seeing what related strands of DNA do in our near relatives. The brain is a genetically expensive organ and it would take more than a single happy mutation to bring about something as complex as language – but it may be possible to track those mutations back through evolution.

CHAPTER SEVEN

STATES OF MIND

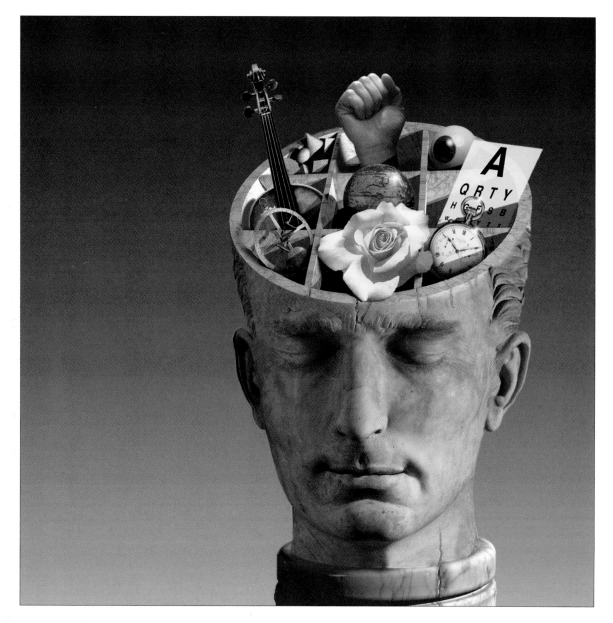

The human brain holds billions of impressions, some fleetingly, some for a lifetime. We call them memories. Just as incoming sensory information is broken down, then rebuilt to form perceptions, so perceptions are broken down again as they pass into memory. Each fragment is sent off to storage in a different part of our vast internal library then pulled out and reassembled when we recall past events. Each run-through etches them deeper into the neural structure until there comes a time when memories and the person who holds them are effectively one and the same.

MEMORY IS MANY DIFFERENT THINGS: it is the picture that comes into your mind when you think of the home you lived in as a child; it is the ability to hop on a bike and pedal away without working out how to do it; the feeling of unease associated with a place where something frightening once happened to you; the retracing of a familiar route and the knowledge you hold that the Eiffel Tower is in Paris. The raw material of memory also provides the building materials for our imagination, especially our visions of the future. We never dream up anything truly novel; just re-configure the bits of experience we have already had, either at first hand or vicariously. Mental creativity consists of smashing up the mosaic of our experience and using the shards to build a new picture.

Not surprisingly, such a complex, multifaceted aspect of brain functioning is hard to pin down. Each different type of memory is stored and retrieved in a different way, and dozens of brain areas are involved in a complex network of interactions. Little by little, though, the geography of human memory is becoming clear.

To understand memory you have to look at individual cells, because that is where memories are made.

Whichever type of memory you consider it consists of the same essential thing: an association between a group of neurons such that when one fires, they all fire, creating a specific pattern. Thoughts, sensory perceptions, ideas, hallucinations – any brain function (save the random activity of a seizure) is made up of this same thing. One pattern – a group of neighbouring neurons firing together in the auditory cortex, say – brings about the experience of a certain note of music. Another pattern, in a different area, brings about the feeling of fear; another, the experience of blue; another, a particular taste – a hint of tannin, say, in a sip of wine. A memory is a pattern like these. The only difference is that it remains encoded in the brain after the stimulation that originally gave rise to it has ceased. Memories form when a pattern is repeated frequently, or in circumstances that encourage it to be encoded. This is because each time a group of neurons fires together the tendency to do so again is increased. Neurons fire in synchrony by setting off each other like particles in a trail of gunpowder. Unlike gunpowder particles, though, neurons can fire again and again. This firing can be fast or slow. The faster a neuron fires, the greater the electrical charge it punches out and the more likely it is to have a knock-on effect on its neighbour. Once the neighbour has been triggered to fire a chemical change takes place on its surface which leaves it more sensitive to stimulation from that same neighbour. This process is called long-term potentiation. If the neighbour cell is not stimulated again it will stay in this state of readiness for hours, maybe days. If the first cell fires again during this period, the neighbour may respond even if the firing rate of cell number one is relatively slow. A second firing makes it even more receptive and so on. Eventually, repeated synchronous firing binds neurons together so that the slightest activity in one will trigger all those that have become associated with it to fire, too. A memory has been formed.

Many things influence whether or not a thought or perception comes to be a memory. Take the taste of tannin. If, when you first taste it, you register it only vaguely as part of a general red winey taste, the association between the neurons that momentarily got together to create the tannin experience will be weak and may in time disappear altogether. If this happens, you will have

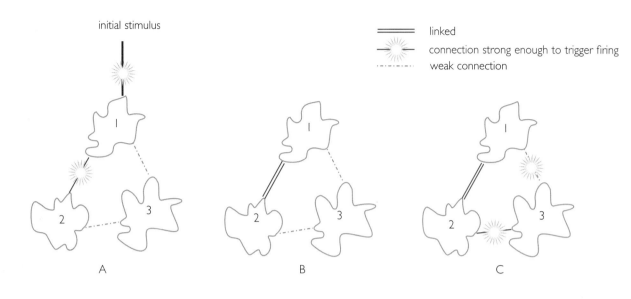

initial stimulus

linked
connection strong enough to trigger firing
weak connection

A   B   C

Memories are groups of neurons which fire together in the same pattern each time they are activated. The links between individual neurons, which bind them into a single memory, are formed through a process called long-term potentiation. (LTP)
A) Cell 1 receives a stimulus which causes it to fire. If it fires fast enough it will set off its neighbour, cell no. 2, which will also fire. Cell no. 2 is chemically changed by this – receptors which are normally hidden inside the cell wall are brought to the surface. These make the cell more responsive to its neighbour. Cell no. 2 stays in this 'standby' state for hours or perhaps days. B) If cell no. 1 fires again during this time, it need do so only weakly in order to trigger a response from cell no. 2. Each time the two cells fire in synchrony the link between them is strengthened. Eventually they are permanently bonded so when one fires the other fires. C) When the two cells fire together their combined energy is enough to trigger any neighbouring cell to which they are both weakly attached. If this happens repeatedly the three cells become bound together in a distinctive firing pattern – a memory.

forgotten the taste, and next time you come across it it will seem as unfamiliar as it did the first time. In practice it is more likely that the tannin neurons will retain some very faint 'special' attraction for one another, so a second tasting will bring a vague sense of recognition.

It would be quite different, though, if – as part of a wine-tasting course, perhaps – you made an effort to distinguish the taste of tannin from all the other flavours in the wine and concentrate on it. In this case the neural pattern created by the tannin will be activated repeatedly, and each time it will be strengthened. Eventually, the association between the neurons will be so strong that they will fire away merrily at the slightest provocation, making the taste familiar and instantly detectable. This will also help to make it likeable. Recognition, particularly of sensory stimuli, is a major part of enjoyment. That is why so many tastes, including tannin, are 'acquired'.

A tannin memory that consists purely of taste is a pretty elementary thing. All it enables you to do is to recognize the taste when you come across it again. If, when you taste it, you link it with its name, however, you will form an association between the neurons that produce the tannin taste pattern and those that produce the tannin word pattern. Your tannin memory will then include both the taste and a label for it. So now when someone says: 'This wine is high in tannin', you will have an idea of how it will taste. You could embellish your tannin memory even more by adding to it the knowledge of its role in wine-making

amygdala   temporal
            lobe   caudate nucleus

THE HUMAN MEMORY SYSTEM

Many different brain areas are involved in memory.
Temporal lobe: long-term memories permanently lodged in
the cortex. Putamen: procedural memories, like riding a bike,
are stored here. Hippocampus: involved in laying down and
retrieving memories, particularly personal ones and those
related to finding your way about. Amygdala: unconscious
traumatic memories may be stored here. Caudate nucleus:
many instincts — which are geneteically encoded memories —
stem from here.

or its chemical structure. The more aspects to it
that a memory has the more useful it becomes and
the easier it is to retrieve because each aspect gives
a separate 'handle' by which to yank out the full
memory from storage. A multifaceted tannin
memory would even equip you to say things like:
'A modest little quaffing wine but firmed up nicely
by a subtle hint of tannin' — should you so desire.

Tannin-type memories generally end up in
what is known as semantic memory, the store of
things that we 'know' independent of our personal

relationship to them. When these are first laid down they are, inevitably, part of a bigger construct that includes the personal. The tannin memory will include, for example, where you were when you first tasted it, who you were with, what was said and so on. But unless these personal elements have some particular significance, in time they will fade so that all you are left with is the knowledge of tannin itself. This is true of all the things you 'know': the shape of a mountain, the capital of the USA, the word for the drape of fabric you draw across a window... Once they were all attached to memories of the circumstances in which you learnt them. But the personal marginalia have long since fallen away, leaving the bare but useful facts.

Memories that remain clothed in personal detail are quite different, and the brain deals with them differently. These recollections, known as episodic memories, are usually cradled in a sense of time and space. They include the memory of 'being there', and are personal in a way that your knowledge that the White House is in Washington is not. When we recall them they recreate much of the state of mind we were in when they were laid down.

A state of mind is an all-encompassing perception of the world that binds sensory perception, thoughts, feelings and memories into a seamless whole. To produce it millions of neural brain patterns fire in concert, creating a stream of new 'mega-patterns' – one for every conscious moment. Say you are sitting overlooking the sea, drinking red wine, listening to music and wondering why your offspring are late back from a sailing expedition. The mega-pattern in your head at any particular moment would be woven from the elementary motifs created by the pattern associated with fear; the pattern associated with the taste of wine, the experience of blue and the sound of a musical note. There might also be a pattern that matches your children's faces or your last sight of them; a pattern relating to some previous late-home incident; a pattern relating to life jackets or coastguards; and probably some complex pattern to do with what you will say to them when they finally return. This constellation of neural activity shimmers with constant change as one thought dies away and another comes forward. But so long as your attention is held by the basic theme, the overall pattern, a sort of mega-mega-pattern, will remain recognizable.

Most mega-patterns of this sort never make it to memory – they fire once then fade away. Even mega-mega-patterns, on the whole, leave only a hazy, sepia-washed impression. Yet there are some that stand out in the sludge of our long-term memory like sharp points of light: a childhood moment on some beach, feeling the hot sand slip through our fingers; a frozen frame from some

Experiences which are destined to be laid down as long-term memories are shunted down to the hippocampus where they are held in storage for two to three years. During this time the hippocampus replays the experiences back up to the cortex, and each rehearsal etches it deeper into the cortex. Eventually the memories are so firmly established in the cortex that the hippocampus is no longer needed for their retrieval. Much of the hippocampal replay is thought to happen during sleep. Dreams consist partly of a rerun of things that have happened during the day, fired up to the cortex by the hippocampus.

A) PROCEDURAL MEMORY – the 'how to' sort like riding a bike, are stored in the cerebellum and putamen. Deeply ingrained habits are stored in the caudate nucleus.

B) FEAR MEMORIES – phobias and flashbacks – are stored in the amygdala.

C) EPISODIC MEMORY – the personal 'filmic' memories which represent our past experience, are encoded by the hippocampus and stored in the cortex. They end up scattered around the cortical areas of the brain. Retrieval, as with semantic memory, then depends on the frontal cortex.

D) SEMANTIC MEMORY – facts are registered by the cortex and end up encoded in cortical areas in the temporal lobe. Retrieval is then carried out by the frontal lobes.

DREAMING UP A MEMORY

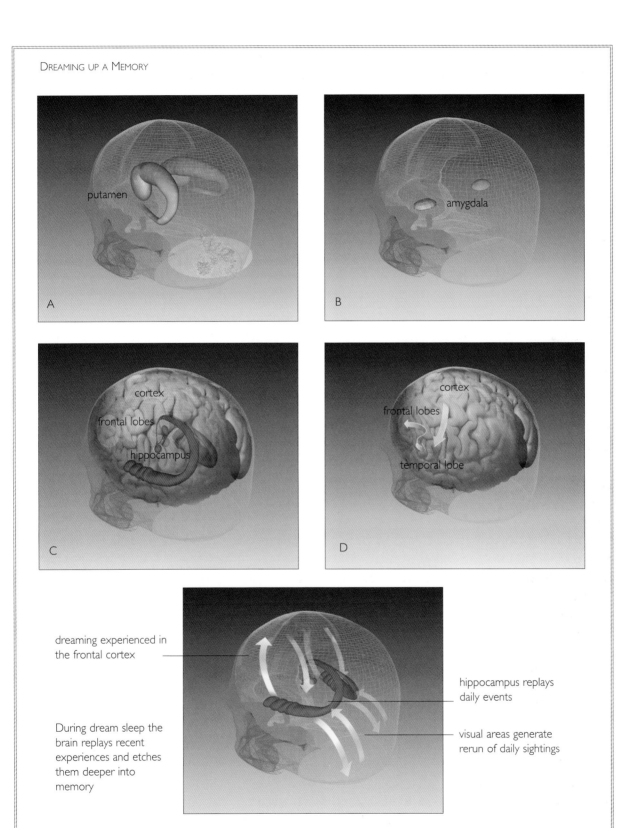

dreaming experienced in the frontal cortex

During dream sleep the brain replays recent experiences and etches them deeper into memory

hippocampus replays daily events

visual areas generate rerun of daily sightings

These pictures show activity in the brain of a person watching a film of navigation through a familiar town. The area lit up is the hippocampus.

distant and otherwise forgotten holiday; the odd, startlingly clear image of a long-dead friend. Why should these brain patterns remain potent while others disappear?

The reason, in most cases, is our old friend emotion. The sort of scenes that stick in our minds are those that, for one reason or another were experienced in a state of emotional excitement. This is because excitement, by definition, is brought about by a surge of excitatory neurotransmitters that increase the firing rate of neurons in certain parts of the brain. This has two

effects, both of which have obvious survival value. First, it increases the intensity of perception, producing that 'crystal clear' feeling and sense of slowed time that people typically report when they are in the midst of a crisis. Second, it boosts long-term potentiation, so events that happen in such a state are more likely to be remembered and avoided (if nasty) or sought after (if nice) in future.

The scenario above is a good candidate for long-term memory because it consists of several striking sensory stimuli: the sight of the sea, the sound of music, the taste of wine, each of which provides a different 'handle'. Any one of those might later cause the entire scene to be retrieved, rehearsed and thus strengthened. More importantly, it is marinated in fear. If the incident ended with your children bustling through the door unharmed, it would probably in time become a mere, faint recollection. But if it ended with a knock on the door and a grim-faced police officer telling you of an accident, you would probably carry the memory of that music, the sight of the sea at that moment, the taste of that wine for ever.

Episodes that are destined for long-term memory are not lodged there straight away. The process of laying them down permanently takes up to two years. Until then they are still fragile and may quite easily be wiped out.

It is this replay from hippocampus to cortex and back again — a process known as consolidation, that slowly turns fleeting impressions into long-term memories.

The regeneration of the original neural patterns etches them deeper and deeper into the cortical tissue, protecting them from degradation until eventually the memories are more or less permanently embedded. They also become linked together independently of the hippocampus. This linkage allows any one aspect of the episode to act as a handle for retrieval of the entire thing. If you had experienced the waiting-for-news episode above, for example, you might find that years

Different aspects of a memory — the things that come to mind when you hear the word 'dog' for instance — are widely distributed and may be linked to millions of extraneous ideas. The image of a dog, for instance, will be stored in the visual part of the brain, along with images associated with the animal — kennels, and dog balls, and bones and terrified cats. The sounds a dog makes — barking and whining — by contrast, will be encoded in the auditory cortex. When you think of 'dog' these various elements are pulled together by the hippocampus and reassembled into a coherent whole.

later the sound of the particular music that was playing then would bring the whole thing flooding back.

Much of the hippocampal replay is thought to happen during sleep. Recordings from hippocampal cells show them engaging in a 'dialogue' with cortical cells, during which they signal one another,

Canadian brain surgeon Wilder Penfield identified the brain regions which produced memories by sticking numbers on the exposed brain during operations.

back and forth, in a call-and-reply formation. Some of this is known to take place during the 'quiet' phase of sleep, when dreaming, if it occurs at all, and is vague and instantly forgotten.[1] Until memories are fully encoded in the cortex they are still fragile and may quite easily be wiped out. And even when they are established they are not fixed. A memory is not, in fact, a recollection of an experience but the recollection of the last time you recalled the experience. Hence our memories are constantly changing and redeveloping. The process by which a memory changes is more or less the same as the consolidation process that lays it down for the first time. As we will see, each time we recall something, it is changed a little because it becomes mixed up with things that are happening in the present. Reconsolidation is a process by which this slightly altered memory effectively replaces the previous one, writing over it, so to speak, rather like re-recording over a rewritable DVD.[2]

Destruction of the hippocampus can have disastrous effects on memory because without it a person cannot take in anything new. If the organ

Right 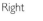 Left

The hippocampus (above, top) *is activated when people are asked to recall personal or 'episodic' memories. Finding your way around a familiar place also involves the hippocampus — but only on the right side* (above, below).

is removed entirely, they may be unable to hold anything in mind for more than a few moments and be effectively frozen in time. Less severe damage may leave them able to learn new facts but unable to lay down personal memories.[3]

The fact that recollection of episodic memories seems to activate more areas of cortex supports the idea that the various elements of these memories are stored in the cortical areas where they were first registered.

The hippocampus does not relinquish all long-term memories to cortical storage areas, however. Unlike facts and childhood recollections, our memories of space remain encoded in the hippocampal neurons, creating internal maps. This was demonstrated in a famous PET study of London taxi drivers. The drivers were put in the scanner, then asked to imagine the routes that would have to be taken to get to and from various points in the city.

As they travelled the familiar routes in their minds their hippocampi lit up — something that did not happen when they were asked to recall other things, including well-known landmarks.[4]

Although the hippocampus is required to encode and retrieve personal memories, there is evidence to suggest that memories of things that once terrified us may, in part at least, be laid down in the amygdala — the limbic nucleus that registers fear. The emotional effect of flashbacks, like those experienced in post-traumatic stress disorder, are thought to stem from this part of the brain, which is why they have the power to rekindle a physical as well as a psychological replay of the original experience.

How reliable are our various memory mechanisms? One way of judging is to look at what happens when memory goes wrong.

Misleading memories

Memories undoubtedly change, and many lie undisturbed for years before popping up unexpectedly. Is it possible, though, for a really intense, *important* event to be buried for decades and then to reappear? Is it, for example, possible for a person to recover the knowledge of childhood trauma after years of forgetfulness? Or are such memories necessarily false — the result of clumsy or sinister suggestion? Most of those involved in the issue would dearly like science to provide a simple either/or answer. But the best evidence yet suggests that both recovered and false memories are real phenomena.

False memories are not unusual. In fact, they are the norm. Falsities creep into almost every mundane recollection but they generally go unnoticed except for the odd puzzlement ('I could have *sworn* I left my keys on the table') and misunderstanding ('It's not ready yet – I said Thursday, not Tuesday'). They arise because human memory does not lay down a fixed record of objective events in the way that a video recorder encodes a film on tape. Instead it creates and recreates the past, producing, like Chinese whispers, a version of events that may in the end bear little resemblance to what actually happened.

The process begins even as we take in the things that are destined for memory. Most sensory perceptions are not registered consciously and only a few of those that are get retained. Of those, most in turn fade from mind within a few hours. This leaves a tiny distillation of the past to take root in long-term memory. This personal selection of life's highlights is distorted both by selection and by our idiosyncratic way of seeing things. If two people look at a busy scene and are later asked to recall what was happening in it their reports will differ according to what struck each of them at the time as most important or intriguing. Depending on which threads are selected and how they are interpreted, the scene may be remembered as amusing or frightening or just muddled. So memories are not 'pure' recordings of what happens to start with – they are heavily edited before they are laid down.

The process of falsification gets another boost each time a memory is recalled. As we go over things that have happened we add a bit, lose a bit, tweak a fact here, tinker with a quote there and fill in any little bits that may have faded. We may consciously embellish the recollection with a bit of fantasy – the biting comment, perhaps, that we wished we had said but that was actually only thought of later. Then this new, re-edited version

is tucked back in storage. Next time it gets an airing it may pop up with the fantasy comment still attached, and this time it will be difficult to distinguish it from the 'genuine' memory. So, by gradual mutation, our memories change.

Given this, it can take very little tampering to create an entirely false memory. Psychologists Elizabeth Loftus and Jacqueline Pickrell at Washington University have shown that false memories can be implanted simply by 'reminding' people of things that never happened. They gave twenty-four volunteers four short accounts of what they claimed were true incidents (supplied by a relative) from the participants' early childhoods. Three of the four were actually true, but the fourth – a tale of getting lost in a shopping mall, crying and eventually getting help from a stranger – was a fabrication. After reading the stories and later being reminded of them, one in four participants was adamant that the false event had really happened.[5]

Even our memory of major, well-documented events can be surprisingly dodgy. In July 2005, a series of near simultaneous terrorist attacks occurred in London, one of which involved the bombing of a bus. The press subsequently carried large photographs of the aftermath, and detailed accounts of what happened from eye witnesses. But the event itself was not recorded on camera.

When a group of people were asked – just a short time after the event – if they had seen CCTV footage of the explosion, however, 84 per cent of people said they had.[6] The psychologists who carried out the study asked the group questions like 'Was the bus moving when the bomb went off?' and received detailed responses such as: 'The bus had just stopped to let two people off when two women got on and a man. He placed the bag by his side, the woman sat down and doors closed. As the bus left there was an explosion and then everyone started to scream'.

Although false memories may seem to be true to the person who experiences them, imaging studies suggest that the brain activity involved in recalling a real event differs from that which produces a false recollection. Daniel Schacter at Harvard University took PET scans of the brains of 12 women while they were shown lists of words, some of which they had seen before and some of which were new to them. As each list was shown the women were asked to recall if they had seen it before. Lists that the women had already seen activated the hippocampal and language areas of the brain, while lists that the women *thought* they had seen, but in fact had not, activated these regions plus the orbito-frontal cortex. This, remember, is the 'uh-oh...something funny here!' bit of the brain that was found to light up when things are not quite 'right'. Its activation during false memory recall suggests that – even though the person may not be conscious of it – at some level the brain 'knows' the memory is not correct and continues to generate cerebral question marks. If this finding turns out to be true for long-term memories as well as the recent ones that were involved in Schacter's study, brain imaging may one day have a role in the courtroom or even in therapy to help determine the reality of our imaginings.[7]

People who habitually tell false stories, a condition called confabulation, may be unconsciously trying to 'fill in' otherwise blank spaces in their past. If they have some other condition – mild temporal lobe epilepsy, perhaps, or dementia – the stories may be fantastic: lurid tales of abductions by aliens and so on. But often the falsehoods are quite banal and their very pointlessness underlines the teller's clear belief that they are true. Sometimes the stories are a mixture of truth and falsehood. One such patient, for example, told his doctor: 'I used to work on an assembly line [correct] putting metal rings on the legs of frozen turkeys [correct] at the Hawkeye Packing Plant [incorrect] in the southwest part of town [incorrect].'[8]

Confabulation of this sort is in some ways similar to the compulsive storytelling often seen in people with Williams syndrome. Both are an attempt to bind things together, to make unrelated thoughts into an integrated whole. We all do this to some extent, our brains are constantly seeking to make neat patterns of the information that comes in, and incomplete or fragmented memories (which we all inevitably possess) do not sit easily in our mental filing system. In order to neaten them up the brain may link inappropriate fragments together to create a hotchpotch of half-truths or complete them in a 'likely' way, much as it completes visual stimuli that do not fall into the expected pattern.

The brain also likes events to follow a standard narrative formula: beginning, middle and appropriate conclusion. Studies have shown that when people recall experiences that do not conform to this pattern they will often edit them in retrospect in such a way that they fit the expected structure. In one a group of people who underwent counselling for an anxiety disorder was asked to keep progress diaries. The diaries showed that the course of therapy was bumpy – they would get a bit better, then a bit worse, then a bit better, and at the end many of them reported feeling no better than when they began. When they were asked about the counselling a year or so later, however, nearly all of them reported a straightforward improvement from start to satisfactory resolution.

Habitual confabulation is different from this normal neatening-up and bringing into-line with expectations that we all do from time to time. Some people tell falsehoods as a matter of course – they spin a dense web of falsehood where their past should be. Such people can rarely maintain stable relationships because they are so untrustworthy and they generally lead very difficult lives as a result.

Confabulation is associated with frontal lobe injury. This raises the possibility that the brain's 'lie-detecting' mechanism does not function in such storytellers, so the person does not feel even a faint glimmer of unease when real memories blur into false ones.[9] Such injuries are seen frequently in Korsakoff's syndrome – a condition brought on by alcohol-induced brain damage. Korsakoff's patients suffer severe memory loss, and their confabulation seems to be an attempt to fill in the large blank spaces where real memories should be.

Lost in time

One of the most extraordinary and most thoroughly investigated cases of total amnesia concerns a man, known only as H.M., who has no memory of anything that has happened to him since he underwent a brain operation for epilepsy nearly 50 years ago. H.M. is the Phineas Gage of memory research in that, like Gage, his misfortune has provided researchers with a rare opportunity to see exactly what happens when a clearly defined and usually well-protected area of a person's brain is completely lost. He also demonstrates how the most profound aspects of human personality and experience are rooted in mere flesh.

H.M. had such severe epilepsy as a young man that eventually an operation to remove the areas where his seizures were focused seemed to hold the only prospect of delivering him some sort of normal life. In fact – for reasons that could not at the time have been predicted – the result of the operation was catastrophic.

The area removed from H.M.'s brain included, on both sides, the front two-thirds of the hippocampus, an area of surrounding tissue about 8 x 6 centimetres in size, and the amygdala.[10]

Time effectively stopped for H.M. while he was on the operating table. When he came round from the surgery his memory of the previous two years or so was found to be eradicated. Everything that happened to him until the age of about 25 he could remember normally, but there was nothing after that.

This in itself would not have been disastrous –

These are scans of people with amnesia – the highlighted areas around the thalamus show abnormal reduction in blood flow. (Based on: *The Thalamus in Amnesia: Structural and Functional Neuroimaging Studies* L.J. Reed et al. Neuroimage, S 630, Vol. 5, No 4 1997)

people who have brain surgery or head injuries frequently have what is known as retrograde amnesia for the period around and before the trauma. As H.M. recovered, however, it became clear that his plight was far more serious than this. He was not just unable to remember the immediate past, he was also unable to lay down anything new. Everything that went into his head stayed put for a few minutes, at most, then faded away...

Try to imagine what this must be like. Normal consciousness feels like a stream – a movement through time. Each moment is made up of a clutch of perceptions, but of themselves these incoming data are meaningless outside of the context of that stream. If you could experience a single moment, entirely uninformed by every moment that has gone before it, you would have no idea what was happening. Our plans, our actions, our thoughts – all these depend on continuity of perception. Even our identity requires a knowledge of who we were a moment before, and the moment before that.

LIES: THE GIVEAWAY BRAIN

The scans below show the difference – according to the manufacturers of the software that processes them – between a brain which is telling the truth (left) and one which is telling a lie (right). The extra activity in the lying brain is thought to result from the extra cognitive effort required to stop telling the truth and to make up a plausible falsehood. The scans suggest that truth-telling is the default position for the human brain, and that lies are a sophisticated development that we still have to work at.

'Lie Detection' brain scans are already in use in some courts and may eventually replace the polygraph test as a way of judging the credibility of a witness. Their use is highly controversial, however, with some people arguing that the artificial laboratory conditions in which the 'lie-detecting' scans have been tested bears little or no relationship to the messy, complicated business of real-life interactions. Nevertheless, it has to be remembered that time-honoured methods of telling whether someone is telling the truth – the use of intuition and judgement by observers and the polygraph – are also pretty unreliable (see for instance: K.E. Sip, A. Roepstorff, W. McGregor, Frith CD. *Detecting deception: the scope and limits.* Trends Cogn Sci. 12(2):48–53) (2008).)

BELIEF AND NON-BELIEF

The human brain treats statements it believes to be true quite differently from those it thinks are false. The first type are likely to guide further thought and action, while the second are likely to be dismissed.

The distinction, in terms of brain function, between 'believing' and 'disbelieving' was examined in a scanning study in which people were presented with a wide range of statements and asked to judge which were true and which were false.

The scans suggested that, although many of the 'high cognition' parts of the brain are likely to be involved in assessing the truth-value of a statement, the final acceptance of a statement as 'true', or its rejection as 'false', seems to rely on more primitive, emotional areas. These include the anterior cingulate cortex – an area concerned with (among other things) melding emotional reactions with thoughts and judgements, and the insula cortex, an area which is sensitive to the 'wholeseomeness' of things. The involvement of the insula suggests that lies might actually disgust us.

The believing brain is active in areas concerned with binding emotions and thoughts, while the skeptical brain sparks up on the edge of the insula, on the deep infold between the frontal and temporal lobes. The insula is sensitive to things which are 'disgusting' – suggesting that falsehood is treated much like an unhealthy substance which the body wants to reject.[11]

8 cm

The brain tissue removed from H.M.'s brain included the hippocampus. With it went his past.

since 1953 — he is always in the company of strangers. He never showed signs of irritation at the constant requests to do the sort of tedious things psychologists learn so much from — tracing a line through mazes, repeating words, naming objects — because to him they were, and remain, all new.

Although each procedure was always unfamiliar to H.M., and his performance on those that require memory function was always uniformly dire, there were some at which he did better each time he tried. Mirror writing, for example — trying to write while monitoring your performance via a mirror — is extremely tricky to do at first, but most people can get quite good at it with practice. H.M., too, became good at it through repeated attempts. But his performance in the later trials surprised him because he had no memory of the previous times he did it. Similarly, he has learned to play new tunes on the piano yet he has no memory of actually being taught them.[12]

The skills that H.M. learnt all involve laying things down in procedural memory — the 'how to' rather than the 'what?' store. He succeeded because this type of memorizing is done in a separate area — a neural loop involving the cerebellum and the subcortical nucleus called the putamen — that was untouched in H.M.'s operation. The 'how-to' mechanism tends to be less subject to degeneration than the hippocampal area and is often preserved in people with severe memory loss. In those with Alzheimer's disease islands of skill — the ability to play golf or to swim the butterfly stroke — may remain when almost all other memory has gone.

The separation of different types of memory is dramatically demonstrated in a curious condition known as 'fugue', or, more formally, psychogenic amnesia. This involves loss of episodic (personal) memory but retention of semantic (facts) memory. This is the good old standby affliction beloved of soap operas in which people say: 'Who am I?' and appear not to know their families. Unlike H.M., people with fugue usually lay down

H.M. does not have the continuity that allows most of us to make meaning of our lives. He is permanently trapped in a single, frozen moment. The stream of his life stopped running when he was 25, so, for him, his identity is suspended there with it. When asked he tells people he is a young man. He talks about his brother and friends, long dead, as though they were still alive. When he is given a mirror to look in his face registers horror as he sees an old man look back at him. The cruelty of inviting him to look at his reflection is mitigated only by the fact that within minutes he has clearly forgotten what he saw.

H.M. is an old man now and is rarely asked to take part in investigations. Over the years, though, he has done exhaustive tests for various psychologists. Some of these researchers spent weeks at a time with him, seeing him each and every day. Yet each session had to begin the same way — with an introduction. H.M. hasn't got to know a person memories all right and have their entire past stored away. It is just that they are unable to gain access to them. These buried memories may show up without the amnesic person realizing what is happening. A preacher called A. Bourne, for example, had a period of fugue in which he adopted the name A. Brown – a curiously similar name. A. Brown was a zealous churchgoer and on one occasion, during a particularly fervent testimony-swapping session, he spoke of a religious experience he had in fact experienced as A. Bourne – even though he claimed not to remember anything that had happened to him in that identity. Another amnesic patient was reconciled with her family when her doctor suggested that she dial a telephone number at random. The number she chose – without knowing why – turned out to be her mother's.[13]

People who suffer a mental or physical trauma may be left amnesic only for the event and the time around it. The abnormal brain activity that gives rise to fugue occurs in the limbic system, and particularly in the hippocampus and the amygdala. This was demonstrated in a brain scanning study that was done on a 22-year-old woman who could not remember anything that had happened to her for four years prior to a traumatic event. The woman reported a dream-like memory of being kidnapped and violated by a masked robber, but this may not have been a true recollection. The researchers gave the woman a series of photographs to look at. Some were of friends from her time at school which pre-dated the four-year 'black out', others were of university friends that she knew during the period she could not recall and a third type were of strangers. Consciously, she recognised the school friends, but not those from university. fMRI images of her brain, taken as she looked at the photos, showed that the sight of her school friends caused a normal degree of activation in the hippocampus and amygdala – the areas that deal with familiar memories – whereas the sight of the university friends elicited a muted

As Alzheimer's disease progresses the brain shrivels and shrinks. Above left shows a slice through a normal brain, above right shows tissue from a patient with severe Alzheimer's disease.

response indistinguishable from the response to the faces of strangers.[14]

Another case involved a man in his 40s who had a complete blank for 19 years of his life prior to a stroke. This period of his life contained many stressful events, and brain imaging showed that when he looked at snapshots from the time, recording events at which he was present, brain regions concerned with the early stages of auto-biographical memory retrieval showed normal activity. However, reduced activity was seen in brain regions concerned with the later stages of recollection when the fragments of memory were brought together and the episode was reconstructed. His brain was simply unwilling to recreate these events because they were associated with too much pain.[15]

The study suggests that this type of blocking-out happens quite early in perceptual processing – long before it starts to impinge on consciousness.

People in a state of fugue often seem to retain an unconscious memory of what happened. A man who had been the victim of a homosexual rape, for example, became very distressed and even attempted suicide after being shown a Rorschach card that is often interpreted as showing one person attacking another from behind. Another rape victim became very agitated when, without her realizing, she was taken back to the scene of the assault. It happened to be a brick path, and the woman had earlier reported that the words 'bricks' and 'path' kept popping into her mind.[16]

Unconscious memories – often called covert recollection – permeate everything we do. Social psychologist Robert Zajonc showed, for example, that people generally prefer things they have seen before, even if they do not remember seeing them. Similarly, our reactions to people are changed by whether we have seen them before, even if we do not remember them. In one experiment volunteers were shown a number of faces in quick succession – too quick for them to register properly. Later the volunteers were asked to rate another lot of faces – some of which had been shown before and some of which were new – for attractiveness. Although the volunteers were unable to remember seeing the pre-exposed faces they consistently rated them more attractive than new ones. In a sophisticated variant of this experiment some of these same volunteers were asked to join two other people, A and B, to decide the gender of the author of some poems. In fact, the exercise was not about this task at all. Person A, though not person B, was among the faces that the volunteers had already (very briefly) seen. The volunteers did not remember seeing A, but when (by arrangement with the researchers) A and B failed to agree on the gender of one of the poets, leaving the volunteer with the deciding vote, the volunteer inevitably sided with the person they had previously glimpsed.

The unconscious recognition of a stimulus is known to psychologists as priming and the stimulus itself – the quickly glimpsed face – is the prime. As the experiments above show, benign or neutral primes are generally endearing. But nasty primes can make people feel scared or aggressive, without them knowing why.

Covert memories involving fear are encoded in the amygdala rather than the cortex and in some cases no amount of thinking about them will bring them to mind because cortical activity tends to depress amygdala activation rather than increase it. This is perhaps why traumatic amygdala-based memories tend to pop into consciousness when we relax and allow our minds to wander, as in the psychoanalytical technique of free association. This clearly has profound implications for the debate about the sort of memories experienced during therapy. Memories that are laid down in a fragmented way in the cortex but burned indelibly on the amygdala might well remain buried until later life. Indeed, in a recent survey of 129 women who had fully documented (in hospital records) histories of sexual abuse, 16 per cent said they had at some stage forgotten about what happened to them and that the memories had later come back to them.[17] These were often fragmentary, and took the form of flashbacks rather like those experienced in post-traumatic stress disorder. This suggests the memories were located in the amygdala rather than the cortex.

In these cases the cortical, conscious memories of trauma may be difficult to access because they were not laid down in the normal way. Prolonged stress has been shown to affect the hippocampus. Vietnam veterans who suffer from post-traumatic stress disorder (once known as shell-shock) have been found to have 8 per cent less hippocampal tissue than comparable veterans, and adult survivors of childhood abuse were found in one study to have 12 per cent less hippocampal tissue. These people were found to have memory deficits both for the traumas they underwent and for more recent events.[18]

The hippocampal damage seen in trauma victims is thought to be brought about by long-term elevation of stress hormones. A single flush of these hormones, as we have seen, helps to form memories. But if the brain is constantly bathed in them it seems the hippocampus may be damaged with deleterious effects on memory recall and consolidation.

Infant trauma, it has been suggested, may also allow the memory to split itself into different compartments, creating what seem to be several different characters within the same brain: causing Multiple personality disorder (MPD). The first recorded case of MPD was in 1817 but the condition came to public attention with the classic story – made into a successful film – of *The Three Faces of Eve* in 1957. At that time even those who believed the condition was genuine thought it very rare. Today, however, some clinicians claim that as much as 1 per cent of the population in the USA is affected by the disorder.

MPD (which is also known as Dissociative Identity Disorder) is another issue in which professional (and public) opinion is polarized. Some psychiatrists think it is nonsense, a factitious condition invariably produced by someone with an overheated imagination and a collusive therapist. Others acknowledge it as a legitimate condition with a clear aetiology and physiological markers. During the 1990s the condition attracted a huge amount of controversy because it was linked almost exclusively to childhood sexual abuse. Since then interest in MPD and the other dissociative disorders has waned, along with the controversy.[19]

The Dissociative Disorders, of which MPD/DID is one, refer to a group of conditions in which a person experiences the world in a fragmented way. In particular, some part of their experience which would they would normally be aware of is blocked out before it reaches consciousness. We all, all the time, edit out some parts of our available experience – if we didn't we would be overwhelmed by the onslaught of perceptions, thoughts, emotions and sensations which constantly assail us. Narrowing our field of consciousness to a small portion of this allows us to function; to ignore incipient hunger pangs in order to finish a bit of work, say, or to put a problem to the back of our mind while we get the children off to school. Even extreme dissociation can, in some circumstances, be useful. A doctor or nurse, for instance, might need to block out their sense of compassion or revulsion in order to do their job. If they felt overwhelming pity whenever they saw someone in pain they might not be able to do anything to help. Sometimes, though, the dissociative mechanism goes into overdrive, getting stuck on permanently (so the doctor loses all sense of pity, even when off the job) or goes into overdrive, cutting out bits of experience that a person really needs to know about.

MPD/DID, like fugue, is a form of dissociation which involves slicing up one's memories so that, instead of a person being able to tap into more or less any part of their autobiographical database, part of it is inaccessible.

In fugue that bit is a particular chunk of time – usually a period that precedes a trauma. In MPD/DID what happens is that a person's memory of who they are is compartmentalised, so at any time part, or parts of it, are missing. The result is that a person may never have their 'whole' personality available, but instead split their autobiographical memories – along with knowledge of who they are – in a succession of 'selves'. Each of these will consist of a different chunk of the whole person – one may be the child self, another an angry self, a third the 'male' part of the self, and so on. Each of them may have no knowledge of, or conscious connection with the others and a person may slip seamlessly from one to another, taking on different names, ages, biographies and characteristics.[20]

When the inner workings of MPD patients' brains are displayed what appears is a pattern that suggests very strongly that 'alters', as the various different personalities are known, are not just performances by the patients. As one set of behaviours disappears and another takes its place the neuronal patterns change to match the altered demeanour. The brain scans even show a change in the memories that are available to each personality.

One study, for example, involved 11 women, each of whom seemed to have two distinct states of being. In one state they claimed to recall some kind of childhood trauma while in the other they denied any such memory. The women's brains were monitored while they listened to tape recordings of someone reading out some of their own, previously related recollections. One of the recordings described the traumatic memory. When the women were in their 'non-traumatised' personality the parts of their brains which would be expected to respond to a personal anecdote remained quiet. In other words, they registered the information as though it was something that had happened to someone else. When they switched to the other personality, however, the trauma story stirred a flurry of activity in the brain areas associated with a sense of self. Instead of just registering what they were hearing, their brains remembered them. Just as the women's behaviour suggested, their two personalities had different autobiographies.[21]

Another imaging study was done on a 47-year-old woman who could switch from one personality to another more or less on cue. During the transition from one to the other the part of the brain that processes memories momentarily 'closed down', as though it was shutting off one 'bag' of memories while switching to another.[22] A third study of personality-switchers found that their brainwave coherence – a measure of which neurons are firing in synchrony – was completely different in each of their personalities. This suggests that the subjects were thinking and feeling quite differently in each state.[23] No such changes were seen in actors trying to mimic the condition, nor in the subjects themselves when they were asked to act out a change of identity. Alters do not just behave differently – their brains think, feel, and recollect things differently too.

Memorising the Future

As well as allowing us to re-experience the past, albeit in a corrupted or fractured way, human memory also provides the foundation for imaging the future.

Our ability to conjure up scenarios which have not actually happened is prodigious. Imaginative capacity runs along a spectrum from the mundane skills required to envisage what your supper might taste like if you combined the onion, mushrooms, and left over chicken in the fridge with some curry sauce, through to the awe-inspiring visions of artists, writers, and excitable children. Even the humblest of these skills outranks the abilities – as far as we can tell – of every other species.

At first sight memory and imagination seem quite distinct: the first is concerned, after all, with what has happened already whereas the second is all about what has not. But recent studies show that imagination is wholly dependant on memory, because memories are its building blocks. When we imagine something happening we root around in our memory and come up with experiences which seem likely to recur, then combine them, chop them, shake them and blend them until they come out as something apparently entirely different. Even the most phantasmagoric scenes derive from things that have already occurred – we simply can't invent something for which we do not already have the ingredients, any more than we can rustle up a dish made of things we do not have in the larder. The skill of people who are especially imaginative is that they chop the memories finer and mix them up more thoroughly. They may also have a tendency to experience more – to suck more information from their surroundings – than those whose imaginations are more down to earth, and to focus more closely on novelty.

Memory, then, is not so much a part of our selves; rather it is the greater part of the stuff that we are made of: our biographies, our recollections, our imaginings and even our personalities. Take it away from a person and they become, as the writer Oliver Sacks described H.M., a 'Lost Mariner' adrift on the ocean of life.

REMEMBERING THE FUTURE

PROFESSOR ELEANOR MAGUIRE,
*Wellcome Trust Centre for Neuroimaging,
London*

What is memory for? Clearly, it allows us to accrue information about the world, to develop conceptual knowledge, and to record significant personal events that contribute to our autobiography and ultimately inform our sense of self. Until quite recently the majority of memory research was oriented to the past, examining how such knowledge and events are recorded and their possible neural substrates. But as Lewis Carroll observed in *Alice in Wonderland*, 'It's a poor memory that only works backwards'. In fact, there is now wide agreement that we and other organisms remember the past so that we can try to predict the future.

If recalling the past and predicting the future are indeed closely linked, then one might expect them to be supported by similar brain structures. This does indeed seem to be the case – patients with damage to the hippocampus (on both sides) are amnesic for past experiences and often unable to recollect any event that happened to them during their lifetime and patients with hippocampal amnesia are also unable to imagine plausible personal future events.

A study in which healthy volunteers were scanned using fMRI found that recalling past experiences and imagining possible future ones activated a network of brain regions in common including the hippocampus. Interestingly, these brain areas are not just engaged by past and future experiences but also by imagined fictitious experiences that are neither past nor future-oriented, while hippocampal amnesic patients are also unable to imagine fictitious events.

Thus recalling or imagining past, fictitious and future episodes seem to have a common neural substrate. In fact, several other cognitive functions – spatial navigation, day-dreaming and aspects of theory of mind – also share many of the same brain regions in common.

This begs the question, how do brain structures like the hippocampus subserve such a diverse range of functions? A clue emerged from the study of hippocampal amnesia patients. The source of their deficit seemed to be an inability to integrate an imagined experience into a coherent whole, manifesting itself most obviously in the discontinuity of the spatial context. This suggests the hippocampus plays a critical role in imagination by binding together the disparate elements of an event or scene. It may perform the same function when supporting the recollection of previous experiences, memories for which have long been known to be malleable and dynamic representations of the past as opposed to perfect fixed records.

A new theory receiving increasing support suggests that the brain areas and cognitive processes common to the diverse functions outlined above can be characterized by the concept of 'scene construction'. Scene or event construction involves the mental generation and maintenance of a complex and coherent scene or event. Scene construction allows for the internal rehearsal of events or scenes, and underpins the process of creating a setting in which a simulated event can unfold whether past, present, future, out of time altogether, or hypothetical.

The ability to pre-experience hypothetical

events gives us a head start in planning for the future. Being able to accurately and richly mentally construct possible future states before making a decision helps to evaluate the desirability of different outcomes and also the planning processes needed to make them happen. But in humans, the use of this scene construction process goes far beyond simply predicting the future, to the general evaluation of fitness for purpose and ultimately creativity. For example, a scriptwriter or novelist who is writing a passage in a film or book may play out the whole scene using their construction system, not with the idea of predicting the future, but instead for the purpose of evaluating its aesthetic suitability. Thus, the construction process, the ability to flexibly recombine stored information in novel ways, arguably sits near the apex of human intellectual abilities. It allows us to be limitlessly creative and inventive even though constrained by a basic set of raw component elements gleaned over a lifetime of experiences.

CHAPTER EIGHT

HIGHER GROUND

The frontal lobes are where ideas are created; plans constructed; thoughts joined with their
associations to form new memories; and fleeting perceptions held in mind until
they are dispatched to long-term memory or to oblivion.
This brain region is the home of consciousness — the high-lit land where the products of the
brain's subterranean assembly lines emerge for scrutiny. Self-awareness arises here, and emotions
are transformed in this place from physical survival systems to subjective feelings.
If we were to draw a 'you are here' sign on our map of the mind,
it is to the frontal lobes that the arrow would point. In this our new view of the brain echoes
an ancient knowledge — for it is here, too, that mystics have traditionally placed
the Third Eye — the gateway to highest point of awareness.

EVERYTHING THE HUMAN BRAIN does is amazing, but not all of it is so special. Computers can calculate better than us; recording machines can rerun the past more accurately; dogs can smell more acutely; birds are better at singing... It is not what we do that makes us so precious (a totally paralysed, mute person is no less a person, after all), it is what goes on inside our heads – the rich and highly developed quality of our consciousness.

You can travel around the brain for a long time without confronting consciousness. Behaviourists, for example, managed to dominate psychology for most of the twentieth century without even admitting that it existed. Now, though, the behaviourists' obsession with rigid objectivity has been replaced by a fervour of interest in subjective experience that is currently engaging some of the greatest philosophers and scientists in the world.

There are two broad schools of thought about consciousness (and by extension mind): one is that it is some transcendent quality beyond understanding. Essentially, this is Cartesian dualism – the idea that the 'spirit' world is separate from the material world in which our brains are rooted. The other is that it is the product of brain activity, a property of the material world that can be explored and will eventually be explained without recourse to the supernatural.

Those who have taken up the challenge of trying to explain consciousness (rather than assuming it to be an impenetrable mystery) are faced with huge questions. Does it have a purpose, or is it just a by-product of neural complexity? Is it a single, continuous stream, or is that feeling of continuity and oneness an illusion? If you could

remove the informational content of a living brain and keep it separate from its body – download it, perhaps, on to a floppy disc – would consciousness go with it? And if so, *where* exactly would it be? What bytes of data could you afford to junk when you take Grandad off-line and still be sure he is able to enjoy his virtual existence?

There are no answers yet to these questions but there are some intriguing clues. In particular, the search for the neural basis of consciousness (the philosopher's stone of brain mapping) is providing fascinating insights into its quarry.

A huge volume of evidence suggests that consciousness emerges from the activity of the cerebral cortex that the particular type of consciousness that includes the sense of self requires activation in the frontal lobes. Ask yourself this: 'Where, precisely, do I feel that "I" am centred?' If you are like most people, you will point to a position just above the bridge of your nose. It is right behind here that you will find the prefrontal cortex – the area of the frontal lobe most closely associated with the generation of consciousness. This region is also responsible for our conscious perception of emotion and our ability to attend and focus. Most important of all, it endows the world with meaning and our lives with a sense of purpose. The symptoms of schizophrenia, depression, mania and Attention Deficit Disorder are mainly due to frontal lobe disorder. Our growing knowledge about this area, and the chemicals that make it tick, holds the best hope of restoring people with these disorders to normal life.

The frontal cortex is the part that mushroomed most dramatically during our transition from hominid to human and it makes up about 28 per

1) *Orbito-frontal cortex: this area inhibits inappropriate actions, freeing us from the tyranny of our urges and allowing us to defer immediate reward in favour of long-term advantage.*

2) *Dorsolateral prefrontal cortex: things are held 'in mind' here, and manipulated to form plans and concepts. This area also seems to choose to do one thing rather than another.*

3) *Ventromedial cortex: this is where emotions are experienced and meaning bestowed on our perceptions.*

4) *Anterior cingulate cortex — helps focus attention and 'tune in' to own thoughts.*

cent of the cortical area of the human brain, a far larger proportion than in any other animal. The back part of the frontal lobe is given over to the parts of the brain that allow us to take physical action. This includes part of the language area (Broca's), which articulates speech, and the motor cortex, which controls movement. Just in front of the motor cortex is a strip called the premotor cortex, or Supplementary Motor Area (SMA). This is where proposed actions are rehearsed before they are actually carried out.

The premotor cortex is an important landmark. It divides the sensing and doing cortex from the area that is given over to man's most impressive achievements – juggling with concepts; planning and predicting the future; selecting thoughts and perceptions for attention and ignoring others; binding perceptions into a unified whole; and, most important, endowing those perceptions with meaning.

Edge forward from the premotor strip and you enter an area known as the prefrontal cortex. This is the only part of the brain that is free from the constant labour of sensory processing. It does not concern itself with the mundane tasks in life such as walking around driving a car, making a cup of coffee or taking in the sensory perceptions from an unremarkable environment. All these can be done adequately without calling on the prefrontal cortex. So long as our mind is in neutral the prefrontal cortex merely ticks over. When something untoward occurs, though, or when we actually think rather than daydream, the prefrontal cortex springs into life and we are jettisoned into full consciousness as though from a tunnel into blazing sunshine.

The frontal lobes are connected by numerous neural pathways to almost all the other cortical areas and also to the limbic region. These paths are two-way – they carry in information from the buried parts of the brain and they also carry signals back. Information must flow in to the frontal lobes in order for them to function, but a heavy input from below can inhibit activity on the surface and vice versa. If a person is asked to concentrate very hard on visual sensations – sorting them into categories, for example, the frontal lobes close down. Conversely if they concentrate on themselves rather than the outside world, the sensation-generating parts of the brain go quiet.[1] This 'see-saw' arrangement means that a sudden flood of emotion may occlude thought, while an arduous cognitive task may dampen emotion. This is why terror can (momentarily at least) wipe a brain clean of thought, while young men who wish to prolong sexual congress are traditionally advised to practice calculus.

Awareness, perception, self-awareness, attention, reflection – these are all separate components of consciousness and the quality of our experience varies according to which and how many of them are present. It is a little like a printing process in which an image is built up by laying down its component colours one on top of the other. The first pass of the ink-jet leaves a vague monochromatic impression, the second gives it greater definition, the third brings a richer and clearer view and so on. At some point the smears of ink become the picture, and at the end of the process, although the image may be formed from just five colours, it can contain thousands of hues. Of course, the picture is the result of many processes that precede its printing: an original painting, text or photograph has to exist first and the original has to be set up for printing either as a digital code (in a computerized system) or as an etching on a metal plate. The equivalent mental processing that precedes consciousness involves many of the neural systems in every brain region. However, just as a final printed image may be built up on the page from just a handful of component colours, so it seems that the penetrating, multifaceted consciousness that normal healthy humans enjoy may be created by the activity of relatively few brain parts.

The paramount importance to consciousness of the frontal lobes was discovered from brain injury studies many decades ago, and cases like that of Phineas Gage further suggested that specific parts of this region are responsible for specific qualities like self-awareness, personal responsibility, purposefulness and meaning. Even so, until functional brain imaging came along it was difficult to imagine that such amorphous concepts could be pinned down to precise clumps of nerve cells. That, though, seems to be the case, and in its short history functional brain imaging has proved spectacularly successful at teasing out the physical loci of our most elevated states of mind.

Although consciousness emerges from the cortex it requires an entire brain to feed it. The brainstem, midbrain and thalamus are essential because they are part of a system that directs and controls conscious attention by shunting neurotransmitters to various parts of the cortex. Activity in these areas alone is sometimes seen in people in deep comas and although it is not sufficient to give rise to consciousness it can produce an eerie simulacrum of conscious behaviour. The patient's eyes may lock on to a moving target, for example, so they may seem to be watching those who pass by. They might clutch at things, too, and grimace if pricked with a pin. These actions are purely reflex but nevertheless deeply disturbing for those who see them.*

What has to happen in the brain for the first smear of consciousness to be laid? A clue to this comes from studies of a curious condition called blindsight, which is a godsend to researchers because it allows them to study what happens on the very edge of consciousness.

---

* There are those who argue that the emergence of consciousness from the cortex cannot be known for certain, and they are right. The evidence is essentially negative in that despite many cases of people claiming to have experienced things while clinically dead (during surgery for instance) no one without a functioning cortex has ever displayed behaviour consistent with consciousness. The assumption that the cortex is essential for experience informs many ethical decisions in current medicine, including turning off life-support machines of brain-damaged patients and taking organs from bodies that are still breathing. To discover it is wrong would remove one of the few lodestones in a notoriously boggy area of morality, and shed an unwelcome new light on past practices. Happily, nothing has emerged from the new imaging studies to suggest that a rethink is in order.

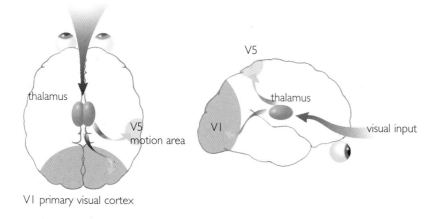

thalamus

V5
motion area

V1 primary visual cortex

V5

thalamus

V1

visual input

Most visual input goes to V1, the primary visual cortex at the back of the brain where sight is consciously experienced. A smaller neural pathway leads direct to V5, however, and this is how some blind people may nevertheless be aware of movement, so-called 'blindsight'.

Blindsight is the ability of people to see things without being conscious that they are seeing them. People experiencing it are fully conscious of all but the blindsight itself, so the fully conscious bit of them can report on how it feels to be aware-yet-not-aware of one element of their brain functioning. The effect is almost as though a fully conscious brain is in telepathic contact with a less conscious one.

Blindsight first came to light on the battlefields of the First World War when blinded soldiers were seen to duck bullets even though they had no idea they were doing so. It has since been methodically investigated in several subjects. Some degree of blindsight can be induced in people with normal vision by using Transcranial Magnetic Stmulation (TMS) to effectively 'turn off' the primary visual cortex (V1). This is the area of the brain where information from the eyes usually impacts first, and starts to be turned into conscious sight. When it is put out of action, people are unable to see in the normal way and report the experience of being blind. But in laboratory tests they can still reach for moving objects, correcting the direction of their grasp as they go.[2] Blindsight is more commonly studied, however, in people who are already blind, or partially blind, due to V1 damage. The neurons in V1 are arranged so that they each respond only to their own part of the visual field. If some neurons are killed by injury, the area of visual field that they formerly registered becomes (or seems to become) a blind spot.

Oxford University's Larry Weiskrantz, the first scientist to investigate blindsight experimentally, found that people with this sort of injury could often point accurately at a target that was moved across their blind area even though they had no conscious awareness of it. Later he found they could often tell the shape and orientation of a target, too. This is the conversation that took place after an experiment in which the subject successfully identified the position of a symbol placed in his blind spot at every attempt. Weiskrantz speaks first:

'Did you know how well you were doing?'

'No, I didn't because I couldn't see anything. I couldn't see a darn thing.'

'Can you say how you guessed? What it was that allowed you to say whether it was horizontal or vertical?'

'No, I could not because I couldn't see anything. I just don't know.'

'So you really didn't know if you were getting them right?'

'No.'[3]

Blindsight is probably brought about by the remnants, in humans, of a primitive visual system that once — in our deep evolutionary past —

Consciousness in the brain

What has to happen in the brain to make an experience conscious? Scanning studies have determined that when a person is consciously aware of a sensation, their brains show a distinct and consistent activation pattern which is different from the activation that occurs when their brain merely registers the stimulus.[4]

It seems there has to be a certain amount of excitatory activity in the brain before consciousness arises and a large number of neurons need to be firing in synchrony. The synchronicity 'binds' separate elements of an experience into a single perception. To produce the experience of looking at the setting sun, for instance, neurons might be oscillating in the brain area concerned with generating the colour red; the area that generates knowledge of shape (an orb) another that is concerned with hooking out memories of sunsets and another that brings up the word 'sunset'. A firing rate of about 40 Hz (40 times each second) is thought to be the minimum level of excitation required. [5]

ATTENTION

The crucial prerequisite for consciousness seems to be attention. The brain started as the body's alarm system, and alertness can be thought of as a special mechanism to ensure that the brain is at its most efficient when danger is about.

If the brain picks up a stimulus that may be a threat – a rustle in the bushes, say, the reticular activating system – a clutch of nuclei in the base of the brain – releases a rush of adrenaline throughout the brain. This closes down all unnecessary activity, so an alert brain shows up on a brain scanner as very quiet. It also inhibits body activity: the heart rate slows and breathing becomes shallow and quiet.

While the brain waits on alert for something to which to react, activity is maintained in the superior colliculus, the lateral pulvinar (a part of the thalamus) and the parietal cortex. These areas are concerned with orienting and focusing. Once a cue comes the appropriate area of the brain springs into activity and shows a greater level of activity than a brain that was not previously alert.

Attention is necessary for thinking, as well as for consciousness of sensations. The brain constantly scans the environment for stimuli. This is done largely by automatic mechanisms in the brainstem. Even people in Persistent Vegetative State show scanning eye movements, which are part of this system.

Damage to the superior colliculus may cause oculomotor apraxia – in which eyes can't lock on to a new target. This makes a person functionally blind. Damage to the parietal cortex may make a person unable to disengage from a stimulus. Focus is brought about by the lateral pulvinar – a part of the thalamus – which operates rather like a spotlight, turning to shine on the stimulus. Once it is locked on, it shunts information about the target to the frontal lobes, which then lock on and maintain attention.

Attention requires three elements: arousal, orientation, focus.

Arousal is dependent on a group of nuclei in the midbrain – the top of the brainstem – called the Reticular Activating System. The core of the brainstem is made up of neurons that have unusually long dendrites stretching up and down. Some of these travel right up to the cortex. Some of them are responsible for consciousness; concussion often results from disturbance of the system, and damage to them may result in permanent coma. Others control the sleep/wake cycle. A third group is responsible for controlling the level of activity in the brain. When they are stimulated they release a flood of neurotransmitters, which set neurons firing throughout the brain. The ones known to be particularly involved in activating the prefrontal lobe are dopamine and noradrenaline. Stimulation of this group of reticular neurons also creates alpha brainwaves – oscillations of electrical activity at 20–40 Hz – which are associated with alertness.

Orientation is done by neurons in the superior colliculus and parietal cortex. The superior colliculus turns the eyes to the new stimulus, while the parietal cortex disengages attention from the current stimulus.

Whether something is consciously perceived or merely registered by the brain depends partly on whether the brain is already primed to attend to it or not. High activation in the dorsolateral prefrontal cortex, which is concerned with directing attention, and the intra-parietal cortex, an area concerned with 'binding' incoming information, seems to put the brain on standby for a conscious perception. A touch on the hand, for instance, was consciously noted by volunteers who showed this pattern of neural activity immediately before the stimulus, where as a touch that was identical in intensity was not noticed by people whose brains were in a different state.[6]

ATTENTION DISORDER

Attention Deficit Hyperactive Disorder is a condition marked by lack of concentration, short attention span and physical restlessness. It is usually diagnosed in children, many of whom are so disruptive that normal play and schooling is impossible for them. Brain imaging studies show clearly that children with this disorder have an underlying neurological dysfunction which almost certainly accounts for their behaviour. The limbic system is working at full steam in these children but the cortical areas which focus attention, control impulses and integrate stimuli are underactive. Although it is generally thought of as a childhood condition, ADHD – characterized by a relative inability to plan ahead, organize and concentrate – is increasingly recognized in adults. Some 70 per cent of people who show the symptoms in childhood continue to show them as adults and brain scanning studies of adults who had ADHD as children show that the executive areas of their brains have less connective tissue than normal people. Drug treatment for ADHD stimulates these underactive areas, causing the brain to concentrate and focus.

Amphetamine-type drugs which raise the level of excitatory neurotransmitters in the cortex reduce Attention Deficit. The activity they produce inhibits the limbic system, substituting thought for action and producing more controlled and focussed behaviour.[7]

shunted all light-borne information to the subcortical areas of the brain that focus attention and trigger appropriate physical reactions to stimuli. It was entirely concerned with the practical business of organizing the animal's behaviour and as such it did not register anything that was not likely to be of immediate physical importance. It was probably similar to the system now observed in, say, a lizard. Anything outside a lizard's own little bit of space is beyond the concerns of a lizard's visual system. It probably cannot register a fly in a distant corner, only a fly within tongue's reach. And stationary objects do not have the same impact on it as moving objects because stationary objects, by and large, do not signify either food or attack. The lizard-level visual system is purely for survival – it is not there to help the lizard appreciate Picasso. And so it once was with us.

Research on blindsight subjects has revealed that it is not just movement that can be reported on – one 'star' blindsighter can tell the shape and colour of a target as well as movement, and even the expression on an 'invisible' face.[8] And sight is not the only sense which can be conscious or unconscious – researchers have also revealed the existence of 'blindtouch' and even 'blindsmell'.

In one experiment, for example, people were asked to smell two phials of liquid, each of which had a very weak odour – one pleasant (amyl acetate, similar to bananas) and the other nasty (butyric acid, a bit like rancid butter). The volunteers claimed to be unable to detect if there was any smell at all – but when prompted to 'guess' which one smelt nice and which was nasty, they were very successful.[9]

Studies such as this suggest that sensory information which does not make it to consciousness may nevertheless influence our behaviour. Places that somehow don't 'feel right'; people who seem curiously attractive for reasons we can't work out – perhaps the

phonological loop

visuo-spatial sketch pad

central executive

THE WORKING MEMORY

Memory used to be regarded as a simple library with a long-term store – childhood memories and so on – and a short-term store – a temporary holder in which information is retained for as long as it is needed, then discarded. As experimental techniques became refined, however, it has become clear that there is no rigid dividing line between a memory and a thought. A new term has therefore crept into use to describe how we juggle perceptions, memories and concepts: working memory.

Professors Alan Baddeley and Graham Hitch have developed a model of working memory based on three parts:

* The Central Executive – co-ordinates information from a number of sources, directs the ability to focus and switch attention, organizes incoming material and the retrieval of old memories and combines information arriving via two temporary storage systems:

* Visuo-spatial sketch pad holds images

* Phonological loop holds acoustic and speech-based information

Brain imaging studies at the Wellcome Department of Cognitive Neurology have found that the three parts are echoed precisely in the activity seen when people carry out cognitive tasks.

Working together these three brain circuits allow us to hold important incoming information in mind while combining it with knowledge we already hold to create a plan of action appropriate for the current situation.

A) PHONOLOGICAL LOOP

Broca's area
(inner speech)

phonological
stage
(inner voice)

central executive

B) VISUO-SPATIAL SKETCH PAD

visuo-spatial
sketch pad

central executive

effect they have on us is due to our unconscious processing of their aversive or attractive odour.

As the cerebral cortex evolved, there came a time, presumably when it became advantageous to shunt information to this new brain as well as to the existing sensory detection system. The cortex — being more complex and flexible than the old brain beneath it — was able to bring about more sophisticated and effective reactions to stimuli. Gradually, the cortex evolved more and better tricks and the brain remoulded itself to take advantage of them. More light-borne information flowed to the cortex, where it stimulated the growth of more grey matter, which in turn thought up more imaginative reactions, which encouraged more light to flow to it and so on. Meanwhile, the old subcortical system became increasingly redundant. Blindsense, however, reveals what this ancient mechanism can do when it is not eclipsed by the cortical sensory system. The ability that some skilled tennis and cricket players have to hit a speeding ball before its existence can possibly be registered by the cortex may also be due to blindsight.

On the face of it blindsight seems no more significant for consciousness than the reflex actions seen in people in vegetative comas. Yet there is evidence that it is a little closer to consciousness than that. When pressed to describe the experience of blindsight some subjects admit to a vague awareness. To quote one: 'I sort of feel that something is there…when it moves it feels as though something is coming towards me — like a billiard cue being aimed at me.' Furthermore, subjects who take part in blindsight experiments get better at them as time goes on.[10] This suggests that, although blindsight may itself be unconscious, it may mark the beginning of a route that leads to consciousness.

The difference between blindsight and the automatic reactions is reflected by a difference in brain activity. Reflex actions do not involve cortical activity — clutching and reacting to pinpricks, for example, is sometimes observed in babies with anencephaly, where no cortex exists.[11] By contrast,

SHORT-TERM MEMORY

ALAN BADDELEY
Professor of Psychology, University of Bristol

My colleague Graham Hitch and I developed our model of working memory in order to account for the results of an experiment in which we tried to interfere with the operation of short-term memory in normal people. We asked students to learn word lists, comprehend prose or do reasoning tests while their short-term memory was occupied with remembering and repeating back telephone numbers. We found that performance was dented but not catastrophically impaired by this simulated 'short-term memory loss'. We suggest that this is because the phonological loop of these patients is impaired by our telephone-number task.

We believe that the phonological loop can be split into two components: a memory store that holds a fast-decaying (one to two seconds) speech-based trace, and a rehearsal system that repeats the trace and registers it in the memory store via non-vocalized speech. Hence a visually presented set of letters can be remembered by saying it to oneself. But because the memory trace fades while the rehearsal is going on we can typically only remember as many words as we can say in two seconds.

Adult patients with pure phonological loop impairment can get by as long as they do not attempt to learn new words. Recent research on a group of eight-year-old children with language deficits found that, while their non-verbal intelligence was appropriate to their age, their language was delayed by two years and their capacity to repeat back an unfamiliar nonsense word by four years. Since this latter task is closely linked with vocabulary development and is a good predictor of future language and reading skills it suggests that the phonological loop has evolved as part of the mechanism for acquiring language.

Less is known about the more complex visuo-spatial sketch pad although the four active regions so far identified by functional imaging are thought to represent 'what', 'where', executive control and possibly image rehearsal.

Working memory allows us to use our memory systems flexibly. It enables us to hold on to information by rehearsing it in our minds, to relate that information to older knowledge and to plan our future actions.

FREE WILL AND THE BRAIN

Back in the mid 1980's, the late Benjamin Libet, then a neuroscientist at the University of California, San Francisco set out to discover the timing of brain events which led to consciously willed actions. In particular he wanted to find out how the timing of a conscious decision related to the brain processes that executed it. Volunteers were fitted with EEG sensors placed to pick up signals from the cerebral cortex and told to make a simple hand movement. The important thing was that the act should be self-initiated, rather than dependent on some outside cue. The EEG measurements were precisely pinpointed by linking them to a timing device, and the timing of the subjects' decisions was arrived at by getting the students to watch a clock and note precisely when the conscious 'urge' to move occurred. Previous experiments[12] had already demonstrated that voluntary actions are preceded by a wave of activity — called the Readiness

Potential (RP) – in the cerebral cortex about half a second before they are carried out. Mere reflex actions – like whipping your hand away from a hotplate, do not produce a RP. Libet arranged his EEG equipment to catch the RP and catch it he did. Each time a hand movement was made the brain processes required to do it were heralded – about half a second before the actual act – by the characteristic fluctuation in neural activity.

If an act of will is something outside the automatic brain processes that actually execute the movement you might expect that the decision to move would come just before, or maybe at the same time as that first, preparatory brain activation. But what Libet found instead was that the students consistently reported making the decision to move their hands after the RP had begun. In nearly every case the subject said the conscious urge, or decision to move occurred about 350–400 milliseconds after the EEG spikes revealed the RP. The movement itself then took place about two tenths of a second after that. [13]

The importance of Libet's finding can hardly be exaggerated. If, as it seems to show, the unconscious brain kicks off a movement, and the conscious decision to make the movement comes in its wake, the implication is that the brain itself is the force that initiates the action. Rather than causing action, consciousness merely reflects what the brain is already doing. If this is true of all actions it follows that our behaviour is simply the end product of automatic brain processes – and our notion of a 'free will' is illusory.

fMRI scans show that a subsection of the visual cortex called V5 – the area that registers movement – lights up during blindsight even though V1 – the primary sensory area that is essential for normal sight – is not active. [14] So blindsight, perhaps, is not entirely unconscious. It brushes the cerebral cortex, and in doing so it may send tiny whispers of that activity up to consciousness via some little-used neural byway, producing the first glimmer of awareness.

This still falls far short of anything we understand as consciousness. To crank that faint awareness up to a full-blown perception a sensory stimulus has to be registered by an area of primary sensory cortex (V1, for example, in the case of vision). These areas kick off the unconscious assembly lines that begin with the raw material of sensory stimuli and end by delivering to the brain's frontal surface well-processed mental constructions. For the perception to be laden with emotional as well as sensory content a parallel processing line must run from the limbic system (especially the amygdala) to the frontal lobe.

To create full consciousness it is not enough for perceptions merely to 'pop up' in the front of the brain. The pattern of brain activity in which this alone happens – high in the back and sides, low in the front – is seen in people who, one way or another, are not quite 'there'. They may, for example, be 'lost' in an experience, asleep or dreaming. This type of pattern is also seen in sleep and in Attention Deficit Disorder. It is also seen in the type of schizophrenia that is characterized by withdrawal and inertia. [15] At its most extreme, low frontal activity may result in catatonia, a state in which people fail completely to respond to their surroundings. One woman who spent months lying in bed without speaking or voluntarily moving later explained how she had felt. She had been aware, she said, of what was going on around her, but none of it prompted any thought. 'I couldn't say anything,' she said, 'because nothing came to mind.'

To bring such a semi-slumbering brain to full, thinking, feeling awareness more activity is required in the frontal lobes. Let us see where it must take place to bring about each component of that state.

The Self

Unlike the woman in a state of catatonia, we do not just bask, thoughtless and uncommenting, in our experience. Rather we experience it through a dense matrix of concepts which we call 'I', or the self.

The 'I' 'owns' and constantly judges our sensations, our emotions and our perceptions, and takes responsibility for our actions. It creates a sensed separation between the thinking, reflective part of our cognition and the rest of our experience, and so allows us to consider and 'do' things with or about our perceptions. It also allows us to know the difference between our own dreams and memories – self-generated experience – and external events. And, crucially, in a social species such as ours, it allows us to see ourselves as objects in the world – something which has its own unique perspective rather than a universal view. This in turn, encourages us to understand that other, similar 'objects' also have an internal world, and their own, different, point of view.

Human beings are not born with a built-in self – it develops, step by step, as we mature.

As we have seen, memories and imaginings are created by the same neural activity that occurs when things really happen. So if you simply imagined or recollected experiences you would not be able to tell if they were happening inside or outside your head. You would therefore be unable conceptually to 'do' anything with what you had brought to mind. You would merely experience it, as though in a trance.

It starts, sensibly enough, with the drawing up of internal 'maps', each one an idea that is encoded in neuronal patterns. The most basic of these is one that tells us where our bodies end and the rest of

DO WE HAVE CONSCIOUS FREE WILL?

PROFESSOR PATRICK HAGGARD
Institute of Cognitive Neuroscience & Dept. of Psychology, University College London

The Libet experiment seems to show that unconscious processes in the brain cause our actions, and we only know about our actions just before we act. Libet's experiment has been widely criticised. Some scientists object to the way Libet tried to time the internal stream of consciousness by asking people to use the clock as an independent external time-keeper. Others suggest that the real act of will is the participant's deciding to volunteer for the experiment or not. Nevertheless, the basic result has been replicated a number of times in recent years.

Libet's finding is not so controversial for neuroscientists, who see conscious experience as a product of brain activity, not as a cause of brain activity. But worryingly, our society, and particularly our legal system, is built on an everyday understanding of volition that modern science seems to reject. The important question is: what are we to make of Libet's results, and what do they mean for our understanding of human nature?

Currently, the dominant view in psychology and neuroscience is a determinist one. According to this view, our behaviour is fully determined by previous experience and by current context. The idea that we freely will and control our behaviour is simply an illusion (Wegner: The Illusion of Conscious Will, MITP 2002). This illusion arises because we retrospectively attribute our actions to be caused by our prior thoughts. So if I have been thinking about the growing darkness in the room, and I notice my hand moving towards the light switch, I will infer that I *willed* the movement of my hand towards the switch. 'Conscious free will' is therefore not really an experience related to the initiation of actions, but part of a narrative that we retrospectively tell ourselves to explain our own behaviour. Many determinists further argue that our behaviours are not voluntarily caused, but are *unconsciously* determined by events in the world around us. For example, several experiments in social psychology show that large and unconscious changes in our behaviour are determined by seemingly tiny features of other people's behaviours. Indeed, we all know how a small departure from conventional behaviour on someone else's part makes us want to move to the next carriage on a train. But showing that our social antennae are finely-tuned tells us little about our individual intentions and their relation to control.

The key question is whether *anything* that we might call volition is left over apart from the retrospective narrative? What function does this experience have, or is it purely epiphenomenal? In my own view, the most striking evidence comes from the unique case of direct stimulation of the human brain during neurosurgical operations. In some cases, direct electrical stimulation of the cortex causes patients to report an 'urge' to move a specific body part. Two key brain areas where stimulation can evoke urges are the pre-Supplementary Motor Area and the parietal cortex. Studies with patients who have focal brain lesions, and with healthy volunteers whose brain activity is temporarily disrupted with transcranial magnetic stimulation, show that the same areas also contribute to judgements of conscious intention in the Libet experiment. What does this artificially-generated experience mean? The urge cannot be a retrospective inference, nor can it be the immediate cause of movement, because it occurs without the patient actually moving. Nor does it seem like an artifactual or random result, because stimulation at the same sites with higher currents often produced actual movement of the same body part. So neuroscience tells us that our conscious volition is not the cause of our actions, but neither is it just a narrative that we make up to explain our actions. It could simply be an epiphenomenon, an irrelevant by-product of activity in particular brain areas. Alternatively, conscious volition could have some function, other than causing the immediately following action.

My personal view is that conscious volition may play an important role in *learning* about the outcome of complex actions. Many of us have an intense memory of saying an unkind word, or even deliberately hitting someone. Our conscious intention to speak, or to hit, doesn't cause us to speak that particular word, or deliver that particular blow. But it can provide a vivid marker of what it felt like to be about to make that particular mistake. This vivid experience can be associated with memory for the consequences of our action: the motor areas of the brain that control our actions appear to receive a brief 'flash' of dopamine at the time of action, perhaps for exactly this purpose. A strong conscious experience of our own volition may be relevant not so much to the action we are performing now, but to the next time we are in a similar situation. Conscious volition on one occasion could provide a strong guide for what we should or should not do on the *next* occasion. I think Libet was therefore right to see an intimate link between conscious volition and inhibitory self-control, though his idea of a brain-independent conscious veto seems to me like an unconvincing 'ghost in the machine'.

<u>SLOW-WAVE SLEEP</u> The entire brain oscillates in a gentle rhythm quite unlike the fragmented oscillations of normal consciousness. Brain scans show less activity in the limbic system.

slow wave sleep

<u>HYPNOSIS</u> Brain scans show increased activity during hypnosis, particularly in the motor and sensory areas suggesting heightened mental imagery. Increased blood flow in the right anterior cingulate cortex suggests that attention is focused on internal events. The brain activation seen in this state is quite different from that seen in normal waking or sleeping.

hypnosis

<u>SCHIZOPHRENIA</u> Lack of activity in the frontal lobes is a feature of states of mind in which consciousness is disturbed or decreased. In chronic schizophrenia the dorsolateral prefrontal cortex is especially hypoactive. This might account for the state's common reduction in planned or spontaneous behaviour and social withdrawal. The anterior cingulate cortex – thought to distinguish between external and internal stimuli – is also underactive, which may be one reason schizophrenics confuse their own thoughts with outside voices.

schizophrenia

<u>DREAMING</u> Vivid visual dreams light up the visual cortex; nightmares trigger activity in the amygdala and the hippocampus flares up from time to time to replay recent events. The areas which seem to be most commonly active are the pathways carrying alerting signals from the brainstem and the auditory cortex; supplementary motor area and visual association areas – all of which produce the 'virtual reality' effect of dreaming. Activity is decreased in the dorsolateral prefrontal cortex, the area of waking thought and reality testing.

dreaming

<u>MEDITATION</u> Scans of people in a self-induced state of 'passive attention' have been shown to 'turn off' areas of the brain normally associated with seeking stimuli, including the parietal, anterior and premotor cortexes.

meditation

the world begins. Later our personal body atlas will contain maps that allow us to know our place – literally, our spatial location – in the world. Finally we develop more abstract 'self' maps, which delineate the mental self, or ego. Each of these is represented in a different area of the brain, with those underpinning our physical self situated mainly in the back areas of the brain and those concerning our abstract self towards the front.

Babies probably do not distinguish between their own body and other objects. They begin to do so only when the body maps in the brain start to take in information from the outside world. These maps are not detailed. The me/not me map, for example, does not necessarily accord faithfully with the baby's actual shape – it is, if you like, just roughly baby-shaped. The body and its internal representation only come to match up perfectly because the brain map gets bashed into place, effectively, as the infant bumps up against the outside world and discovers, sometimes painfully, where its actual boundaries lie. With each bump the child learns a little more about its real shape, and revises the internal map accordingly.

Normally these two things – the internal map of the body and the body itself – end up being perfectly matched. But it is quite possible for them to be different. If an early accident causes a child to lose a limb, for example, the map and the body may end up askew and the person feels what is known as a phantom limb – a subjective feeling that they have a body part which is not, in fact, there. Phantom limbs may fade or disappear as the map is overwritten by learning, but sometimes they continue to be felt for life. Conversely, the internal map may 'lose' a limb or two, leading the person to feel that the real flesh and blood limb is not really part of them. This may explain the odd cases of people who have persuaded surgeons to amputate their healthy limbs.

The creation of a mental idea of one's body is closely followed by the development of an idea of

The same stimulus activates different brain areas according to whether the subject is paying attention to it or not. The scans above show, left: *the brain of a person who is hearing speech, but concentrating on their breathing. The auditory cortex is responding, but few other areas of the brain are active.* Right: *Now the subject is actively listening to the words – note how many other areas of the brain have come alive.*

one's self as a mental entity. One of the earliest manifestations of this is the development of an individual point of view.

In order to have one's own perspective, it is first necessary to recognize that it is a perspective – a particular view, rather than the only view of the world. This means that one has to grasp the idea – and acknowledge the irritating consequences – that other people have their own views too, and that they are not the same as our own.

Once we have developed a sense of self all the experiences we can report are filtered through it. Most of the time we do not realise this – it is only when we deliberately reflect on our selves that the sense of self becomes part of our conscious experience.

Thinking

The nuts and bolts of thinking – holding ideas in mind and manipulating them – takes place in a region of cortex on the dorsolateral (upper side) prefrontal cortex. This is also the location of the closely related activity called working memory. Planning takes place in this area, and it is here that choices are made between various possible actions.

Von Economo neurons (VENs) are long spindly cells which have been found only in human brains and those of some other primates and which seem to be crucial for social intelligence. They occur in the anterior cingulate cortex (ACC) and, in humans, in the insula. The ACC is active when people assess their own actions, especially in a social context and when we experience empathy, trust, guilt and deceit. It seems to measure what a person is doing, and the results of the action, against their goals, providing a feedback mechanism that alerts people speedily to their errors so that they can alter their actions. VENs bridge the upper part of the limbic system at the bottom of the ACC, and the cortex, and are thought to ensure that information about one's visceral reactions to what is going on are communicated to the cortex so that they can be taken into account as the conscious brain works out what to do. They are one of the mechanisms which seem to give rise to the sense of self. In the insula, which is concerned with the visceral self (monitoring our body's boundaries, and information from the internal organs) VENs may carry out a similar 'bridging' function.

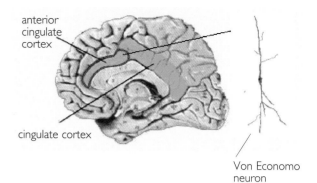

anterior cingulate cortex

cingulate cortex

Von Economo neuron

One part of the brain which is particularly concerned with monitoring our own internal states lies within the inside front edge of the longitudinal fissure, the deep chasm that runs from the front of the brain to the back. This, the anterior cingulate cortex, is sensitive to information from the body and seems to play a part in labelling stimuli as coming from outside or in. It lights up fiercely when a person feels pain, and it also becomes active when we are conscious of emotion.[16] Indeed, the picture generated by a brain experiencing physical pain is in some ways similar to one feeling emotional pain — one reason, perhaps, why the words we use to describe the two states are so often the same.

Novel actions that require choice involve more brain activity than routine ones. The scans below, left show the brain of a person choosing which words to say. The areas that are lit up are those concerned with making decisions and focusing attention. In the scans in the middle, the person has practised until the task has become routine and these areas remained switched off. On the right the person is choosing new words, so the activity returns.

Some studies suggest that each type of information has its own special temporary storage niche. An area in the upper reaches of the right hemisphere prefrontal lobe, for example, has been found to light up when a person holds information about objects that are temporarily out of sight. Another spot nearby seems to hold the memory of how many times you have done a thing before. This may be part of a sort of metamemory – the ability to 'know what you know' and to recognize when a particular activity has been 'done to death' – both of which are skills that often seem to be missing in people with frontal lobe damage.[17]

Damage to this part of the prefrontal lobe undermines a person's ability to monitor their own performance and to learn from their mistakes. It may also wreck their working memory, making them absent-minded and unable to do tasks like adding figures or doing two or three things in succession. Long-term memory may not be affected, however – it is the ability to juggle memories, not to recall them, that is likely to be worst hit.

One way in which this sort of damage may show up is by bringing about a sort of mental stasis. People in this condition have slow and blunted thought processes. They seem to be rooted in mind-ruts, unable to move in a fresh direction, even when old ways repeatedly fail to bring reward.

A test called the Wisconsin Card Sorting Task shows up this state very clearly. It involves getting participants to sort differently marked and coloured cards into categories. They are first asked to start sorting but are not told how to do it – whether by colour, shape or into equal piles. When they start putting things in piles, using whatever method they choose, the investigator at first feeds them approval. But after a while the investigator starts saying they are doing it wrong, even though the sorter is still sorting the same way. Normal people soon abandon the original sorting method and try another, at which point the inves-tigator again rewards them for a while, and then starts saying they are doing it wrong. The normal person then shifts to yet another tack, showing an overall strategy that maximizes approval. People with frontal lobe injury often fail to do this. Once they have received approval for sorting in one way they keep doing it that way even when they are told it is no longer correct. It does not take much imagination to see how the mindset that causes this will create problems for them in their daily life.

The ability to make a plan of action is useless without the ability to carry it through. One of the things that contributed to the downfall of Phineas Gage after his accident was that he made a dozen plans a day and was unable to follow any of them through. The essential requirement for following through a plan is to put aside things that are immediately attractive in favour of those that further long-term strategy. This ability seems to be located in the orbito-frontal cortex – the region that lies behind the bridge of the nose and continues beneath the bottom curve of the brain, running backwards towards its core.

As we have seen, the basic drives, urges and desires that motivate behaviour come from the unconscious brain and are essentially reflexive: automatic responses to environmental stimuli. If you see food, for example, and your hypothalamus is registering hunger, your unconscious brain prompts you to eat it.

In practice we suppress most of these urges in favour of more complicated (and ultimately beneficial) behaviour. We don't eat when we see food – we wait until we have bought it, or until it has been served on a plate and put before us on a table. If we are trying to lose weight, we may resist the temptation to eat it altogether. That way we attain long-range aims: to stay out of prison; to maintain a civilized lifestyle; to get into last year's jeans.

Children find it more difficult to resist their impulses, partly because they have yet to learn that self-control is generally a useful strategy, and also because the prefrontal lobes are very slow to

Neglect — a partial view

The patient had been left half-paralysed by a stroke, but seemed not to know it. This is a (condensed) conversation that took place between him and his doctor:

Doctor: Would you clap both your hands together, please?
(Patient lifts right hand and makes clapping motion in air, then puts it back on bed. Smiles, apparently satisfied.)
Doctor: That was just your right hand. Could you raise your left hand and do it again with them both, please?
Patient: My left hand? Oh. It is a little stiff today. My arthritis.
Doctor: Could you try to lift it though, please?
(Pause. The patient does not move.)
Doctor (repeats): Could you try to lift your left hand, please?
Patient: I did. Didn't you see it?
Doctor: I didn't. Do you think you moved it?
Patient: Of course I did. You can't have been looking.
Doctor: Would you lift it again for me, please?
(Patient does not move.)
Doctor: Are you moving it now?
Patient: Of course I am.
Doctor (indicating left hand lying on bed): What is that then?
Patient (looking): Oh, that. That is not my hand. It must belong to someone else.

The weird refusal to face facts shown by that patient is a well-recognized condition called anosognosia — a word meaning 'lack of knowledge of illness'. It is caused by damage to an area of the brain that is concerned with paying attention to one's own body. Anosognosia is

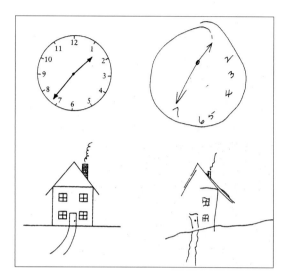

People with certain types of brain injury fail to acknowledge half of the world — everything to one side (usually the left) of their centre line of vision is ignored. The pictures above right show attempts by such a patient to reproduce the pictures on the left.

fairly common among patients who have strokes that cause left-sided paralysis. This is because the area that is affected in anosognosia nestles very close to the motor cortex, and strokes (or other injuries) that affect the right motor cortex (therefore the left body side) often affect the area that is associated with anosognosia, too. Sometimes this peculiar dissociation from half of the body comes about when there is no paralysis. Patients just behave for all the world as though everything to one side of a vertical mid-body line has ceased to exist. They forget to move the limbs on that side. If they walk, they drag the neglected leg behind them. They do not comb one side of

Brain activity switches from one hemisphere to the other as subjects turn their attention from side to side. The scans show the changes in a subject's brain as they look (left) at a visual stimulus on their left (right hemisphere lights up) and then (right) to one on their right.

their hair. Sometimes – to the extent that it is practically possible – they even forget to put clothes on half their body. The condition is one form of an intriguing condition known as neglect.

Neglect may just be for the left half of the body or it may extend to involve everything in one half of the visual field. Again, the left side is usually the half that is blanked off.

Patients with this form of neglect do not appear to see or be aware of anything to their left. They leave food on the left side of their plate, ignore people who approach them from the left and turn only to the right. If they are asked to draw a clock, they will typically draw a vague right-handed hemisphere, with all the numbers crowded on to one side.

The one-sidedness usually continues even in the person's imagination. If they are asked to close their eyes and imagine walking down a familiar street they will describe, from memory, the buildings on the right but make no mention of those on the other side. The only way to get them to describe the other side of the street is to get them to turn around in their mind's eye and walk back up the other way.[11]

To all intents and purposes people with neglect are 'blind' to half the world. But this is no ordinary blindness. The parts of the brain that deal exclusively with visual input (the primary visual areas) are invariably intact and can be seen on scans to be processing incoming images in the normal way. The blindness is at a higher level in the brain – the level at which sensory input becomes a concept rather than just a stimulus.

People with neglect do not think: 'I cannot see to my left.' Their left simply does not exist in their minds as something to think about at all. Whereas a person with 'normal' half-hemisphere blindness would compensate by turning their head and body towards the blind side in order to bring it into sight, a person with neglect never feels the need to do this. When they read they tend to start each line from the middle of the page and continue to do this even when the text is plainly nonsensical as a result. It just does not occur to them that there is anything 'leftward' to look at.

Neglect is best understood as a defect of attention – an inability of the brain to be conscious of some part of the outside world. What you are not conscious of you cannot miss – hence the patients' airy disregard for their condition. We all have a touch of visual neglect. There is a blind spot in the normal visual field that corresponds with the area of the retina where the optic nerve leaves the eye. There are no light-sensitive neurons in this spot, so there is no way that light falling on it can be registered by the brain. The disc of blankness this creates is quite big – big enough to obliterate five or six degrees of the visual field. When we look at things with both eyes each eye 'covers' for the other's blind spot. But if you shut one eye your field of vision has a blind area right in the middle.

You can demonstrate this by looking, with one eye only, at one of the crosses below. If you move the book towards your nose at some point the other cross will disappear. This does not, however, produce any conscious awareness of blindness. The impression is that the visual field is complete – an intact page, but one that does not have a cross on it.

+   +

Magicians sometimes use their knowledge of the blind spot to trick people right under their noses. In fact, it is only 'under their noses' that such disappearing tricks work because at greater distances the blind spot takes up too little of the visual field, and is too well covered by the other eye, to provide effective camouflage. They are also experts at directing attention away from things they do not want you to see, creating a temporary form of neglect.

Some cases of neglect may arise from damage to the parietal lobe, where it is thought we carry an internal map both of our own body and of the outside world. It is a sort of conceptual amputation. Others seem to be caused by a failure of attention and are asociated with damage to the frontal lobe, the cingulate cortex (the area within the deep fissure between the two hemispheres) and parts of the basal ganglia concerned with controlling movement. The particular aspect of attention that seems to be affected in neglect is the automatic turning towards a stimulus, known as orienting. Like many unconscious processes, orienting is mainly carried out by the right hemisphere of the brain. One way in which this hemisphere may specialize in orienting is by being equipped to turn attention either to the left or to the right. Therefore left-hemisphere damage generally leaves left–right orienting intact. The left hemisphere, by contrast, is thought to orient exclusively to the right, so right-brain damage leaves a person without any left-orienting facility. This is thought to be why people with right-sided brain lesions are more likely to develop neglect than those with left-hemisphere damage.

The most extreme form of anosognosia is a refusal to acknowledge total blindness. This condition is known as Anton's delusion, and people with it blunder about, apparently contained in a visual world entirely of their own construction.

At the other end of the spectrum there are subtle forms of neglect that apply to us all. The stereotypical absent-minded professor who fails to notice he is wearing non-matching socks; the workaholic husband who is staggered to return home one day to find his wife has left him; the feckless debtor who appears not to see the mounting piles of red bills – all these are examples of conceptual neglect that may have a neurological basis.

Just as a person who sees shapes more than colours may do so because they have fewer colour-sensitive neurons and more shape-sensitive ones, so the professor probably has fewer neurons in the area of brain associated with self-grooming and more in the area concerned with abstract problem solving. The workaholic may also have a neural deficit. Or perhaps he is short of the neurotransmitter (oxytocin, probably) that would stimulate the area concerned with home and family. The person who runs into debt may have less activity than others, and perhaps fewer brain cells, in their frontal lobes. Their behaviour stems directly from the way they see things.

If prompted, people can usually turn their attention to these areas — just like people with mild left-hemisphere neglect can be forced to attend to the blank side by continual challenge of the 'clap your hands' type. 'Look at it my way' is a more literal figure of speech than it at first appears to be. But unless prompted time and again, it is unlikely that the professor will think about his socks for longer than it takes to change them or that the workaholic will attend to his wife for much longer than it takes to get her back. Most of us make little effort consciously to change our view of the world, and as time goes by we allow our areas of neglect to solidify. Our view of the world may not be entirely internally generated, like people with Anton's delusion. But we are all just a little like them.

mature. Until the prefrontal lobes are fully working – which may not be until a person is in their twenties – the limbic system is the stronger force. It is therefore accurate to say that a child does not have as much free will as an adult.

The orbito-frontal cortex has rich neural connections to the unconscious brain where drives and emotions are generated. The down signals from the cortex inhibit reflex clutching and grabbing, and if you take away that control — as happens sometimes in frontal lobe injury — the unconscious retakes the body. This is seen in a bizarre condition called magnetic apraxia. Patients with this disorder automatically scan the environment for anything that catches their attention. When something does, they reach out and grasp it. Sometimes they are unable to let it go.

Orbito-frontal cortex seems, then, to be the area of the brain that bestows a quality we may refer to as free will.

Yet even this heady endowment does not make consciousness complete. Its most important component is not the ability to plan, or choose, or follow through a strategy despite the insistent urgings of our unconscious brain to chase each passing shadow. Rather it is the intuitive sense of meaning that binds our perceptions into a seamless whole and makes sense of our existence.

Can that, too, be pinpointed?

Astonishingly, it seems that it can. Meaningfulness is inextricably bound up with emotion. Depression is marked by wide-ranging symptoms but the cardinal feature of it is the draining of meaning from life. People in a severe state of depression fail to see life as a unified pattern and start instead to see it as a fragmented, incomprehensible sequence of pointless events. Social bonds are severed, normal activities seem purposeless — everything seems to be falling apart. By contrast, those in a state of mania see life as a gloriously ordered, integrated whole. Everything seems to be connected to everything else and the smallest events seem bathed in meaning. A person in this state is euphoric, full of energy and flowing with love. They are also in a state of high creativity – the connections they see between things, which are often invisible or overlooked by others, are often used by them to make new concepts.

The area of the brain that is most noticeably affected in both depression and mania is an area on the lower part of the internal surface of the prefrontal cortex – the ventromedial or subgenual cortex.[18] This, as we have seen, is the brain's emotional control centre. It is exceptionally active during bouts of mania, and inactive (along with other prefrontal areas) during depression. The connections between this region and the limbic system beneath it are very dense, closely binding the conscious mind with the unconscious, and this configuration is probably what gives it its special status: it is, if you like, the part that best incorporates the whole of our being, making sense of our perceptions and binding them into a meaningful whole.

Problems up front

Between them the various regions of the prefrontal cortex produce those qualities that we think of as most essentially human: the ability to plan, to feel emotion, to control our impulses, to make choices, and to endow our world with meaning. What, then, of those whose frontal lobes do not function as they should?

The story of Phineas Gage echoes through history because it was the first well-reported case to raise the awkward possibility that morality, free will and responsibility for one's actions were rooted literally in flesh and could be removed without removing the whole person. Since then plenty of other Gages have been discovered, though none has come about their injuries in quite such a sensational way. Most of them, in fact, are victims of common or garden cerebral accidents like strokes. There are also many cases of people who never gain the 'higher' qualities of mind because of developmental brain damage.

J.P. is a classic case. As a young boy he had a normal IQ and could, when he wanted to, do most things – including school work – as well as any other boy of his age. His social behaviour, however, was monstrous. He lied, cheated and stole. Once he borrowed a glove, defecated into it, then returned it to its owner. He seemed to have no grasp of the fundamental concepts of sportsmanship. As he grew up his behaviour took him predictably in and out of various prisons and psychiatric hospitals, picking up the usual labels – schizophrenia, mania, psychopath – along the way.

When he was about twenty J.P. came to the attention of neurologists S.S. Ackerly and Arthur Benton. They noted he had a complete absence of anxiety, incapacity for insight and an inability to learn from punishment. They described him as having 'an unawareness of his total life situation involving todays and tomorrows'.

Brain imaging – using a now obsolete technique in which air was injected into the brain to show up any cavities and an exploratory operation revealed something very much amiss in J.P.'s brain. His left frontal lobe was severely shrunken – and the right lobe was missing altogether. Ackerly and Benton followed J.P. for 30 years. Their final report, written when J.P. was 50, described him as 'the same uncomplicated, straightforward, outrageously boastful little boy he was at 20'. They concluded that their patient was 'a very simplified human organism with only rudimentary mechanisms for social adjustment'. Their final words were: 'J.P. has been a stranger in this world, without knowing it.'[19]

Catastrophic frontal lobe injury like that found in J.P. is rare, but prefrontal dysfunction is common to many conditions. Depression and mania, as we have seen, are marked by changes of activity in this area and so is schizophrenia. Indeed, scans of depressed people and withdrawn schizophrenics have many similarities as do those of schizophrenics and people with acute mania.[20] Mania –

Could a Computer Ever Understand?

Sir Roger Penrose
*Rouse Ball Professor of Mathematics,
University of Oxford*

Few would claim that the machines we use today have much, or even any, understanding – but there are many who argue that it is only a matter of time before computers, or computer-controlled robots, will possess genuine intelligence and therefore really know what they are doing. Indeed, those who hold to what has come to be known as 'strong Artificial Intelligence' (AI) think that machines will eventually possess all the attributes – consciousness, self-awareness, the ability to reflect and so on – that we now think of as essentially human. If they are right, it would mean that understanding, along with all those other human qualities, is something that can be achieved by working things out rather than as a result of some other process or phenomenon.

It seems clear to me that understanding is something that requires awareness – to be fully aware of a situation is the first step to understanding it. A lot of number-crunching may create the appearance of understanding and, conversely, true understanding may circumvent a lot of computation – but the two things are no substitute for one another, rather they are complementary.

I do not think that non-biological machines can ever cross the chasm between computation and understanding. To explain understanding I believe we have to step outside the conventional framework of our present day material world and look to a new physical picture that incorporates the quantum universe – a state whose mathematical structure is largely unknown. This does not mean that understanding has no connection with the brain – in fact, I think there is a specific component of brain tissue that gives rise to it.

The human body contains structures called microtubules – tiny tubes that are especially prevalent in nerve cells. Those in brain cells could, I propose, give rise to a stable quantum state that would bind the activity of brain cells throughout the cerebrum and in doing so give rise to consciousness. Such a state could not be replicated in a computer.

The arguments that underlie my proposal are complicated and some are admittedly speculative. Beneath the technicality I have a strong feeling that it is obvious that the conscious mind cannot work like a computer. That feeling, which comes more easily to children than adults, is surely something that a computer could never have.

CONSCIOUSNESS —
NOT A THING BUT A PROCESS

FRANCIS CRICK
*Salk Institute of Biological Studies,
San Diego*

Francis Crick was awarded the Nobel Prize in 1962 for his discovery, with James Watson, of the molecular structure of DNA. Since then he has turned to another huge scientific challenge.

The explanation of consciousness is one of the major unsolved problems of modern science. Indeed, the overwhelming question in neurobiology today is the relation between the mind and the brain. In the past the mind (or soul) was regarded as something separate from the brain but interacting with it in some way. But most neuroscientists now believe that all aspects of the mind, including its most puzzling attribute, consciousness or awareness, are likely to be explainable in a more materialistic way as the behaviour of large sets of interacting neurons. As William James, the father of American psychology, said a century ago: consciousness is not a thing but a process.

Until recently, however, most cognitive scientists and neuroscientists felt that consciousness was either too philosophical or just too elusive to study experimentally. But in my opinion, such timidity is ridiculous. I believe that the only sensible approach is to press the experimental attack until we are confronted with dilemmas that call for new ways of thinking.

The major question that neuroscience must answer is as follows: What are the differences between the active neuronal processes in our heads that correlate with consciousness and those that don't? Are the neurons involved of any particular type? What — if anything — is special about their connections and firing?

Although, in the long run, an all-embracing theory taking in emotion, imagination, dreams, mystical experiences and so on will be necessary, my work assumes that all the different aspects of consciousness employ a basic common mechanism (or perhaps a few such mechanisms). I hope that understanding the mechanism for one aspect will go most of the way to helping us understand them. So my colleague Christof Koch and I, thinking it wise to begin with the aspect of consciousness likely to yield most easily, selected the mammalian visual system because firstly humans are very visual animals and secondly because so much work has already been done on it.

I hold that the biological usefulness of visual consciousness in humans is to produce the best current interpretation of the visual scene in light of past experience (either our own, or that of our ancestors embodied in our genes), and to make this interpretation directly available for a sufficient time to the parts of the brain that contemplate and plan voluntary motor output such as movement or speech.

But there actually seem to be two systems: the rapid acting 'on-line' or unconscious system and the slower, conscious 'seeing system'. To be aware of an object or even an event the brain has to construct a multilevel (for example, lines, eyes, faces), explicit, symbolic interpretation of part of the visual scene. A representation of an object or event will usually consist of representations of many of the relevant aspects of it, which are likely to be distributed over different parts of the visual system. Much neural activity is needed for the brain to construct a representation, most of which is probably unconscious.

The term 'visual consciousness' almost certainly covers a variety of processes. When one is actually looking at a visual scene the experience is very vivid, whereas the visual images produced by trying to remember the same scene are much less vivid or detailed. I am concerned here mainly with the normal, vivid, experience. Some form of very short-term memory seems almost essential for consciousness but this memory may be very transient, lasting for only a fraction of a second. Psychophysical evidence for short-term memory suggests that if we do not pay attention to some aspect of the visual scene, our memory of it is very transient and can be overwritten by subsequent visual stimulus.

Although working memory expands the time frame of consciousness it is not obvious that it is essential. Rather it seems to be a mechanism for bringing an item or a small sequence of items into vivid consciousness, by speech or silent speech. In a similar way, episodic memory, enabled by the hippocampal system, is not essential for consciousness but a person is severely handicapped without it.

Consciousness, then, is enriched by visual attention, though attention is not essential for visual consciousness to occur. Attention is either caused by sensory input or by the planning parts of the brain. Visual attention can be directed to a location in the visual field or to one or more moving objects. The exact neural mechanisms that achieve this are still being debated. But in order to interpret visual input the brain must arrive at a coalition of neurons whose firing represents the best interpretation of the visual scene, often in competition with other possible but less likely interpretations.

in behavioural terms – is the 'sunny' side of paranoia – a state in which everything seems to be linked together in some grand scheme. The paranoid delusions of schizophrenia also revolve around mysterious linkages, but the grand scheme is usually sinister rather than glorious. Autism, too, is associated with abnormal prefrontal activity. More controversially frontal lobe dysfunction has been linked to aggressive and violent behaviour. Imaging studies of prisoners have found that a significant number have abnormalities in these lobes – and psychiatrist Itzhak Fried, of the University of California Los Angeles Medical School, has proposed that prefrontal dysfunction might explain the behaviour of men who turn into monsters. As he wrote in The Lancet:

'Repeatedly throughout history, groups of individuals, usually young men, have violently attacked other members of society often with the approval of and encouragement from, those in authority. The victims are usually defenceless and are no direct threat to the attackers. Some of the notable manifestations of the phenomenon in this century are the killing of Armenians by Turks in 1915–1916, of European Jews during World War II, of Cambodians during the Pol Pot regime and the ethnic killings in Rwanda in the 1990s. Civil strife, extreme conditions, and ethnic conflict have often had a role in these events, much as poverty and lack of hygiene lead to outbreaks of infectious disease. Yet these events would not have happened without a distinct transformation in the behaviour of individuals.'[21]

Fried suggests that the transformation, which he dubs Syndrome E, is brought about by spasms of overactivity in the orbito-frontal and medial prefrontal cortices. This creates heavy neural down traffic from the cortex, which inhibits the amygdala and prevents emotion from rising to consciousness. In this state people with Syndrome E – typically young men, according to Fried – can carry out horrific acts of violence without being assailed by normal feelings of fear and disgust.

After the spasm of hyperarousal the prefrontal cortex falls back, exhausted, into a state of underarousal that precludes normal reflection and self-awareness and thus prevents those with the syndrome from acknowledging the awfulness of what they have done.

The involvement of prefrontal dysfunction in monstrously aberrant behaviour like that cited by Fried is as yet unproven. It is, however, known to cause a certain type of compulsiveness, which can lead to antisocial acts. French neurologist François L'Hermitte has investigated a number of people with damaged or partially missing frontal lobes and all of them, he reports, have one thing in common: when confronted by some cue that suggests they should do something, they seem to be compelled to go ahead and do it. In many of them this shows up as a compulsion to steal: if a purse is left lying unguarded, or a car unlocked, it is, to them, just *demanding* to be taken.

L'Hermitte christened this type of compulsion 'environment dependency syndrome'. In an imaginative series of experiments with two frontal lobotomy patients, he demonstrated just how extreme this automatic obeisance to outside stimuli can be.

In one experiment L'Hermitte invited two of the patients to his home and, without explanation, ushered the first one, a man, into a bedroom. The bed was made up with the top sheet turned down ready for use as in a hotel room. When the patient saw this he immediately got undressed (including removing his toupee), got into bed and prepared to go to sleep, even though it was the middle of the day.

When the patient had been gently persuaded to get up again, L'Hermitte ushered a second patient, a woman, into the room. When she saw the (by now rumpled) bed she, too, went straight to it. But instead of getting in she started to make it. In neither case had the patients' actions been suggested by any word of encouragement or instruction. The actions seemed to be the result of pre-programming. The fact that the first patient got in the

bed while the second patient made it presumably reflected something about male/female role playing rather than a fundamental difference in information processing!

In another study, L'Hermitte took one of the patients to another room and said, just before he opened the door, the single word 'museum'. As soon as the patient entered he started to examine the paintings on the wall, just as if he were in a museum. Halfway down the wall there was an obvious gap, where a picture was missing. Nearby L'Hermitte had placed a hammer, nails and, leaning on the wall beneath, the missing picture. The patient, again without any conversation or instruction, picked up the hammer, banged a nail in the wall and hung the picture.[22]

Although people with frontal lobe damage respond to cues in idiosyncratic or preconditioned ways, some reactions are very common. Men with frontal damage (particularly to the part of the brain just above the eyes) often exhibit sexual inhibition or aggression in response to what they see as sexual cues. A recent, rather touching, case of this occurred in a man who was injured in a road accident and was subsequently unable to stop himself proposing to women. He asked one woman to marry him within three days of meeting her and another woman received a proposal during their first telephone call. The judge who heard the man's subsequent claim for damages described him as having changed from a loveable and gentle man to a 'sexual, over-forceful pest who will not take no for an answer'. He also noted that the man had become totally irresponsible with money – buying things like a child, then casting them aside. The £2-million compensation he was awarded is held for him by a state-appointed guardian.[23]

Clearly, these modern-day Phineas Gages do not choose their fate – it is foisted on them by accident or illness. By any normal meaning of the word they cannot be said to possess free will.

So can – or should – they be held responsible

for their actions?

The debate (mad or bad?) is ancient and well rehearsed. Does this new science of brain exploration add anything new to it? Surely, yes.

At the moment our legal and moral code is founded on the assumption that each of us contains an independent 'I' – the ghost in the machine that controls our actions. This notion is essentially the same as the dualism first formalized by Descartes. It has endured largely because it *feels* right – how else could mere flesh and blood produce experiences like love, meaning, passion and reverence?

So long as our feelings and actions emerged as though by magic from the black box of our brains it was inevitable that the intuitive explanation of mind would prevail, and as a working hypothesis it has done us proud for centuries. But now that the black box has been opened dualism is fast becoming difficult to sustain. As the studies in this book show, when we look inside the brain we see that our actions follow from our perceptions and our perceptions are constructed by brain activity. In turn, that activity is dictated by a neuronal structure that is formed by the interplay of our genes and the environment. There is no sign of some Cartesian antennae tuned into another world.

Many people baulk at the idea that our actions are entirely mechanistic and some envisage a doomsday scenario if it ever caught on. If people could not be held responsible for their behaviour, they argue, we would all abandon any attempt at responsibility and fall into passive fatalism, acting carelessly on every urge without constraint.

One answer to this is that yes, perhaps we would – if we *could*. But the machine does not work that way. As we have seen, some illusions are programmed so firmly into our brains that the mere knowledge that they are false does not stop us from seeing them. Free will is one such illusion. We may accept rationally that we are machines but we will continue to feel and to act as though the essential part of us is free of mechanistic imperatives.

The illusion of free will may have evolved because it functions as an internal police force. By creating the sense of a self-determining 'I', it encourages us to punish those who offend us, and also to see brain dysfunctions as weaknesses of some non-material 'self' rather than as illnesses of the body. These distorted views were probably useful once because they would have driven antisocial and ailing people away from the tribe. Now they just cause pain.

It seems unlikely to me that we will continue to punish people for misconduct when the crossed wires that spark their behaviour become as clear to see as a broken bone. Rather, I hope (and expect) we will use our knowledge of the brain to develop treatments for sick brains that will be infinitely more effective than the long-winded, hit-and-miss psychological therapies we use today. Restraint could then be used only when such treatment fails, or for those who would rather lose their liberty than their old habits.

I also hope that the ability to modulate brains will be used more widely to enhance those mental qualities that give sweetness and meaning to our lives, and to eradicate those that are destructive. Such an idea reeks of hubris today but future generations, I think, will be less frightened of taking control of our minds as we now seek to control our bodies. Far from diminishing human existence, I believe that this could make our lives immeasurably better.

The findings outlined in this book give only the sketchiest impression of the landscape of the mind – the task of creating a detailed picture stretches far into the future. Yet I believe one thing is already clear: there is no ghost in this place, no monsters in the depths, no lands ruled by dragons. What today's mind voyagers are discovering is instead a biological system of awe-inspiring complexity. There is no need for us to satisfy our sense of wonder by conjuring phantoms – the world within our heads is more marvellous than anything we can dream up.

References

Chapter One

1. George Coombe, *Elements of Phrenology* (MA, Marsh, Capen and Lyon, 1834)
2. Itzhak Fried, 'Electrical current stimulates laughter', *Nature*, 391:6668 (1998), 650
3. Carlyle Jacobsen and John Fulton, Yale University, lecture at the Second International Congress of Neurology, London, 1935
4. Edward Shorter, *A History of Psychiatry; From the Era of the Asylum to the Age of Prozac* (New York, John Wiley, 1997), 228
5. Ibid.
6. H. Mayberg, A. Lozano, V. Voon, H. McNeely, D. Seminowicz, C. Hamani, J. Schwalb, S. Kennedy. *Brain Stimulation for Treatment-Resistant Depression.* Neuron, 45 (2005), 651–660
7. B. D. Greenberg, D. A. Malone, G. M. Friehs, A. R. Rezai, C. S. Kubu, P. F. Malloy, S. P. Salloway, M. S. Okun, W. K. Goodman & S. A. Rasmussen. *Three–Year Outcomes in Deep Brain Stimulation for Highly Resistant Obsessive-Compulsive Disorder.* Neuropsychopharmacology 31 (2006), 2384–2393
8. M. A. Persinger. *The Neuropsychiatry of Paranormal Experiences.* The Journal of Neuropsychiatry & Clinical Neurosciences. 13 (2001), 515–524
9. E. S. Bromberg-Martin & O. Hikosaka. *Midbrain Dopamine Neurons Signal Preference for Advance Information about Upcoming Rewards.* Neuron. 63 (2009), 119–126
10. R. Marsh, A. J. Gerber & B. S. Peterson. *Neuroimaging studies of normal brain development and their relevance for understanding childhood neuropsychiatric disorders.* Journal of the American Academy of Child and Adolescent Psychiatry. 47 (2008), 1233–1251
11. Daniel Pendick, 'The New Phrenologists', *New Scientist*, 155:2091 (1997), 34–47
12. J. S. Peper, R. M. Brouwer, D. I. Boomsma, R. S. Kahn & H. E. Hulshoff Pol. *Genetic Influences on Human Brain Structure:A Review of Brain Imaging Studies in Twins.* Human Brain Mapping. 28 (2007), 464–473
13. F. N. Haque, I. I. Gottesman & A. H. C. Wong. *Not Really Identical: Epigenetic differences in Monozygotic Twins and Implications for Twin Studies in Psychiatry.* American Journal of Medical Genetics Part C: Seminars in Medical Genetics 151C (2009), 136–141
14. J.M. Tanner, *Foetus into Man; Physical Growth from Conception to Maturity* (Ware, Castlemead Publications, 1989), 113
15. British Nutrition Foundation, Institute of Food Research report, January 1998
16. G. K. Beauchamp & J. A. Mennella. *Early Flavor Learning and its Impact on Later Feeding Behaviour.* Journal of Pediatric Gastroenterology and Nutrition. 48 (2009), 25–30
17. S. Baron-Cohen, S. I. Lutchmaya & R. Knickmeyer. *Prenatal Testosterone in Mind: Amniotic Fluid Studies – the effect of prenatal levels of testosterone on development and behavior up to age 4.* MIT Press, 2006
18. R. Seidl, B. Bidmon, M. Bajo, B. C. Yoo, N. Cairns, E. C. LaCasse & G. Lubec. *Evidence for Apoptosis in the Fetal Down Syndrome.* Journal of Child Neurology. 16 (2001), 438–442
19. S. J. M. C. Palmen, H. van Engeland, P. R. Hof & C. Schmitz. *Neuropathological Findings in Autism.* Brain. 127 (2004)
20. Joseph LeDoux, *The Emotional Brain* (New York, Simon and Schuster, 1996)
21. Ibid.
22. P. O. McGowan, A. Sasaki, A. C. D. Alessio, S. Dymov, B. Labonte, M. Szyf, G. Turecki & M. J. Meaney. *Epigenetic regulation of the glucocorticoid receptor in human brain associates with childhood abuse.* Nature Neuroscience. 12 (2009), 342–348
23. Tanner, *Foetus into Man*
24. A. D. Friederici. The neural basis of language development and its impairment. Neuron. 52 (2006), 941–952
25. M. Beckman. *Crime, Culpability and the Adolescent Brain.* Neuroscience. 305 (2004), 596–599
26. C.D Frith, K.J. Friston, P.F. Liddle, & R.S. J. Frackowiak, Willed action and the prefrontal cortex

in man: a study with PET. Proceedings of the Royal Society of London, Series B, 244, (1991) 241-246

27. J & B. Wilgus. Face to Face with Phineas Gage. Journal of the History of the Neurosciences . 18 (2009) 340–345

28. J.M. Harlow, 'Recovery from the passage of an iron bar through the head', Publications of the Massachusetts Medical Society, 1868, cited in Antonio R. Damasio, *Descartes' Error: Emotion, Reason and the Human Brain* (London, Picador, 1995)

29. The Edwin Smith Surgical papyrus, discovered in Luxor, 1862

30. W. Penfield and P. Perot, 'The brain's record of auditory and visual experience', *Brain*, 86 (1963), 595–696

Chapter Two

1. J. P. Szaflarski, S. K. Holland, V. J. Schmithorst & A. W. Byars. *An fMRI study of language lateralization in children and adults*. Human Brain Mapping. 27 (2006) 202–212

2. Sally P. Springer and Georg Deutsch (eds.), *Left Brain / Right Brain*, 4th edn (New York, W.H. Freeman, 1993)

3. H. W. Huang, C. L. Lee & K. D. Federmeier. *Imagine that! ERPS provide evidence for distinct hemispheric contributions to the processing of concrete and abstract concepts*. Institute of Neuroscience. 49 (2009), 1116–1123

4. Marthe J. Farah, *Visual Agnosia: Disorders of Object Recognition and What They Tell Us About Normal Vision* (Cambridge, MA, MIT Press, 1991)

5. R.C. Gur et al, 'Differences in the distribution of gray and white matter in human cerebral hemispheres', *Science*, 207:4436 (1980), 1226–8

6. M. A. S. Boksem, R. Smolders & D. De Cremer. *Social power and approach-related neural activity*. Social cognitive and affective neuroscience. 10 (2009), 1–5

7. M. Hobbs, 'A randomized controlled trial of psychological debriefing for victims of road traffic accidents', *British Medical Journal*, 313:7070 (1996), 1438–9

8. R. A. Mayou, A. Ehlers & M. Hobbs. *Psychological debriefing for road traffic accident victims. Three-year follow-up of a randomised controlled trial*. British Journal of Psychiatry. 176 (2000), 589–93

9. T. Ohnishi, H. Matsuda, T. Asada, M. Arugal, M. Hirakatal, M. Nishikawa, A. Katoh & E Imabayashi. *Functional Anatomy of Musical Perception in Musicians*. Cerebral Cortex. 11 (2001), 754–760

10. Michael S. Gazzaniga, *Nature's Mind: The Biological Roots of Thinking, Emotions, Sexuality, Language and Intelligence* (Harmondsworth, Penguin Books, 1992)

11. Richard Nisbett and Timothy Wilson, 'Telling more than we can know – verbal reports on mental processes', *Psychological Review*, 84 (1977), 231–59

12. R.W. Sperry, 'Hemispheric specialization: scope and limits', in F.O. Schmitt and Frederic G. Worden (eds.)

13. Matthew 25: 33, 34, 41

14. P.G. Hepper et al, 'Handedness in the human foetus', *Neuropsychologia*, 29:11 (1991), 1107–11

15. Luigi Gedda, Director, Gregor Mendel Institute, Rome, quoted by Lawrence Wright in 'Double mystery', *New Yorker*, 7 August 1995

16. C. Francks. *LRRTM1 on chromosome 2p12 is a maternally suppressed gene that is associated paternally with handedness and schizophrenia*. Molecular Psychiatry. 12 (2007),1129–1139

17. S. Coren and D.F. Helpern, 'Left-handedness: a marker for decreased survival fitness', *Psychological Bulletin*, 109 (1991), 90–106

18. C. S. Ruebeck, J. E. Harrington & R. Moffitt. *Handedness and Earnings*. National Bureau of Economic research Working Paper No. 12387* July 2006

19. R.W. Sperry, 'Hemisphere disconnection and unity in conscious awareness', *American Psychologist*, 23 (1968), 723–33

20. Alan J. Parkin, *Explorations in Cognitive Neuropsychology* (Oxford, Blackwell, 1996)

21. Alan J. Parkin, 'The alien hand', in Peter W. Halligan and John C. Marshall (eds.), *Method in Madness: Case Studies in Cognitive Neuropsychiatry* (Hove, Psychology Press, 1996)

22. Parkin in Halligan and Marshall

23. R. Leiguardia, S. Starkstein, M. Nogues, M. Berthier and R. Arbelaiz, 1993, cited in Halligan and Marshall

24. Joseph LeDoux, D.H. Wilson and Michael Gazzaniga, 'A divided mind', *Annals of Neurology*, 2 (1977), 417–21

25. R.W. Sperry, 'Brain bisection and consciousness', in

John C. Eccles (ed.), *How the Self Controls Its Brain* (New York, Springer-Verlag, 1966)

26. Savic et al, *PET and MRI show differences in cerebral asymmetry and functional connectivity between homo- and heterosexual subjects*, PNAS , pp.106 (51), (2009)

Chapter Three

1. Peter Chadwick, *Schizophrenia – the Positive Perspective* (London, Routledge, 1997)
2. E. Gerard & B. S. Peterson. *Developmental processes and brain imaging studies in Tourette syndrome.* Journal of Psychosomatic Research. 55 (2003), 13–22
3. R. S. Baltimore & H. B. Jenson. *Infectious diseases and immunization: Pediatric autoimmune neuropsychiatric disorders associated with streptococci (PANDAS).* Current Opinion in Pediatrics. 21 (2009), 127–130
4. Richard Restak, *Brainscapes: An Introduction to What Neuroscience Has Learned About the Structure, Function and Abilities of the Brain* (New York, Hyperion, 1995), 106
5. Tourette newsgroup posting on the Internet, January 1998
6. Obsessive–compulsive disorder (OCD) newsgroup posting on the Internet, January 1998
7. Restak, *Brainscapes*, 107
8. OCD newsgroup posting on the Internet, January 1998
9. Frederick Toates, *Obsessional Thoughts and Behaviour* (Thorsons, 1990)
10. Phyllida Brown, 'Over and over', *New Scientist*, 155:2093 (1997), 27
11. Kenneth Blum et al, 'Reward deficiency syndrome, *American Scientist*, 84 (1996)
12. John J. Ratey and Catherine Johnson (eds.), *Shadow Syndromes* (London, Bantam Press, 1997)
13. C-Y. Li, X. Mao, L. Wei. *Genes and (Common) Pathways Underlying Drug Addiction.* PLoS Computational Biology. 4 (2008), 28–34
14. WHO Global Obesity forecast, 2005
15. A. Rothenberger et al, 'What happens to electrical brain activity when anorectic adolescents gain weight', *European Archives of Psychiatry and Clinical Neurosurgery*, 240:3 (1991), 144–7
16. Wagne et al: *Altered Reward Processing in Women Recovered from Anorexia Nervosa* Am J Psychiatry 164:1842–1849, December 2007

17. Kaye Weltzin, 'Serotonin activity in anorexia and bulimia', *Journal of Clinical Psychiatry*, 52, supplement (1991), 41–8
18. Wallin G. van der Ster et al, 'Selective dieting patterns among anorectics and bulimics', *European Eating Disorders Review*, 2 (1994), 221–32
19. Y. Oomura, S. Aou, Y. Koyama and H. Yoshimatsu, 'Central control of sexual behaviour', *Brain Research Bulletin*, 20 (1988), 863–870
20. B. R. Komisaruk, C. Beyer & B. Whipple. *Orgasm.* The Psychologist. Volume 21 Part 2 February 2008
21. B. R. Komisaruk, C. Beyer-Flores & B. Whipple. *The science of orgasm.* Baltimore, MD: Johns Hopkins University Press. (2006)
22. J. R. Georgiadis, R. Kortekaas, R. Kuipers, A. Nieuwenburg, J. Pruim, A. A. T. S. Reinders & G. Holstege. *Regional cerebral blood flow changes associated with clitorally induced orgasm in healthy women.* European Journal of Neuroscience. 24 (2006), 3305–3316
23. A. Bartels & S. Zeki. *The Neural Correlates of Maternal and Romantic Love.* Neuroimage. 21 (2004), 1155–1166
24. Jerome Goodman, Columbia University, quoted by Michael S. Gazzaniga, *Nature's Mind: The Biological Roots of Thinking, Emotions, Sexuality, Language and Intelligence* (Harmondsworth, Penguin Books, 1992), 155
25. Simon LeVay, *The Sexual Brain* (Cambridge, MA, MIT Press, 1994), 102
26. Ibid.
27. D. L. Cohen & J. Belsky. *Avoidant romantic attachment and female orgasm: testing an emotion-regulation hypothesis.* Attachment & human development. 10 (2008), 1–10
28. Savic et al PET and MRI show differences in cerebral asymmetry and functional connectivity between homo- and heterosexual subjects PNAS July 8, 2008 vol. 105 no. 27 9403–9408
29. Louis R. Franzini and John Grossberg (eds.), *Eccentric and Bizarre Behaviours* (New York, John Wiley, 1995)
30. F.R. Farnham, 'Pathology of love', *The Lancet*, 350:9079 (1997), 710
31. R. Swerdlow & J. Burns. University of Virginia in Charlottesville, USA case report to American Neurology Association meeting New York, October 2002

32. Susan Greenfield (ed.), *The Human Mind Explained: The Control Centre of the Living Machine* (London, Cassell, 1996)

33. A. Nystrand, 'New discoveries on sex differences in the brain', National Institute of Ageing, NIH Bethseda, *Lakartidningen* 93:21 (1996), 2071–3

Chapter Four

1. Antonio R. Damasio, *Descartes' Error: Emotion, Reason and the Human Brain* (London, Picador, 1995)

2. J. Coid, *Prevalence and correlates of psychopathic traits in the household population of Great Britain*, International Journal of Law and Psychiatry, Volume 32, Issue 2, pp. 65–73 (2009)

3. Jackson et al, *How do we perceive the pain of others? A window into the neural processes involved in empathy*, NeuroImage, Volume 24, Issue 3, pp. 771–779 (2005)

4. Tamietto et al. Proc. Natl Acad. Sci. USA http://dx.doi:10.1073/pnas.0908994106 (2009)

5. Paul Ekman, quoted in *New Scientist* 'Emotions' supplement, 150:2027 (1996), 11.

6. Paul Frank and Paul Ekman, 'Behavioural markers and recognizability of smile of enjoyment', *Journal of Personality and Social Psychology*, 64:1 (1993), 83–93

7. B. Kolb et al, 'Developmental changes in the recognition and comprehension of facial expression: implications for frontal lobe function', *Brain and Cognition*, 20 (1992), 74–84

8. J.S. Morris et al, 'A differential neural response in the human amygdala to fearful and happy facial expressions', letter to *Nature*, 383:6603 (1997), 812–15

9. Tranel, Gullickson, Koch, Adolphs, Cogn Neuropsychiatry (3), pp.219–32, University of Iowa College of Medicine (2006)

10. Ekman, *New Scientist*

11. Ibid.

12. U. Hess et al, 'The facilitative effect of facial expression on the self-generation of emotion', *International Journal of Psychophysiology*, 12:3 (1992), 251–65

13. Interview on *Woman's Hour*, BBC Radio 4, 25 February 1998

14. Ibid

15. *Can you be blamed for sleepwalking crimes?*, New Scientist, 24 November 2009

16. Claudio Bassetti, The Lancet, *SPECT during sleepwalking*, Vol. 356, Issue 9228, pages 484–485, (August 2000)

17. Milad et al, *Fear extinction in rats: Implications for human brain imaging and anxiety disorders*, Biological Psychology, Volume 73, Issue 1, pp. 61–71 (2006)

18. Andrew Young and Kate Leafhead, 'Cotard's delusion' in Peter W. Halligan and John C. Marshall (eds.), *Method in Madness: Case Studies in Cognitive Neuropsychiatry* (Hove, Psychology Press, 1996)

19. E. A. Murray, *The amygdala, reward and emotion*, Trends in Cognitive Sciences Volume 11, Issue 11, pp. 489–497, (2007)

20. Drevets et al, *Subgenual prefrontal cortex abnormalities in mood disorders* Nature 386, pp. 824–7, (1997)

21. Mayberg HS, Brannan SK, Tekell JL, Silva JA, Mahurin RK, McGinnis S, Jerabek PA. *Regional metabolic effects of fluoxetine in major depression: serial changes and relationship to clinical response*, Biol Psychiatry 48, pp 830–43 (2000)

22. Mayberg et al, *Deep brain stimulation for treatment-resistant depression*, Neuron 45, pp. 651–60, (2005)

23. Michael Posner and Marcus E. Raichle (eds.), *Images of Mind* (New York, W.H. Freeman, 1994)

24. Wayne Drevets et al, 'Subgenual prefrontal cortex abnormalities in mood disorder', letter to *Nature*, 386: 6527 (1997), 824–7

Chapter Five

1. V. S. Ramachandran, D. Brang. *Tactile-emotion synesthesia*. Neurocase. 14 (2008), 390–399

2. Daniel J Levitin. *This is Your Brain on Music*. Atalantic Books. 2008

3. P. Schneider, M. Scherg, H. G. Dosch, H. J. Specht, A. Gutschalk & A. Rupp. *Morphology of Heschl's gyrus reflects reflects enhanced activity in the auditory cortex of musicians*. Nature Neuroience. 5 (2002), 688–694

4. D. L. Strait, N. Kraus, E. Skoe & R. Ashley. *Musical experience and neural efficiency – effects of training on subcortical processing of vocal expressions of emotion*. European Journal of Neuroscience. 29 (2009), 661–668

5. Nabakov, Vladimir, *Speak, Memory* (London, 1967, Weidenfeld & Nicolson)

6. S. Witelson, D. Kigar, T. Harvey. *The exceptional brain of Albert Einstein*. The Lancet. 353 (1999), 2149–2153

7. A.M. Sillito in Richard L. Gregory (ed.), *The Oxford Companion to the Mind* (Oxford University Press, 1987)

8. Spector et al, *Synaesthesia, a new approach to understanding the development of perception*, Development Psychology (2009) Vol. 45, pp175–189

9. J. Ward, D. Thompson-Lake, R. Ely & F. Kaminski. *Synaesthesia, creativity and art, what is the link?* British Journal of Psychology. 99 (2008), 127–141

10. M. J. Banissy & J. Ward. *Mirror-touch synesthesia is linked with empathy*. Nature Neuroscience. 10 (2007), 815–817

11. K. Patterson and J. Hodges in Alan D. Baddeley et al (eds.), *Handbook of Memory Disorders* (Chichester, John Wiley, 1996)

12. Glyn W. Humphreys and M. Jane Riddoch, *The Fractionation of Visual Agnosia in Visual Object Processing* (London, Lawrence Erlbaum Associates, 1997)

13. L.D. Kartsounis and Tim Shallice, 'Modality specific semantic knowledge loss for unique items', *Cortex*, 32:1 (1996), 109–19

14. G. Gainotti et al, *Cognitive Neuropsychology*, 13 :3 (1996), 357–89

15. Prosopagnosia website

16. J.E. McNeil and E.K. Warrington, 'Prosopagnosia: a reclassification', *Quarterly Journal of Experimental Psychology, A*, 43:2 (1991), 267–87

17. Tim Shallice, *From Neuropsychology to Mental Structure* (Cambridge University Press, 1989), 390

18. G. Gianotti. *Face familiarity, the right temporal lobe and the possible underlying neural mechanisms*. Brains Research Reviews. 56 (2007) 214–235

19. G. Blount, 'Dangerousness of patients with Capgras syndrome', *Nebraska Medical Journal*, 71 (1986), 207

20. T. Canli. *Functional Brain Mapping of Extraversion and Neuroticism: Learning From Individual Differences in Emotion Processing*. Journal of Personality. 72 (2004), 1105–1132

21. R. Melzack. *Phantom limbs and the concept of a neuromatrix*. Trends in Neurosciences. 13 (1990), 88–92

22. R. Melzack, 'Phantom limbs', *Scientific American* supplement, 7:1 (1997), 84

23. Steven Rose, *The Making of Memory: From Molecules to Mind* (London, Bantam Press, 1993), 103

24. Morton Schatzman, *The Story of Ruth* (London, Gerald Duckworth, 1980)

25. V. S. Ramachandran & E. L. Altschuler. *The Use of Visual feedback, in particular mirror visual feedback, in restoring brain function*. Brain. 132 (2009), 1693–1710

26. Oliver Sacks, *The Man Who Mistook His Wife for a Hat* (New York, Summit Books, 1985), 135

27. C.D. Frith, 'Functional imaging and cognitive abnormalities', *The Lancet*, 346:8975 (1995), 615–Louis R. Franzini and John Grossberg (eds.), *Eccentric and Bizarre Behaviours* (New York, John Wiley, 1995)

28. Paul Sieveking, 'Then I saw her face', *Sunday Times*, 2 November 1997

29. D. Westen et al. Emory University, report to the Annual Conference of the Society for Personality and Social Psychology Jan. 28, 2006

Chapter Six

1. Oliver Sacks, *Seeing Voices* (London, Picador, 1991), 40

2. G. Konopka, J. M. Bomar, K. Winden, G. Coppola, Z. O. Jonsson, F. Gao, S. Peng, T. M. Preuss, J. A. Wohlschlegel & D. H. Geschwind. *Human-specific transcriptional regulation of CNS development genes by FOXP2*. Nature. 462 (2009), 213–217

3. J. F. Battey et al. *Words Gestures are Translated by same brain regions*. Proceedings of the National Academy of Sciences. (2009)

4. Robert Finn, 'Different minds', *Discovery*, June 1991

5. Ursula Bellugi, 'Williams syndrome and the brain', *Scientific American*, December 1997, 42–7

6. Keysers et al. Neuron. 42 (2004), 335–346. (image ref)

7. M. Iacoboni, I. Molnar-Szakacs, V. Gallese, G. Buccino, J. C. Mazziotta & G. Rizzolatti. *Grasping the Intentions of Others with One's Own Mirror Neuron System*. PLoS Biology. 3 (2005), 1–7

8. Uta Frith, 'Autism', *Scientific American*, special issue, April 1997, 92

9. M. Dapretto et al. Nature Neuroscience. 9 (2006), 28–31

10. Hadjikhani et al. Neuroimage. 22 (2004), 1141–1150

11. Paul Fletcher et al, 'Other minds in the brain – a

functional imaging study', *Cognition*, 57 (1995), 109–28

12. Simon Baron-Cohen, 'Is there a language of the eyes?', *Visual Cognition*, 4:3 (1997), 311–31

13. Lorna Wing, 'The autistic spectrum', *The Lancet*, 350:9093 (1997), 1762

14. John J. Ratey and Catherine Johnson (eds.), *Shadow Syndromes* (London, Bantam Press, 1997), 230

15. L.W. Olsho, 'Infant frequency discrimination', *Infant Behaviour and Development*, 7 (1984), 27–35

16. Jaak Panksepp, reported in *New Scientist* 'Emotions' supplement, 150:2027 (1996)

17. A.C. North et al, 'In-store music affects product choice', *Nature*, 390:6656 (1997), 132

18. D. Strait, E. Skoe, R. Ashley & N. Kraus. *Musical Experience Promotes Subcortical Efficiency in Processing Emotional Vocal Sounds*. Annals of the New York Academy of Sciences: Neurosciences and Music III. 1169 (2009), 209–213

19. V. Gazzola, L. Aziz-Zadeh & C. Keysers. *Empathy and the somatotopic auditory mirror system in humans*. Current Biology. 16 (2006), 1824–1829

20. M. Bangert, T. Peschel, G. Schlaug, M. Rotte, D. Drescher, H. Hinrichs, H. J. Heinze & E. Altenmüllera. *Shared networks for auditory and motor processing in professional pianists: Evidence from fMRI conjunction*. NeuroImage. 30 (2006), 917–926

21. B. Mampe, A. D. Friederici, A. Christophe & A. Wermke. *Newborns' cry melody is shaped by their native language*. Current Biology. 19 (2009)

22. (1) G.A. Donnan et al, 'Identification of brain region for co-ordinating speech articulation', *The Lancet*, 349:9047 (1997), 221; (2) J.R. Binder et al, 'Human brain areas identified by fMRI', *Journal of Neuroscience*, 17:1 (1997), 353–62

23. D.V.M. Bishop, 'Listening out for subtle deficits', *Nature*, 387:6629 (1997), 129

24. J. Graham Beaumont (ed.), *The Blackwell Dictionary of Neuropsychology* (Oxford, Blackwell, 1997)

25. Alan J. Parkin, *Explorations in Cognitive Neuropsychology* (Oxford, Blackwell, 1996), 133

26. H. Goodglass and D. Kaplan, *The Boston Diagnostic Aphasia Examination* (Philadelphia, Lea and Febiger, 1983)

27. M. Kinsbourne and E.K. Warrington, 'Jargon aphasia', *Neuropsychologia*, 1 (1963), 27–37

28. Christine Temple, *The Brain* (Harmondsworth, Penguin Books, 1993), 90

29. Stephen M. Kosslyn and Oliver Koenig, *Wet Mind: The New Cognitive Neuroscience* (New York, Free Press, 1992)

30. Ralph, Sage and Ellis, 'Word meaning blindness: a new form of acquired dyslexia', *Cognitive Neurology* 13:5 (1996), 617–39

31. E. Paulesu, U. Frith et al, 'Is development dyslexia a disconnection syndrome?', *Brain*, 119 (1996), 143–7

32. Margaret Donaldson, *Human Minds: An Exploration* (Harmondsworth, Penguin Books, 1992)

33. Russ Rymer, *Genie: A Scientific Tragedy* (Harmondsworth, Penguin Books, 1993)

34. Oliver Sacks, *Seeing Voices*

35. K.H.S. Kim et al, 'Distinct cortical areas associated with native and second languages', letter to *Nature*, 388:6538 (1997), 171

Chapter Seven

1. A. Takashima, K. M. Petersson, F. Rutters, I. Tendolkar, O. Jensen, M. J. Zwarts, B. L. McNaughton & G. Fernandez. *Declarative memory consolidation in humans: A prospective functional magnetic resonance imaging study*. PNAS 103 (2006), 756–761

2. K. Nader & O. Hardt. *A Single Standard for memory: the case for reconsolidation*. Nature Reviews Neuroscience. 10 (2009), 224–234

3. Farana Vargha-Khadem et al, 'Differential effects of early hippocampal pathology on episodic and semantic memory', *Science*, 277:5324 (1997), 376–80

4. E. Maguire et al, 'Recalling routes around London: activation of the right hippocampus in taxi drivers', *Journal of Neuroscience*, 17 (1997), 7103–10

5. Elizabeth F. Loftus, *The Myth of Repressed Memory* (New York, St Martin's Press, 1994)

6. J. Ost, P-A. Granhag, J. Udell, E. R. af Hjelmsater. *Familiarity breeds distortion: The effects of media exposure on false reports concerning media coverage of the terrorist attacks in London on 7th July 2005*. Memory. 16 (2008), 76–85

7. David Schacter et al, 'Recognition memory for recently spoken words', *Neuron*, 17:2 (1996), 267–74

8. Alan D. Baddeley et al (eds.), *Handbook of Memory Disorders* (Chichester, John Wiley, 1996)

9. D. Stuss and D. Benson, 'Neuropsychological studies of the frontal lobes', *Psychological Bulletin*, 95, 3–28

10. Yadin Dudai, *The Neurobiology of Memory: Concepts, Findings, Trends* (Oxford University Press, 1989)
11. S. Harris. *Functional Neuro-imaging of Belief, Disbelief, and Uncertainty.* Annals of Neurology. 63 (2008), 141–147
12. Philip J. Hilts, *Memory's Ghost: The Nature of Memory and The Strange Tale of Mr M* (New York, Simon and Schuster, 1996)
13. Baddeley et al, *Handbook of Memory Disorders*
14. J. C. Yang, G-W. Jeong, M-S. Lee, H-K. Kang, S-J. Eun, Y-K. Kim & Y-H. Lee. *Functional MR Imaging of Psychogenic Amnesia: A Case Report.* Korean Journal of Radiology. 6 (2005), 196–199
15. A. Costello, P. C. Fletcher, R. J. Dolan, C. D. Frith & T. Shallice. *The origins of forgetting in a case of isolated retrograde amnesia following a haemorrhage: evidence from functional imaging.* Neurocase. 4 (1998), 437–446
16. Baddeley et al, *Handbook of Memory Disorders*
17. L.M. Williams, 'Recovered memories of abuse in women with documented sexual victimization histories', *Journal of Traumatic Stress*, 8, 649–73
18. J.D. Bremner et al, 'MRI-based measurement of hippocampal volume in post-traumatic stress disorder', *Biological Psychiatry*, 41 (1997), 23–32
19. G. Harrison, Pope. Jr., S. Barry, A. Bodkin & J. I. Hudson. *Tracking Scientific Interest in the Dissociative Disorders, a Study of Scientific Paper outputs 1984–2003.* Psychotherapy and Psychosomatics. 75 (2006) 19–24
20. R. Carter, *Multiplicity – the new science of Personality*, Little Brown, (2008)
21. S. Reinders, E. R. S. Nijenhuis, A. M. J. Paans, J. Korf, A. T. M. Willemsen & J. A. den Boer. *One Brain, Two selves.* NeuroImage. 20 (2003) 2119–2125
22. G. E. Tsai, D. Condie, M. T. Wu & I. W. Chang. *Functional Magnetic Resonance Imaging of Personality Switches in a Woman with Dissociative Identity Disorder.* Harvard Review of Psychiatry. 7 (1999), 119–122
23. A. Hopper, J. Ciorciari, G. Johnson, J. Spensley, A. Sergejew & C. Stough. *EEG Coherence and Dissociative Identity Disorder.* Journal of Trauma and Dissociation. 3 (2002), 75–88

Chapter Eight

1. I. I. Goldberg. *When the Brain Loses Its Self: Prefrontal Inactivation during Sensorimotor Processing.* Neuron. 50 (2006), 329–339
2. M. S. Christensen, L. Kristiansen, J. B. Rowe & J. B. Nielsen. *Action-blindsight in healthy subjects after transcranial magnetic stimulation.* PNAS. 105 (2008), 1353–1357
3. Lawrence Weiskrantz, *Blindsight: A Case Study and Its Implications* (Oxford, Clarendon Press, 1986)
4. A. Schurge, F. Pereira, A. Treisman & J. D. Cohen. *Reproducibility Distinguishes Conscious From Nonconscious Neural Representations*, Science. 2009
5. S. M. Doesburg, J. J. Green, J. J. McDonald & L. M. Ward. *Rhythms of Consciousness: Binocular Rivalry Reveals Large-Scale Oscillatory Network Dynamics Mediating Visual Perception.* PLOS. 4 (2009)
6. M. Boly, E. Balteau, C. Schnakers, C. Degueldre, G. Moonen, A. Luxen, C. Phillips, P. Peigneux, P. Maquet & S. Laureys. *Baseline brain activity fluctuations predict somatosensory perception in humans.* M. PNAS. 104 (2007), 12187–12192
7. N. Makris, S. L. Buka, J. Biederman, G. M. Papadimitriou, S. M. Hodge, E. M. Valera, A. B. Brown, G. Bush, M. C. Monuteaux, V. S. Caviness, D. N. Kennedy & L. J. Seidman. *Attention and Executive Systems Abnormalities in Adults with Childhood ADHD: A DT-MRI Study of Connections.* Cerebral Cortex. 2007
8. C. A. Heywood & R. W. Kentridge. *Affective blindsight?* Trends in Cognitive Sciences. 4 (2000), 125–126
9. T. Radil. *Anosmic and Hyposmic Olfaction – a blindsight-like phenomenon.* Towards a Science of Consciousness. Abstract no 169. (2000)
10. Daniel C. Dennett, *Consciousness Explained* (Harmondsworth, Penguin Books, 1993), 331
11. Marshall Miles, 'A description of various aspects of anencephaly', Lafayette College, USA, http://www.lafayette.edu/~loerc/miles.html
12. Kornhuber, Hans and Deeke, Luder, Hirnpotentialänderungen bei Willkürbewegungen und passiven Bewegungen des Menschen: Bereitschaftspotential und reafferente Potentiale, Pflügers Archiv für die Physiologie des Menschen und Tiere. 284 (1965), 1–17.
13. B. Libet. *Do We Have Freewill?* Journal of

Consciousness Studies. 6 (1999), 47–57.

14. J.L. Barbur et al, 'Conscious visual perception without V1', *Brain*, 116 (1993), 1293-302

15. C.D. Frith, *Schizophrenia* (Hove, Psychology Press, 1997)

16. Michael Posner and Marcus E. Raichle (eds.), *Images of Mind* (New York, W.H. Freeman, 1994)

17. D. Stuss in *The Blackwell Dictionary of Neuropsychology* (Oxford, Blackwell, 1997), 350

18. Wayne Drevets et al, 'Subgenual prefrontal cortex abnormalities in mood disorder', letter to *Nature*, 386:6527 (1997), 824-7

19. S.S. Ackerly and Arthur Benton, 'Report of a case of bilateral frontal lobe defect', *Publication of Association for Research in Neurology and Dental Disease*, 27, 479–504, cited in Antonio R. Damasio, *Descartes' Error: Emotion, Reason and the Human Brain* (London, Picador, 1995)

20. R.A. O'Connell, 'SPECT imaging study of the brain in acute mania and schizophrenia', *Journal of Neuroimaging*, 2 (1995), 101–4; also Ian Daly, 'Mania', *The Lancet*, 349:9059 (1997), 1157–9

21. Itzhak Fried, 'Syndrome E', *The Lancet*, 350:9094 (1997), 1845–7

22. François L'Hermitte, 'Human autonomy and the frontal lobes', *Annals of Neurology*, 19 (1986), 335–4

23. *Daily Telegraph* report, 8 November 1997

PICTURE CREDITS

American Journal of Neuroradiology: page 38; Corbis/ Brooks Kraft: page 125; Chris Frith: page 170; Elsevier: page 87 (both images), page 105, page 127; page 141, page 142 (top two images); page 149; MedicalRF.com/ Science Photo Library: page 196; National Academy of Sciences, U.S.A: page 20, page 26; Nature Publishing Group: page 143, page 111, page 109; Roger Harris/ Science Photo Library: page 85, page 88.
While every effort has been made to trace copyright holders, if any have inadvertently been overlooked the publishers would be happy to acknowledge them in future editions.

BIBLIOGRAPHY

Books

Aleksander, Igor *The World in My Mind, My Mind in the World: Key Mechanisms of Consciousness in People, Animals and Machines* (Exeter, Imprint Academic, 2007)

Baddeley, Alan D. *Your Memory: A User's Guide* (London, Carlton Books, 2004)
The Blackwell Dictionary of Neuropsychology (Oxford, Blackwell, 1997)
Blakemore, Colin *The Mind Machine* (London, BBC Books, 1988)
Baron-Cohen, Simon et al *Understanding Other Minds: Perspectives from Autism* (Oxford, Oxford University Press, 1999)
Broks, Paul *Into the Silent Land: Travels in* Neuropsychology (London, Atlantic Books, 2004)

Calvin, William H. *How Brains Think* (London, Weidenfeld and Nicolson, 1997)
Chadwick, Peter *Schizophrenia – The Positive Perspective* (London, Routledge, 1997)
Coombe, George *Elements of Phrenology* (MA, Marsh, Capen and Lyon, 1834)
Cytowic, Richard *Synaesthesia: A Union of the Senses* (New York, Springer-Verlag, 1989)

Damasio, Antonio R. *Descartes' Error: Emotion, Reason and the Human Brain* (London, Picador, 1995)
Dennett, Daniel C. *Consciousness Explained* (Harmondsworth, Penguin, 1993)
Donaldson, Margaret *Human Minds: An Exploration* (Harmondsworth, Penguin, 1992)
Dudai, Yadin *The Neurobiology of Memory: Concepts, Findings, Trends* (Oxford, Oxford University Press, 1989)

Eccles, John C. (ed.) *The Evolution of the Brain: Creation of the Self* (London and New York, Routledge, 1989)

Farah, Marthe J. *Visual Agnosia: Disorders of Object Recognition and What They Tell Us About Normal Vision* (Cambridge, MA, MIT Press, 1991)
Fine, Cordelia *A Mind of its Own: How the Brain Distorts and Deceives* (London, Icon Books, 2007)
Frackowiak, Richard et al (eds.) *Human Brain Function* (New York, Academic Press, 1998)
Frank, Lone *Mindfield: How Brain Science is Changing Our World* (Oxford, Oneworld, 2009)
Franzini, Louis R. and Grossberg, John (eds.) *Eccentric and Bizarre Behaviours* (New York, John Wiley, 1995)
Freeman, Walter J. *Societies of Brains: A Study in the Neuroscience of Love and Hate* (Hillsdale, NJ, Lawrence Erlbaum Associates, 1995)
Frith, Chris *Making Up the Mind: How the Brain Creates our Mental World* (Oxford, Blackwell Publishing, 2007)
Frith, Uta *Autism: Explaining the Enigma* (Oxford, Basil Blackwell, 1989)

Gardner, Howard *Frames of Mind: the Theory of Multiple Intelligences* (New York, Basic Books, 1993)
Gazzaniga, Michael S. *Nature's Mind: The Biological Roots of Thinking, Emotions, Sexuality, Language and Intelligence* (Harmondsworth, Penguin, 1992)
Goodglass, H. and Kaplan, D. *The Boston Diagnostic Aphasia Examination* (Philadelphia, Lea and Febiger, 1983)
Greenfield, Susan (ed.) *The Human Mind Explained: The Control Centre of the Living Machine* (London, Cassell, 1996)
Gregory, Richard L. (ed.) *The Oxford Companion to the Mind* (Oxford University Press, 1987)
Gregory, Richard L. *Eye and Brain,* 4th ed. (Oxford, Oxford University Press)

Halligan, Peter W. and Marshall, John C. (eds.) *Method in Madness: Case Studies in Cognitive Neuropsychiatry* (Hove, Psychology Press, 1996)
Hilts, Philip J. *Memory's Ghost: The Nature of Memory and The Strange Tale of Mr M* (New York, Simon and Schuster, 1996)
Humphreys, Glyn W. and Riddoch, M. Jane *The Fractionation of Visual Agnosia in Visual Object Processing* (London, Lawrence Erlbaum Associates, 1997)

Kosslyn, Stephen M. and Koenig, Oliver *Wet Mind: The New Cognitive Neuroscience* (New York, Free Press, 1992)
LeDoux, Joseph *Synaptic Self: How Our Brains Become Who We Are* (Penguin Books, 2003)

LeVay, Simon *The Sexual Brain* (Cambridge, MA, MIT Press, 1994)

Loftus, Elizabeth F. *The Myth of Repressed Memory* (New York, St Martin's Press, 1994)

Luria, Aleksandr *The Mind of a Mnemonist* (London, Jonathan Cape, 1969)

McGilchrist, Iain *The Master and his Emissary* (Yale University Press, 2010)

Metzinger, Thomas (ed.) *Conscious Experience* (Exeter, Imprint Academic, 1999)

Mithen, Steven *The Pre-History of the Mind* (London, Thames and Hudson, 1996)

Morton, William H. *The Cerebral Code* (Cambridge, MA, MIT Press, 1996)

Nabokov, Vladimir *Speak, Memory* (London, Weidenfeld and Nicolson, 1967)

Ojemann, G.A. *Subcortical Language* in H.A. Whitaker (ed.), *Studies in Neurolinguistics*, vol. 1 (New York, Academic Press, 1976)

Parkin, Alan J. *Explorations in Cognitive Neuropsychology* (Oxford, Blackwell, 1996)

Penrose, Roger *The Emperor's New Mind* (Oxford, Oxford University Press, 1989)

Piatelli-Palmarini M. *Inevitable Illusions* (New York, John Wiley, 1994)

Posner, Michael and Raichle, Marcus E. (eds.). *Images of Mind* (New York, W.H. Freeman, 1994)

Ratey, John J. and Johnson, Catherine (eds.) *Shadow Syndromes* (London, Bantam Press, 1997)

Redfield Jamison, Kay *Touched with Fire: Manic-depressive Illness and the Artistic Temperament* (New York, Free Press, 1995)

Rose, Steven *The Making of Memory: From Molecules to Mind* (London, Bantam Press, 1993)

Rymer, Russ *Genie: A Scientific Tragedy* (Harmondsworth, Penguin, 1993)

Sacks, Oliver *An Anthropologist on Mars* (London, Picador, 1995)

Sacks, Oliver *The Man Who Mistook His Wife for a Hat* (New York, Summit Books, 1985).

Sacks, Oliver *Seeing Voices* (London, Picador, 1991)

Schacter, Daniel, L. *The Seven Sins of Memory: How the Mind Forgets and Remembers* (New York, Mariner Books 2002)

Schatzman, Morton *The Story of Ruth* (London, Gerald Duckworth, 1980)

Schmitt, F.O. and Worden, Frederic G. (eds.) *Neuroscience: Third Study Program* (Cambridge, MA, MIT Press, 1974)

Shallice, Tim *From Neuropsychology to Mental Structure* (Cambridge, Cambridge University Press, 1989)

Shorter, Edward *A History of Psychiatry: From the Era of the Asylum to the Age of Prozac* (New York, John Wiley, 1997)

Silk, Kenneth R. *Biological and Neurobehavioural Studies of Borderline Personality Disorder* (Washington, American Psychiatric Press, 1994)

Springer, Sally P. and Deutsch, Georg (eds.) *Left Brain / Right Brain*, 4th ed (New York, W.H. Freeman, 1993)

Tanner, J.M. *Foetus into Man: Physical Growth from Conception to Maturity* (Ware, Castlemead Publications, 1989)

Temple, Christine *The Brain* (Harmondsworth, Penguin, 1993)

Toates, Frederick *Obsessional Thoughts and Behaviour* (Thorsons, 1990)

Weiskrantz, Lawrence *Blindsight: A Case Study and Its Implications* (Oxford, Clarendon Press, 1986)

Wolf, Maryanne *Proust and the Squid: The Story and Science of the Reading Brain* (Harper Perennial, 2008)

Articles and Reports

Barbur, J.L. et al 'Conscious visual perception without V1', *Brain*, 116 (1993), 1293–302

Baron-Cohen, Simon 'Is there a language of the eyes?', *Visual Cognition*, 4:3 (1997), 311–31

Bellugi, Ursula 'Williams syndrome and the brain', *Scientific American*, December 1997, 42–7

Binder, J.R. et al 'Human brain areas identified by fMRI', *Journal of Neuroscience*, 17:1 (1997), 353–62

Bishop, D.V.M. 'Listening out for subtle deficits', *Nature*, 387:6629 (1997), 129

Bisiach, E. and Luzzatti, C. 'Unilateral neglect of representational space', *Cortex*, 14, 129–33

Blount, G. 'Dangerousness of patients with Capgras syndrome', *Nebraska Medical Journal*, 71 (1986), 207

Blum, Kenneth et al 'Reward deficiency syndrome', *American Scientist*, 84 (1996)

Brambilla, Riccardo et al 'A role for the Ras signalling pathway in synaptic transmission and long-term memory', *Nature*, 390:6657 (1997), 281

Bremner, J.D. et al 'MRI-based measurement of

hippocampal volume in post-traumatic stress disorder', *Biological Psychiatry*, 41 (1997), 23–32

British Nutrition Foundation, Institute of Food Research report, January 1998

Brown, Phyllida. 'Over and over', *New Scientist*, 155:2093 (1997), 27

Cohen, Philip 'Hunting the language gene', *New Scientist*, 157:2119 (1998)

Coren, S. and Helpern, D.F. 'Left-handedness: a marker for decreased survival fitness', *Psychological Bulletin*, 109 (1991), 90–106

Cotton, Ian 'Dr Persinger's God machine', *Independent on Sunday*, 2 July 1995

Cytowik, Richard. 'Synaesthesia: phenomenology and neurophysiology', *Psyche*, 2:10 (1995)

Daily Telegraph report, 8 November 1997

Damasio, Antonio R. 'Neuropsychology: towards a neuropathology of emotion and mood', *Nature*, 386:6527 (1997), 769

Donnan, G.A. et al 'Identification of brain region for co-ordinating speech articulation', *The Lancet*, 349:9047 (1997), 221

Drevets, Wayne et al 'Subgenual prefrontal cortex abnormalities in mood disorder', letter to *Nature*, 386:6527 (1997), 824-7

Farnham, F.R. 'Pathology of love', *The Lancet*, 350:9079 (1997), 710

Finn, Robert 'Different minds', *Discovery*, June 1991

Fischer and Frederikson 'Extraversion, neuroanatomy and brain function – a PET study of personality', *Personality and Individual Differences*, 23, 345–52

Fletcher, Paul et al 'Other minds in the brain – a functional imaging study', *Cognition*, 57 (1995), 109–28

Forstl, H. and Beats, B. 'Charles Bonnet's description of Cotard's delusion and reduplicative paramnesia in an elderly patient (1788)', *British Journal of Psychiatry*, 160 (1992) 416–18

Frank, Paul and Ekman, Paul 'Behavioural markers and recognizability of smile of enjoyment', Journal of Personality and Social Pychology, 64:1 (1993), 83–93

Fried, Itzhak 'Electrical current stimulates laughter', *Nature*, 391:6668 (1998), 650

Fried, Itzhak 'Syndrome E', *The Lancet*, 350:9094 (1997), 1845–7

Frith, C.D. et al 'Functional imaging and cognitive abnormalities', *The Lancet*, 346:8975 (1995), 615–20

Frith, Uta 'Autism', *Scientific American*, special issue, April 1997, 92

Gainotti, G. et al *Cognitive Neuropsychology*, 13:3 (1996), 357–89

Gur R.C. et al 'Differences in the distribution of gray and white matter in human cerebral hemispheres', *Science*, 207:4436 (1980), 1226–8

Hepper, P.G. et al 'Handedness in the human foetus', *Neuropsychologia*, 29:11 (1991), 1107–11

Hess, U. et al 'The facilitative effect of facial expression on the self-generation of emotion', *International Journal of Psychophysiology*, 12:3 (1992), 251–65

Hobbs M. 'A randomized controlled trial of psychological debriefing for victims of road traffic accidents', *British Medical Journal*, 313:7070 (1996), 1438–9

Hohman, G. et al 'Some effects of spinal cord lesions on feelings', *Psychophysiology*, 3 (1966), 143–56

Kartsounis, L.D. and Shallice, Tim 'Modality specific semantic knowledge loss for unique items', *Cortex*, 32:1 (1996), 109–19

Katz, Joel 'Phantom limb pain', *The Lancet*, 350:9088 (1997), 1338

Kim, K.H.S. et al 'Distinct cortical areas associated with native and second languages', letter to *Nature*, 388:6538 (1997), 171

Kinsbourne, M. and Warrington, E.K. 'Jargon aphasia', *Neuropsychologia*, 1 (1963), 27–37

Kolb, B. et al 'Developmental changes in the recognition and comprehension of facial expression: implications for frontal lobe function', *Brain and Cognition*, 20 (1992), 74–84

L'Hermitte, François 'Human autonomy and the frontal lobes', *Annals of Neurology*, 19 (1986), 335–43

Lane, R. Letter in *Journal of Neurology, Neurosurgery and Psychiatry*, 63:2 (1997)

LeDoux, Joseph, Wilson, D. H. and Gazzaniga, Michael 'A divided mind', Annals of Neurology, 2 (1977), 417–21

Loftus, Elizabeth F. 'Creating false memories', Scientific American, September 1997, 51–5

Maguire, E. et al 'Recalling routes around London: activation of the right hippocampus in taxi drivers', *Journal of Neuroscience*, 17 (1997), 7103–10

McNaughton, N. et al 'Reactivation of hippocampal ensemble memories during sleep', *Science*, 19 July

1994, 676–9

McNeil, J.E. and Warrington, E.K. 'Prosopagnosia: a reclassification', *Quarterly Journal of Experimental Psychology*, A, 43:2 (1991), 267–87

Melzack, R. 'Phantom limbs', *Scientific American* supplement, 7:1 (1997), 84

Miles, Marshall 'A description of various aspects of anencephaly', Lafayette College, USA

Mineka, S. et al 'Observational conditioning of snake fear in rhesus monkeys', *Journal of Abnormal Psychology*, 93 (1984), 355–72

Morris, J.S. et al 'A differential neural response in the human amygdala to fearful and happy facial expressions', letter to *Nature*, 383:6603 (1997), 812–15

New Scientist 'Emotions' supplement, 27 April 1996

Nisbett, Richard and Wilson, Timothy 'Telling more than we can know – verbal reports on mental processes', *Psychological Review*, 84 (1977), 231–59

North, A.C. et al 'In-store music affects product choice', *Nature*, 390:6656 (1997), 132

Nystrand, A. 'New discoveries on sex differences in the brain', National Institute of Ageing, NIH Bethesda, *Lakartidningen* 93:21 (1996), 2071–3

O'Connell, R.A. 'SPECT imaging study of the brain in acute mania and schizophrenia', *Journal of Neuroimaging*, 2 (1995), 101–4; also Ian Daly, 'Mania', *The Lancet*, 349:9059 (1997), 1157–9

Olsho, L.W. 'Infant frequency discrimination', *Infant Behaviour and Development*, 7 (1984), 27–35

Oomura, Y., Aou, S., Koyama, Y. and Yoshimatsu, H. 'Central control of sexual behaviour', *Brain Research Bulletin*, 20 (1988), 863–870

Pantev, C. et al 'Increased auditory cortical representation in musicians', *Nature*, 392:6678 (1998), 81

Paulesu, E. et al 'The physiology of coloured hearing', *Brain*, 118 (1995), 661–76

Paulesu, E., Frith, U. et al 'Is developmental dyslexia a disconnection syndrome?', *Brain*, 119 (1996), 143–7

Pendick, Daniel 'The New Phrenologists', *New Scientist*, 2091 (1997), 34–47

Penfield, W. and Perot, P. 'The brain's record of auditory and visual experience', *Brain*, 86 (1963), 595–696

Phillips, M.L. et al 'A specific neural substrate for perceiving facial expressions of disgust', letter to *Nature*, 389:6550 (1997), 495–7

Putnam, F.W. 'Dissociative phenomena', *American Psychiatric Press Review of Psychiatry*, 10, 145–60

Raine, A. et al 'Brain abnormalities in murderers indicated by positron emission tomography', *Biological Psychiatry*, 42 (1997), 495–508

Ralph, Sage and Ellis 'Word meaning blindness: a new form of acquired dyslexia', *Cognitive Neurology* 13:5 (1996), 617–39

Reading, P.J. and Will, R.G. 'Unwelcome orgasms', *The Lancet*, 350:9093 (1997)

Rees, G. 'Too much for our brains to handle', *New Scientist*, 158:2128 (1998), 11

Rothenberger, A. et al 'What happens to electrical brain activity when anorectic adolescents gain weight', *European Archives of Psychiatry and Clinical Neurosurgery*, 240:3 (1991), 144–7

Sieveking, Paul 'Then I saw her face...', *Sunday Times*, 2 November 1997

Sperry, R.W. 'Hemisphere disconnection and unity in conscious awareness', *American Psychologist*, 23 (1968), 723–33

Stuss, D. and Benson, D. 'Neuropsychological studies of the frontal lobes', *Psychological Bulletin*, 95, 3–28

Tiihonen, J. et al 'Increase in cerebral blood flow in man during orgasm', *Neuroscience Letters*, 170 (1994), 241–3

Van der Ster, Wallin G. et al 'Selective dieting patterns among anorectics and bulimics', *European Eating Disorders Review*, 2 (1994), 221-32

Vargha-Khadem, Farana 'Differential effects of early hippocampal pathology on episodic and semantic memory', *Science*, 277:5324 (1997), 376–80

Weltzin, Kaye 'Serotonin activity in anorexia and bulimia', *Journal of Clinical Psychiatry*, 52, supplement (1991), 41–8

Williams, L.M. 'Recovered memories of abuse in women with documented sexual victimization histories', *Journal of Traumatic Stress*, 8, 649–73

Wing, Lorna 'The autistic spectrum', *The Lancet*, 350:9093 (1997), 1762

Wright, Lawrence 'Double mystery', *New Yorker*, 7 August 1995

INDEX

Page numbers in *italic* refer to the illustrations

acetylcholine (ACh), 29, 69
Ackerly, S.S., 202
addiction, 20, 62, 64, 68–9, *69*, 105
adrenaline, 84
adult attention deficit disorder, 67
advertising, 42
ageing, 23, 71
aggression, 72, 94, 205
agnosia, 116–18
alcoholism, 62, 69
alexithymia, 85–6
alien hands, 49–50, *53*
alpha brainwaves, 186
Alzheimer's disease, 21, 29, 172, *173*
amnesia, 169–76, *169*, *172*, 178
amphetamines, 68–9
amputation, phantom limbs, 125, *126–7*, 195
amygdala, 15, *15*, *16*, 32, 61, *96*; depression, *102*; and drug addiction, 68; emotions, 22, *82*, 84–5, *84*, *85*, *88*, 91, 92–6, 99, 103, *121*; face recognition, *121*; and facial expressions, 87–9; fears and phobias, 99, 100–1; flashbacks, 128; memory, 100, 101, 102, *161*, *163*, 166, 169, 173, 174; nightmares, 194; psychopathic behaviour, 94–6; sense of smell, 114; and sexual behaviour, *53*, 72, 75; Syndrome E, 205
analgesics, 114
anatomy, 14–16, *14–16*
androgens, 71, 72, 79
anger, 55, 91–6
angular gyrus, *138*, *152*, 153–4, *153*
animals: consciousness, 98; depression, 107; language, *138*; noises, *145*
anorexia, 64–5
anosognosia, 36, 146, 198–201, *198*
anterior cingulate cortex, 171; attention, *182*; depression, *102*, *105*, 106; emotion, 196, *196*; hypnosis, 194; neglect, 200; obsessive-compulsive disorder (OCD), 59, 61; and pain, 114, 196, *196*; Tourette's syndrome, *57*
anterior commissure, *45*, 48, 71, *71*
antidepressants, 16, 68, 106, 107
Anton's delusion, 200
anxiety, 41, *61*
aphasia, 151–2
apoptosis, 21
apperceptive agnosia, 116
appetite control, 64–6, *65*

Aron, Arthur, 105
art, 42, 108
artificial intelligence (AI), 203
Asperger's syndrome, 78, 79, 142, *143*, 145–7
association areas, 108, 111
associative agnosia, 116
attention, 128, 185–7, *195*, 198, *199*, 205
Attention Deficit Hyperactive Disorder (ADHD), 67, 181, 187, 191
auditory cortex, 101; attention, *195*; dreams, 194; hallucinations, *129*; hearing, 113; and language, *147*, 150; music, 108, *147*, *149*; speech, 150, *150*, *155*; tinnitus, 126–7, *129*; word deafness, 151
Australopithecus africanus, 32
autism, 21, 77–9, 142–7, *143*, *149*, 205
autokinetic effect, 130–1
automatic movements, 57
automatic thinking, 60
autoscopic delusions, 127–8
axons, 14, *14*, 16, 38, *40*

babbling, 156
babies: bonding with, 76, 149; brain development, 20–3, *20*, *21*, *22*; fear, 97; internal map, *195*; 'prejudices', 131; sex differences in brain, 79; speech development, 155–6; *see also* children
Baddeley, Alan, 188, 190
Baron-Cohen, Dr Simon, 77–9, 145
basal ganglia, 57, *57*, 60, 61, 200
basolateral nucleus, amygdala, 72, 96
Bayes, Thomas, 122
Baysien induction, 122
behaviour: determinist view, 192; psychopathic, 83–4, 91–2, 94–6; sexual, 66–76, *70*, 206; urge-driven, 56–64
behaviour therapy, 90–1
behavioural pharmacology, 63
belief–disbelief, 171, *171*
Benton, Arthur, 202
benzodiazepines, 69
birdsong, *145*
Blakemore, Colin, 95–6
Blakemore, Sarah-Jayne, 31
blind spot, 199–200
blindness, 112–13; Anton's delusion, 200; blindsight, 86–7, 184–91, *184*; neglect, 200
Blum, Kenneth, 62, 63
body: awareness of, 115; bodily hallucinations, 127; body language, 89–90, 145; effects of emotion, 81
body dismorphic disorder, 60, 67

bonding, 76, 149
Bonnet, Charles, 103
Bourne, A., 173
Brack, Charles, 52
Braille, 153
brainstem, 15, 20; attention, 185, 186; and consciousness, 183; dreams, 194; and sexual behaviour, 73
brainwaves, 27
Brambilla, Riccardo, 102
Broca, Pierre, 11, *12*, 27
Broca's aphasia, 152–3
Broca's area, 23, 25–7, *138*, 150, *150*, 151, 152, *152*, 153, *153*, 156, 182
Broks, Paul, 17
Brown, Lucy, 105
bulimia, 65

Capgras' delusion, 123, *123*
Carroll, Lewis, 178
Cartesian dualism, 25, 181, 207
catatonia, 67, 191–2
category-specific recognition failure, 116–18
caudate nucleus, *15*; memory, *161*; obsessive-compulsive disorder (OCD), 59, 60–1, *61*, *62*
cells: glial cells, 15; programmed cell death, 21; *see also* neurons
cerebellum, 14, *16*, 20; evolution, 32; memory, *163*, 172; and speech, *155*
cerebral cortex, 14; baby's brain, 20; as cause of actions, 193; consciousness, 181–3, *182*; emotions, *81*, 82, *82*, 83, 84, 92–4; evolution, 32; and facial expressions, 85, 87; grey matter, 38; mapping, 27–30; memory, *163*, 164–6; sense of touch, 76; sensory processing, 107–8; sex differences, 79; and sexual behaviour, 72–6; thought, 120
cerebrum, 14
Chadwick, Peter, 55
Charles Bonnet syndrome, 121
children: eidetic (photographic) memory, 125, 126; emotional development, 93–4; imaginary friends, 126, 128; language development, 139, 155–6; *see also* babies
choices, making, *196*
Chomsky, Noam, 108, 146, 151
Chugani, Harry, 94
cingulate cortex *see* anterior cingulate cortex
cingulate gyrus, 69
cocaine, 68, 69
cochlear nucleus, *113*
codeine, 114
cognitive illusions, 131–4

cognitive therapy, 41–2
colour: sensory processing, 108; synaesthesia, 21, *109*, *111*
coma, 19, 183, 186
Comings, David, 62, 63
communication, 136–57; body language, 89–90, 145; gestures, 89, 97, 137, 139; music, 147–9; reading, *152*, 153, *155*; speech, 150–7; theory of mind, 143, 144; writing, 153; *see also* language
compulsions, 206
computers, 181, 203
concussion, 186
conditioned fear, 99–100, 102
confabulation, 168–9
conscious brain: emotions, 85, *88*, *91*, 98, *98*; facial expressions, 85; recognition, 111
conscious volition, 193
consciousness, 16, 180–207; computers and, 203; free will, 192–3, 201, 207; meaningfulness, 201; planning, 197; self-awareness, 23, 156, 183, 191, 203; split-brain experiments, 53; thinking, 195–202
convergence zones, 135
Cool, Nadean, 167, 174
coprolalia, 55
Coren, Stanley, 47
corpus callosum, *16*, *38*; alien hands, 49–50; communication between hemispheres, 15, 40–1, *40*, *45*; and homosexuality, 73; sex differences, 71, *71*, 79; split-brain experiments, 44, *44*
cortex *see* cerebral cortex
corticomedial nucleus, amygdala, 72
Cotard's delusion, 103, 106
counselling, 41–2
covert memories, 174
creativity, 104, 202
Crick, Francis, 204–5
Cytowic, Richard, 107

Damasio, Antonio, 81, 82, 135
deafness, 113–14, 137, 138
death, delusions of, 102–3, 106
deduction, 111
dementia, 16, 116; *see also* Alzheimer's disease
dendrites, *14*, 16, 186
depression, 41, 127, 181; animals, 107 ; anterior cingulate cortex, *102*, *105*, 106; and creativity, 104; dopamine and, 67, 104–5; frontal lobe, *100*, *101*, 202; loss of meaningfulness, 201; parietal lobe, 106; prefrontal lobe, *102*, 107; and rejection, 104–5; temporal lobe, 106
Descartes, René, 25, 207
determinism, 192
dichotomania, 35

diencephalon, *65*
Diffusion Tensor Imaging, 26, *26*, *111*
disgust, facial expressions, *87*, 90, 91
dispositional representations, 135
dopamine, 16, 39; and addiction, 64, 67, *67*, 68, 69, *69*; attention, 186; dysfunction, 67, *67*; functions, 29, 67; hallucinations, 29, 128; and love, 52, 76; and memory, 193; pathways, 29; pleasure, 103; and recognition, 123; and satisfaction, *62*, *63*; and schizophrenia, 107; and sexual behaviour, 68; and Tourette's syndrome, 55–6
doppelgangers, 127–8, *129*
dorsolateral prefrontal cortex, *182*, 194, 195
dorsomedial nucleus, hypothalamus, 73
Down's syndrome, 21, 140
dreams, 130, *163*, 165, 194, *194*
drugs: addiction, 20, 62, 64, 68–9, *69*; analgesics, 114; antidepressants, 16, 68, 106, 107; control of urge-driven behaviour, 63; hallucinations, 121, 128
dualism, 25, 181, 207
Duchenne, Guillaume, *85*
Duchenne smile, *85*, 87
Dürer, Albrecht, *51*
dyslexia, *152*, *153*, 154

eating disorders, 62, *62*, 63, 64–6
echolalia, 153
Ecstasy, 68
Egypt, ancient, 25
eidetic memory, 21, 125–6
Einstein, Albert, 108–10, *109*
Ekman, Paul, 90
electricity, sensory processing, 107
electroencephalography (EEG), 27, *27*, 66
emotions, 80–105; anger, 91–6; baby's brain, 21–2; communication between hemispheres, *45*, 48; complex emotions, 85; controlling, 92–3, 97; depression, *100*, *101*, 102–7; differences between hemispheres, 36, 41; emotional recognition system, 123–4, *123*; expressing, 85–91; facial expressions, 86–91, 145; feeling, 81–2; happiness, 103; limbic system, 15, 32; and memory, 164; 'mirroring' in others, 140–2; moral judgements, 82–3; music and, 148–9; psychopathic behaviour, 83–4, *84*, 94–6; psychotherapy, 41–2; and sense of smell, 114; sex differences, 71; split-brain experiments, 48, *48*; as survival mechanism, 84, 98
empathy, 140–2, 146
endorphins, 29, 69, 76
enkephalins, 29, 69, 114
environment dependency syndrome, 206
epilepsy, 11, 27, 44, 73, 76, 95, 128, 169
episodic memories, 162, *163*, 166, *166*,

173, 205
erotomania, 74
Event-Related Potentials (ERPs), 27
evolution, 32–3, *32*, 63, 64, 157, *157*
expressions, facial, 86–91, 145
extroverts, 124
eyes: attention, 186; brainstem and, 19; 'language of the eyes', 142, 145; *see also* vision

Face Recognition Units (FRU), 121–2
faces: differences between hemispheres, *51*; expressions, 86–91, 145; face blindness, 118–19; hallucinations, *129*; recognition, 37–8, *117*, 121–2, *121*, *125*, 131, *133*
false memories, 166–9
fear, 87, 92, 96–102
fear memories, *163*, 174
feedback, *18*, 19; facial expressions, 90; and stuttering, *155*
fight or flight response, 84, 92, 99
fish brain, 32, *32*
Fisher, Helen, 104–5
flashbacks, 128, *163*, 166, 174
foetal development, 20–1, *20*, 79
foreign languages, 156
fovea, 112
free association, 174
free will, 190–1, 192–3, 201, 202, 207
Fregoli's delusion, 119–23
Freud, Sigmund, 97, 98
Freudian psychoanalysis, 42, 55
Fried, Itzhak, 205–6
Frith, Chris, 23, 120–1
Frith, Uta, 144
frontal lobe, 14; ageing, 71; confabulation, 169; consciousness, 180, 181–3; depression, *100*, *101*; development of, 22; dreaming, *163*; dysfunction, 202, 205–6; emotions, *82*, 92; evolution, 32; and facial expressions, 87; hallucinations, *129*; language cortex, 138, 150; language development, 156, 157; memory, *163*; mirror neurons, *141*; neglect, 200–1; obsessive-compulsive disorder (OCD), *59*, 60; psychopathic behaviour, *93*; schizophrenia, 194; sense of smell, 114, *114*; sense of taste, 114; and sexual behaviour, 74–5; thought, 192
fugue, 173–6
functional brain scanning, 12
Functional MRI (fMRI), 26, *26*, 28
future, imagining, 176–9

Gage, Phineas, 24, *24*, 169, 183, 197, 202
Gall, Franz, 11
'gay brain', 73
Gazzaniga, Michael, 43, 48, 50–1
genetics: and alcoholism, 69; brain development, 19, 20–1; and depression, 107;

genetic engineering, 63–4; and homosexuality, 73; language development, 157
gestures, 33, 89, 97, 137, 139
ghosts, 128–30, *129*
glial cells, 16
glutamate, 29
God, *129*
gossip, 157
gourmand syndrome, 114
grammar, 156, 157
grapheme-colour synaesthesia, *109, 111*
Gregory, Richard L., 120
grey matter, *20*, 38
grief, 41
guilt, cognitive illusions, 132–3
gyrus, 14, *20*

Haggard, Patrick, 192–3
hallucinations, 29, 67, 120–1, 124–30, *129*
hallucinogenic drugs, 68
Hamer, Dean, 73
hands: alien hands, 49–50; gestures, 89, 97, 137, 139; handedness, 46–7
Happé, Francesca, 144
happiness, 103
Harlow, John, 24
Hauser, Marc D., 108–9
hearing: deafness, 113–14, 137, 138; hallucinations, 121, *129*; sensory processing, *35*, 107, 113–14, *113*; synaesthesia, 21, 107, 108, 110; tinnitus, 126–7, *129*
heart disease, 114
hemispheres: alien hands, 49–50, *53*; anatomy, 14–16, *16*; brain damage, 36, 37–8, *37*; communication between, 40–1, *45*, 47–8; differences between, 34–53, *39*, *41*; divergent politics, 52; dominance, 49; hearing, 113–14, *113*; and homosexuality, 53; language, 138, 139, *154*, *155*; and left-handedness, 46–7; neurotransmitters, 39; orienting, 200; split-brain, 43–53, *43–4*; working methods, 35–42; *see also* frontal lobe; occipital lobe; parietal lobe; temporal lobe
Hermann's grid, *132*, 134
heroin, 69
Heschl's gyrus, *113*
hippocampus, 15, *15*, *16*; ageing, 71; dreams, *163*, 194; evolution, 32; memory, 22, 99, 100, 101, *161*, *163*, 164–6, *164*, *166*, 169, *172*, 175, 178, 205; sex differences, 71; spatial ability, 37
Hitch, Graham, 188, 190
Holstege, Gert, 70
homosexuality, 53, 73
hormones: emotions, *82*; maternal bonding, 149; sex differences, 20–1, 71, 72, 79; and sexual behaviour, 72, 74, 76; stress hormones, 69, 102, 175; unconscious memories, 100, 102

humour, 11, 36–7, 111
hunches, 41
hunger, 64–6
hypnosis, 194, *194*
hypochondria, 60, *67*
hypothalamus, 15, *15*, *16*; eating disorders, *62*, 64–5; emotions, *82*, 92, 99; evolution, 32; sex differences, 71; and sexual behaviour, 66, 71, 72, 73, 76
hypotheses, and vision, 120, 122

idiot savants, 111
illusions, 130–5, *130–3*
impotence, 74
'in two minds', 49–53
inferior colliculus, *113*
information: communication, 136–57; sensory processing, 107–8
instincts, 60, 97, *161*
insula, 150, *152*, 196; falsehoods, 171, *171*
introverts, 124
intuition, 21

James, William, 204
Jamison, Kay Redfield, 104
jokes, 36–7, 111

Kandinsky, Wassily, *109*
Kawabata, Hideaki, 18
Klein, Rüdiger, 102
Kluver-Bucy syndrome, 75
Koch, Christof, 204
Korsakoff's syndrome, 169
Kyushu University, 66

language, 137–40; aphasia, 151–2; development of, 137–9, 146, 155–6; dyslexia, *152*, *153*, 154; foreign languages, 156; and left-handedness, 46; and memory, 138; phonological loop, 190; reading, 153, 154, *155*; speech, 150–7; split-brain experiments, 48–9, 50–1; Tourette's syndrome, 55, 59; Williams syndrome, 139–40; writing, 153
language areas, 11, *12*, 23, 25–7, *28*, 33, 138, *138*, 139, *147*, 150, *150*, *152*, 156; response to words, *148*
language cortex, 138, 150, 151, 153
Lashley, Karl, 25
lateral geniculate body, 112
lateral inhibition, *132*
lateral nucleus, hypothalamus, 64, 65, 66
lateral pulvinar, 185, 186
lateral thinking, 39
learning, 120; *see also* memory
LeDoux, Joseph, 48, 50–1, 84, 92, 98, 99, 100–1
left-handedness, 46–7
leucotomy, 12, *12*
LeVay, Simon, 73

L'Hermitte, François, 206
Libet, Benjamin, 190–1, 192, 193
lie detection, 90, 169, 170, *170*
limbic system, 15, *15*, *16*, 196; child development, 22; communication between hemispheres, 48; consciousness, 182, 191; and drug addiction, 68; eating disorders, 64–6; emotions, *81*, 82, 84–5, 92, *98*; evolution, 32; and facial expressions, *86*; hallucinations, *129*; and happiness, 103; motor skills, *58*; music, 148; psychopathic behaviour, *93*; recognition, 111, *123*; sense of smell, 114, *114*; sensory processing, 107; sexual behaviour, 72, 74; sleep, 194; and stimuli, *63*; urges, *63*
lobotomy, 12, 206
locus coeruleus, 29
Loftus, Elizabeth, 167
long-term memory, *163*, 164–6, 197
long-term potentiation (LTP), 159, *160*, 164
loop-back system, *18*, 19
lordosis, *70*, 72, 74
love, 76
LSD, 68

macaque monkeys, 66, 72
magic mushrooms, 68
magnetic apraxia, 201
Magnetic Resonance Imaging (MRI), 12, 25, 26, *26*, *28*, 66
Magnetoencephalography (MEG), 27, *27*
Maguire, Eleanor, 178–9
mammalian brain, 15, 32, *32*
mania, 67, 104, 107, 181, 201–5
manic-depressive illness, 104
maps, internal, *164*, *166*, 192–5, 200
Mark, Vincent, 96
marriage, autism and, 147
'mass action' theory, 12
massa intermedia, 71, *71*
mathematics, 111
Maynard Smith, John, 157
meaning: and consciousness, 201; in mania, 67, 107, 201–2
medial geniculate body, *113*
medial prefrontal cortex, 31
medial preoptic area, hypothalamus, 66, *70*, 71, *71*, 72
meditation, 115, 194, *194*
medulla, *16*
memory, 158–77; and ageing, 71; Alzheimer's disease, 172, *173*; amnesia, 169–76, *169*, *172*, 178; brain regions, *165*; conditioned fear, 97, 102; and dopamine, 193; dreams, *163*; eidetic (photographic) memory, 21, 125–6; emotions, 22; false memories, 166–9; flashbacks, 128, *163*, 166, 174; imagining the future, 176–9; language and, 138; long-term memory, *163*, 164–6, 197; neural

connections, 19, 159–66; oxytocin and, 76; recognition, 111, 117–18; recovered memories, 100, 165–6, *165*, 167; short–term, 169–72, 205; smells and, 114; state of mind, 162–4; storage, 30, 159–66, *160*, *163*, *165*; unconscious memories, 100–1, 174; working memory, 188–9, *188–9*, 195, 197, 205

mentalising, 31

microtubules, 203

midbrain, *16*; attention, 186; and consciousness, 183

migraine, 128

mirror neurons, 86, 140–2, *141*, *142*, 143, 146, *149*

modular brain theory, 12

modules, 14–15, 111

Mona Lisa, 89

Mondrian, Piet, *109*

Moniz, Egas, 12

monkeys, 66, 72, 97, 141, 146

moral judgements, 82–3, 108–9

morality, 202; and emotion, 82–3; moral faculty theory, 108–9

morphine, 69, 114

motor cortex, 23, 76, 182; anosognosia, 198; dopamine pathways, 67; motor skills, 57; and sexual behaviour, 73; and speech, 152

mouth cortex, *155*

movement, *28*; automatic, 57

multiple personality disorder (MPD), 175–6

music, 42, 108, 147–9, *147*, *149*, 172

myelin, 15, 20, *20*

myelinization, 22, 23

Myers, Ronald, 44

Nabokov, Vladimir, 110

natural selection, 19, 137

Near-Infra-red Spectroscopy (NIRS), 26, *26*

neglect, 198–201, *198*

neocortex, 32

neural Darwinism, 19

neural networks, 19, *21*

neurogenesis, *21*

neurons, 16, *18*; baby's brain, 20, *21*; brainstem, 186; connections, 13; differences between hemispheres, 38–9; firing, 13–19, *18*; memory, 159–66, *160*; microtubules, 203; mirror neurons, 86, 140–2, *141*, *142*, 143, 146, *149*

neurotransmitters, 16, 28–9, *28*; attention, 186; and consciousness, 183; dopamine dysfunction, 67, *67*; drug addiction, 68–9, *69*; eating disorders, 65; Tourette's syndrome, 55–6; unconscious memories, 100; *see also individual neurotransmitters*

nicotine, 69

nightmares, 194

noradrenaline, 16, 29, 39, 68, 69, 186

nose, sensory processing, 107

nucleus accumbens, 68

Obama, Barack, *125*

obesity, 64

obsessive-compulsive disorder (OCD), 59–64, *59*, *61*, *62*, 67, *67*

occipital lobe, 14

occipito-parietal area, *129*

oestrogen, 72

olfactory bulb, 72

opioids, 69, 114

optic chiasma, 112

optic nerve, 199

orbito-frontal cortex, 18, *59*, 61, *182*, 197, 201, 205

orgasm, 66–72, 73, *73*, 76

orientation, 185, 186, 200

out-of-body experiences, 115

oxytocin, 29, 76, 149, 200

pain, 13, 69, 114, 196

painkillers, 114

panic attacks, 100

Panksepp, Jaak, 148

paranoia, 107, 202–5

Parfit, Derek, 17

parietal lobe, 14; ageing, 71; artificial urges, 193; attention, 185, 186; depression, 106; development of, 22; hallucinations, *129*; language cortex, 150; meditation, 194; neglect, 200; recognition, 111; and sexual behaviour, 76; spatial processing, 37

Parkinson's disease, 16, 29, 56, 67, 127

Pavlov, Ivan, 99

Penfield, Wilder, 27–30, *165*

penis, *70*, 73

Penrose, Sir Roger, 203

perception *see* sensory processing

Persinger, Michael, 13

Persistent Vegetative State, 185–6

personality, multiple personality disorder (MPD), 175–6

phantom limbs, 125, *126–7*, 195

phobias, 96–102, *163*

phonological loop, working memory, 188, *188–9*, 190

photographic memory, 21, 125–6

phrenology, 11, *11*

Pickrell, Jacqueline, 167

pineal gland, 15, 25

Pinker, Steven, 151

pituitary gland, 15

planning, 197

pleasure, 56, 63, 103

poets, 104

pons, *16*

Positron Emission Topography (PET), 23, 26, *26*, 66

post-traumatic stress disorder (PTSD), *88*,

100, 128, 175

prefrontal lobe: adolescence, 31; attention, 186; consciousness, 181, *182*; depression, *102*, 107; and drug addiction, 68; dysfunction, 24, 202–6; emotional development, 93; evolution, 32; face recognition, *121*; functions, *182*; and happiness, 103; obsessive-compulsive disorder (OCD), *59*; self-determination, 24; theory of mind, 143, *143*; thought, 197; Tourette's syndrome, *57*

pregnancy, 20–1

prehistoric man, 32–3, 46, 157

prejudices, 131–3

premotor cortex, *58*, 60, *182*, 194

priapism, 73

primates, 66, 139, 157

priming, 174

procedural memory, *163*, 172

proprioception, 115

prosopagnosia, 116, 118–19

psychiatry, biological, 11

psychoanalysis, 42, 55, 91

psychopaths, 91–2, *93*, 94–6, 108

psychotherapy, 41–2

putamen, *15*; automatic movements, 57; memory, *161*, *163*, 172; motor skills, *58*; obsessive-compulsive disorder (OCD), 60, *61*; tics, 56–9, *62*

racism, 52

Raine, Andrew, 93

Ramachandran, Vilayanur S., *127*, 146

Ras-GRF, 102

Ratey, John, 147

rationalization, 42–3

Readiness Potential (RP), 190–1

reading, *150*, *152*, 153, *155*

recognition, 111–16, *117*; 'acquired' tastes, 159–62; agnosia, 116–18; emotional recognition system, 119–24, *123*; faces, 118–24, *121*, 131, *133*

recovered memories, 100, 165–6, 167

reflex actions, 183, 191

rejection, 104–5

religious beliefs, 13, 62

reptilian brain, 15, 32, *32*

Restak, Richard, 91

Reticular Activating System, 185, 186

reticular formation, 23

retina, 112, 130, 199

reward deficiency syndrome, 62–3

right-handedness, 46

Rimbaud, Arthur, *109*

rituals, 56, 59–60

Rizzolatti, Giacomo, 141, 146

Rolls, E.T., 61

Romanian orphans, 93–4

romantic love, 52, 68, 76, 104–5

Royal Academy, 104

saccades, 112
Sacks, Oliver, 119, 138, 177
satisfaction, 62, 63
scanning, 25, 26–7, 26–7
scene construction, 178–9
Schacter, Daniel, 168
Schatzman, Morton, 126
schizophrenia: auditory hallucinations, 121, 127; dopamine and, 67; frontal lobe in, 181, 194, 194; negative symptom schizophrenia, 191; paranoia, 107
Schumann, Robert, 104
Science, 73
self, sense of, 192–5
self-awareness, 23, 156, 183, 192, 203
self-determination, 23–4
semantic memory, 161–2, 163, 173
sensation, 28, 114
senses: pain, 114; sixth sense, 115; smell, 35, 107, 114, 114, 127; taste, 107, 114; see also hearing; vision
sensory cortex, 75, 76
sensory processing, 106–35, 115; hallucinations, 120–1, 124–30, 129; illusions, 130–5, 130–3, 133; learning, 120; recognition, 111–16, 117; synaesthesia, 107
septum, 68, 73
serotonin, 16; and drug addiction, 68; eating disorders, 65; functions, 28; gourmand syndrome, 114; pathways, 28; and sexual behaviour, 68
sex differences, 71, 71, 77–9, 77–9; depression, 100; hormones and, 20–1, 79; sexual behaviour, 72
sex hormones, 71, 72, 74
sexual behaviour, 66–76, 70, 206
short-term memory, 169–72, 205
Shostakovich, Dmitri, 126–7
sight see vision
sign language, 137, 138, 139
simultagnosia, 129
sixth sense, 115
skull: evolution, 32, 157; phrenology, 11, 11, 12
sleep, 165, 194, 194
'smell brain', 32
smell, sense of, 35, 107, 114, 114, 127
smiles, 85, 86, 87, 89, 89, 90, 91
snakes, fear of, 96, 97, 99
social brain, 31
social integration, 140
social intelligence, 196
social organization, 42
somatosensory cortex, 23, 30, 126
soul, 17
sound: hallucinations, 126–7; hearing, 113–14, 113; music, 147–9; synaesthesia, 21, 107, 108, 110
spatial ability, 37, 77, 79
spatial memories, 164, 166

specific language impairment (SLI), 151
speech, 148, 150–7; Broca's area, 23, 25–7, 138, 150, 151, 182; development of, 155–6; and emotion, 85
Sperry, Roger, 44, 48, 53
spinal cord, 15, 16
spirituality, 13
split-brain experiments, 43–53, 44
stalkers, 74
state of mind, 162–4
statistics, cognitive illusions, 133–4
stimuli, 56
stress hormones, 69, 81, 101, 102, 175
stroke, 16; agnosia, 116; anosognosia, 146, 198; effect on emotions, 36; and language, 27, 150, 153
stuttering, 155
subgenual cortex, 202
subjective experiences, measuring, 18
suicide, 103, 104
sulcus, 14, 16, 20
superior colliculus, 185, 186
supplementary motor area (SMA), 155, 182, 194; artificial urges, 193
surgery: leucotomy, 12, 12; lobotomy, 12
survival strategies, 19, 42, 92, 98, 107
synaesthesia, 21, 107–11
synapses, 14, 16, 31
Syndrome E, 205
syntax, 151

Tan, 27
taste, 107, 114; 'acquired', 159–62; phantom, 127
tegmentum, 128
Temple, Christine, 153
temporal lobe, 14; ageing, 71; delusions of death, 103; depression, 106; and drug addiction, 68; hallucinations, 129; language cortex, 138, 150; memory, 161; recognition, 111; sense of smell, 114; and sexual behaviour, 73, 75–6
testosterone, 20, 72, 74, 79
thalamus, 15, 15, 16, 20; attention, 185; and consciousness, 183; depression, 102; emotional stimuli, 96, 99; evolution, 32; memory, 169; speech recognition, 150; vision, 112, 112
theory of mind, 143, 144
thinking, 28
Third Eye, 180
thought, 195–202; lateral thinking, 39; working memory, 188–9, 188–9, 195, 197, 205
tics, 56–7, 57, 62, 67
tinnitus, 126–7, 129
tone-deafness, 148
tongue, sensory processing, 107
touch, sense of, 35, 75, 76
Tourette, Georges Gilles de la, 55

Tourette's syndrome, 55–9, 57, 62, 67, 67
tranquillizers, 69
Transcranial Magnetic Stimulation (TMS), 184
trauma: post-traumatic stress disorder (PTSD), 88, 100, 128, 175; unconscious memories, 100–1
twins, 19–20, 46

unconscious brain: anger, 91–2; emotions, 21–2, 82; magnetic apraxia, 201; memories, 100–1, 174; see also limbic system
urges, 56–64, 63, 197; artificially generated, 193

vasopressin, 76
ventral tegmental nucleus, 29, 68, 105
ventromedial cortex, 103, 182, 202
ventromedial nucleus, hypothalamus, 64, 66, 70, 74, 75
Virgin Mary, 130–1
vision and visual cortex, 112–13, 112, 118; autokinetic effect, 130–1; blind spot, 199–200; blindsight, 184–91, 184; differences between people, 108; dreams, 194; emotional stimuli, 96, 99; hallucinations, 121, 124–30, 129; and hypotheses, 120, 122; illusions, 130–5, 130–3, 133; reading, 150; sensory processing, 28, 35, 43, 108; split-brain experiments, 45–7, 48; synaesthesia, 21, 107, 109, 111; visual agnosia, 116; visual association area, 153, 194; visual consciousness, 204–5
visionaries, 128
visuo-spatial sketch pad, working memory, 188, 188–9, 190
voices, hallucinations, 121, 127, 129
von Economo neurons, 196

Wang, A.T., 31
Weiskrantz, Larry, 184
Wellcome Department of Cognitive Neurology, 144, 189
Wernicke, Carl, 11, 12
Wernicke's aphasia, 151–2
Wernicke's area, 23, 25–7, 138, 150, 151, 152, 153, 153, 155
Whistler, James McNeill, 109
white matter, 38
Williams syndrome, 139–40, 168
Wisconsin Card Sorting Task, 197
withdrawal symptoms, and drug addiction, 69
word deafness, 151
working memory, 188–9, 188–9, 195, 197, 205
writing, 153

Zaidel, Eran, 48
Zajonc, Robert, 174
Zeki, Semir, 18